Olivia O'Neill spent her childhood on a Welsh hill farm but several members of her family served in the Indian Civil Service during the last century, which has led to a lifelong fascination with India. Miss O'Neill worked for a magazine before marrying a journalist wh
him all over the world,
whenever possible.

Also by Olivia O'Neill:

DISTANT THUNDER

IMPERIAL NIGHTS

Olivia O'Neill

Dragon Star

Futura
Macdonald & Co
London & Sydney

A Futura Book

First published in Great Britain in 1981
by Macdonald Futura Publishers

This edition 1983

ISBN 0 7088 1881 1

Reproduced, printed and bound in Great Britain by
Hazell Watson & Viney Ltd, Aylesbury, Bucks

Futura Publications
A Division of
Macdonald & Co (Publishers) Ltd
Maxwell House
74 Worship Street
London EC2A 2EN

Today we hold
the long rope in our hands.
When shall we put bonds
upon the grey dragon?

Mao Tse-tung: *Poem of the Battle of Mount Liupan*

PROLOGUE

Like a figure carved in ivory, the small skinny boy crouched in the ruined temple's darkest corner, listening to the far-away screams of the warlord's women. He wanted to run away down the hill, into the forest, anywhere that would be out of earshot of those terrible screams, but fear and the habit of obedience held him still. Third Aunt had told him to hide here. She said he would be safe among the broken stone statues with their rolling eyes and lolling tongues. When all was quiet and the bandits had gone away, she would come and fetch him.

The boy didn't much like Third Aunt, who was fat and shrill and domineering, but he had promised his mother that he would obey her. She was his last link with the days of ease and plenty before the Japanese imperialists had come in the night and taken his father with them.

Even before that happened, his mother had seen the way things were going, and she had begged his father to divorce her, for their son's sake. She was only the secondary wife, nothing but a burden and expense in these days of uncertainty, and after a little hesitation her husband had agreed that she should return to her own family. His Number One wife had been delighted. She was proud of her own position and had always resented the shy secondary wife. So she raised no objection to Wen Hsui's divorce, since she did not know the real reason for it.

Wen Hsui's family were angry with her for bringing disgrace upon them. They made her life a misery and soon she felt that even among her own kin her precious son was not safe.

She knew how clever the Japanese were at worming out secrets which Chinese people might wish to hide. They had murdered her father and two of her brothers who opposed them, and seized possession of her Manchurian homeland as well as her husband. One day those devil dwarfs might learn she had a son, and they would send secret agents to kidnap him and drag him off to join his father as their prisoner.

After long thought and many tears she had faced the decision to part with the boy. She had made her sister Wen Yu, who was also a Manchu princess and not footbound, though of high birth, promise that she would take the boy and travel south to the protection of the powerful warlord Ma Yenying. He would teach her son the arts of war, so that when the boy reached manhood he could fight to avenge his ancestors whom the Japanese had killed, and win back his homeland.

So his mother planned. She could not know that in Ma Yenying's domain three successive harvests would fail and cause the worst famine of two famine-ridden centuries. Now the warlord's own stronghold was under attack by a rabble of desperate starving peasants, and Third Aunt – her fat face as white as rice-flour and her voice shaking – had pushed the boy out of the peace gate and told him to run up the overgrown path that led to the ruined temple.

She thrust two rice-cakes into his hand, but these he had eaten long since. Now his stomach growled with hunger. The sun was slanting low. Soon it would be gone, and he shivered at the thought of spending the dark hours here among the evil spirits of unappeased ancestors and the fierce mountain demons who wail all night on wild hill-sides.

Why didn't she come? He was sorry now that he had so often troubled Third Aunt, and had screamed out that he hated her when he found she had sold the Shining Moon. She had taken the jade treasure from his bundle in order to buy foreign medicine for him. In Shanghai, on their journey south, he had been very ill with a fever that sent him strange visions, and he had not known of the Shining Moon's disappearance until he was well enough to reach out his hand for him, and found him missing. Then he'd raved and screamed with angry sorrow, because he alone knew the secret of Shining Moon. He was very old and rare. A foreign devil had made him long ago as a gift to the Son of Heaven of that day, who had declared that if the Shining Moon were lost, ill-luck would fall on the Middle Kingdom, and barbarians triumph over the Sons of Han.

Inside the boy's silk jacket, safe in a soft leather pouch, the tiny gold key was stowed. He glanced fearfully round at the deepening shadows, then slipped open the drawstring and drew it out, caressing the metal's comforting smoothness, just as he used to stroke Shining Moon himself.

It was all Third Aunt's fault that trouble had followed them since they left Shanghai. If she hadn't sold his treasure, perhaps the rains would have fallen and the empty rice-husks swelled, so that the peasants could pay their taxes to Ma Yenying, instead of besieging his citadel with axes and hoes in their skeletal hands. Then he might be eating apricots in the courtyard now, or playing with the gatekeeper's son instead of shivering here in the dark, hungry and scared.

The boy flinched and his palms around the key were suddenly slippery with sweat as the faraway screams rose to a crescendo. A moment later the thump of an explosion rocked the floor he sat on, sending protesting pheasants squawking from their roosts. He could guess what that meant. Unable to break open the heavy stone doors of the granary, the hungry peasants had blown it apart. Perhaps that would satisfy them. Perhaps they would also find the gold treasure which Ma Yenying's guards had been throwing down a dry well as he was hustled away. Perhaps . . .

His quick ear caught the sound of feet shuffling over dead leaves; the rasp of laboured breath. It must be Third Aunt. That was how she had shuffled and panted when she first brought him up here, to play in the ruined temple no one else came near, just as she and her sisters had played when she was small. The heavy door creaked open and a sliver of late sunlight pierced the gloom.

The shuffling steps came near – hesitated as if their owner's eyes had not adjusted to the dimness, then came on again. She was searching for him. An imp of mischief stirred in the boy. Should he hide and frighten her into thinking he'd run away? How worried she would be! How she'd chatter and scold when he showed himself!

No, he decided reluctantly. Third Aunt had had a troubled day and a steep climb. Her temper would not be at its sweetest.

'Here I am,' he called, standing up in the shadows. 'Have you brought me any food?'

There was a sharp intake of breath: an utter stillness.

'And who might you be?' exclaimed a deep, rough voice. A big burly ruffian with a closely shaven head, his belt stuck full of weapons, lunged forward and caught the boy by the shoulder. 'Hey, comrades, come here! Look what I've caught,' he shouted.

'Let me go. You're hurting!' The boy squirmed like a worm on a hook. Other men gathered round, staring at his pigtail, his black embroidered jacket and silk robe.

Their leader pushed his way through the throng. 'Who are you, little grasshopper?' he asked, not unkindly. 'What are you doing here? Are you alone? Come on, answer me. I won't eat you.' He had a broad, weatherbeaten face seamed with deep creases about the eyes and a wide, laughing mouth. He wore a stained and faded cotton tunic jacket with four patch pockets, and a peasant's plaited straw sandals. But what held the boy's eyes was his cap – a shapeless grey bag with a crumpled peak, adorned with a single red star.

He shivered. These weren't ordinary bandits, come to plunder the temple, nor out of work soldiers with full guns and empty bellies. These were the dreaded Red bandits who killed landlords and warlords, instead of holding them to ransom in the traditional way and, having killed them, divided their land and wealth among the peasants. What if they had killed Third Aunt?

'Lost your tongue, little grasshopper?' said the bandit leader, giving him a friendly shove. 'Go on, then; run away home.'

'I – I can't,' muttered the boy, still staring at the red star which seemed to glow in the gloom.

'Why not? Where is your home?'

'In Tientsin,' he said forlornly.

The bandits burst into incredulous laughter. 'Tientsin! That's a thousand *li* from here!'

The boy didn't care for their coarse laughter. His pride rebelled, and he drew himself up very straight. 'I've come south to join the army and fight against the wicked Japanese imperialists,' he declared in his high, childish voice. The men exchanged amused glances.

'What army is that, youngest brother. Which of our brave generals uses children to fight his battles?' asked the leader.

'Ma Yenying, of course,' was the scornful answer.

'Oho, so he's another of that devil's spawn,' growled a tall, slit-eyed ruffian, fingering his pistol. 'I thought we'd killed the last of them down in the valley.'

'Killed them? Oh, not Third Aunt!' Despair gripped him. He broke from the bandit's restraining grip and dashed through the open door. Immediately, he saw that it was true. Billows of rolling smoke hid the place where the citadel had stood, and from its midst shot enormous tongues of flame. No one could have survived such a blaze.

'Stir-fried the lot of them,' said Slit-eyes with satisfaction. 'Here, what's that you've got in that bag?'

He grabbed the pouch that hung round the boy's thin neck and pried away the fingers that tried to protect it.

'Give it back – it's mine!' he screamed, torn between fear and fury.

The bandit laughed and upended the pouch, shaking the gold key into his grimy palm. 'Look at that, now,' he exulted. 'So that old devil of a warlord sent you up here to hide the key to his jewels, did he? Come on, let's see what else you've got . . .'

As his rough hands grabbed at the boy, a sudden violent buffet knocked him sprawling to the temple floor.

'Red fighters don't steal from children, Lin Hsi-sing,' said the red-starred leader grimly. He twitched the key from the fallen man's hand and returned it to its owner. 'Put that safe round your neck again, youngest brother,' he ordered, 'and keep close to me. I'll have to look after you now. We want to fight the Japanese invaders, too, you know. If you'll come along with us we'll teach you to be a Little Red Devil and give you a star to wear on your cap, just like mine. What d'you say to that?'

The boy's hands closed tightly round the key, and he

raised trusting slanted eyes to the blunt craggy features surmounted by the faded red star.

'I'll come with you,' he whispered.

CHAPTER ONE

In the long, high-ceilinged dining room of the Garrick Club, in the heart of London's bustling theatreland, two men shared a corner table on a mild, damp March evening in 1934. The Garrick is a friendly club, which has always encouraged conversation during meals, but this pair of diners seemed preoccupied and ate in near-silence, apart from the elder man's occasional instructions to a waiter. They looked as if they knew each other too well to feel the need for small talk.

At last Sir Charles Curtis eased back his chair and clasped stubby, spatulate fingers round his brandy glass, staring into the amber spirit as if it was a soothsayer's crystal ball. From their carved and gilded frames above the table, David Garrick as Othello and Mrs Jordan in the garb of a shepherdess looked down with amused curiosity to learn what London's leading financier had on his mind.

'This is my problem,' said Sir Charles. 'For how long should we – the British – continue to cast bread on the waters in the hope that it will return transformed into caviare sandwiches?'

'How much good money should we throw after bad?' suggested his companion. Though he was twenty years Sir Charles' junior, fair and spare where the other was dark and heavy, the two men's expressions were curiously similar: shrewd, wary, and self-assured.

Stephen Russell was in his late twenties; he had a bony, intelligent, strong-featured face, with a long nose and jaw which could look severe in repose, an effect contradicted when his well-shaped, sensitive mouth stretched sideways in its unexpectedly charming grin. No one could feel in awe of Stephen when he smiled. He had shrewd, rather narrow grey eyes under straight level brows, and a high forehead from which his smooth fair hair grew back in a tidy wave. He was the youngest and by far the cleverest of three sons whose family had owned land in the Cotswolds for generations, and had also been a successful amateur jockey until a bad fall had forced his retirement from racing the previous year. Very soon afterwards, tragic accidents killed both his elder brothers and made him heir to the family's handsome Georgian house, Longmarsh Park, with its three thousand fertile acres in the Vale of Evesham. It was to this imposing – indeed, daunting – home that he had recently brought his young Irish bride.

The life of a gentleman farmer, however, was not enough to occupy Stephen's brain. He had soon decided to rely on his agent and bailiff for the day-to-day running of the Longmarsh estate, while he continued his work as assistant to Sir Charles Curtis, who was, among other things, a financial adviser to the Treasury. Recently, Sir Charles had been taking an unexpected interest in Chinese affairs; Stephen realized he was now about to learn why.

'Yes, good money after bad. That is the crux of the matter. As you heard at today's meeting, China – that is to say, Generalissimo Chiang Kai-shek – has asked the British government for yet another large loan for the purposes of internal pacification: in plain speech, the suppression of Chinese Communism. Nobody wants China to turn Communist, do they?' He threw Stephen a challenging glance from beneath his bushy eyebrows.

'No, sir,' said Stephen equably, refusing the bait.

'Good. Our government is therefore, like the Americans, inclined to give the Generalissimo what he asks for. More money, more arms with which to fight Communism. But I . . .' He paused.

'You,' guessed Stephen, 'are beginning to wonder if we'll ever see our money back.'

'I'm wondering if we've backed the right man,' said Curtis slowly. 'I'm beginning to think that Chiang may be leading us all up the garden path. Consider the facts. China is now – or very soon will be – completely bankrupt. She already can't pay her war indemnities or service her foreign loans. She can't maintain her armies or modernize her industries. She's got nothing left. Her reserves of silver bullion have been draining out of the country like blood from a main artery. You saw the figures today. Yet Chiang and his brothers-in-law and his ministers and generals are getting richer and richer. It's quite obvious that his whole regime is blatantly corrupt,' said Sir Charles disgustedly.

'That worries you, sir?' Stephen raised a sardonic eyebrow.

'Corrupt *and* inefficient,' amended Curtis, unruffled. 'I may not share your particular brand of impractical idealism, Stephen, but you must not suppose me devoid of business ethics.'

'I promise you I'll make no such mistake,' said Stephen with a perfectly straight face. 'Anyway, for the record, I put my idealism – as you call it – behind me some time ago . . . So Chiang Kai-shek's regime is both corrupt and inefficient?'

'The worst possible combination. I know it's by no means the first time the British government has put money into the hands of crooks, but to subsidize a government composed of knaves *and* fools is bad business for a nation of shopkeepers,' said Sir Charles gloomily.

'What has Chiang got to recommend him, then?'

Curtis spread out his strong, stubby fingers, ticking off the points. 'One: powerful family connections, through his wife. Two: a working relationship – to put it mildly – with the Shanghai gangs and secret societies. Three: Presence. He's got the knack of treating Western journalists like scum and they usually find it impressive. Four: the gift of tongues. You and I might think his speeches sound like a poodle with hysterics, but it goes down well with his fellow-countrymen.

'As far as we're concerned, Chiang's argument is that since he's the only man prepared to fight Communism in China, the West should continue to finance his battle. But where does the money go? It certainly doesn't end up in his soldiers' pockets. Nor, in spite of repeated loans, has he managed to stamp out the handful of Communist bandits who are causing all the trouble. That's why I question whether we should agree to make this latest loan.'

Stephen regarded him thoughtfully. Ever since 1929,

when Chiang Kai-shek had risen to prominence as the leader of the Nationalist party, the Kuomintang, on the death of its founder Dr Sun Yat-sen, and had routed and massacred the Communist trade unionists who were disrupting work at Shanghai's foreign-owned factories, he had been hailed by both Britain and the United States as China's one hope of national salvation. The strong man who would lead his country out of feudal chaos into the modern world, and save her from the menace of Communism.

Chiang had promised to protect Western trade in China, and preserve the foreigners' rights to cheap labour and exemption from taxes. His popularity in the West knew no bounds. Western money poured into his coffers – and vanished.

Now here was shrewd, hard-headed Sir Charles, the least hidebound of all the Treasury advisers, questioning the whole Chiang myth. Stephen was intrigued.

'Is there any alternative to the Generalissimo, sir?'

Curtis sipped his brandy and shook his head. 'No, that's the trouble. There's half a dozen warlords of roughly equal standing, each as bad as the other. All venal, all unreliable. If I could suggest an alternative to Chiang Kai-shek I'd have a better case to put to the Treasury. As it is, I'm alone with my doubts: a voice crying out in the wilderness.'

Stephen concealed a smile. Sir Charles might regard himself as a prophet, but no one could look less like John the Baptist.

'And that, my dear boy, is where you come into it,' said his host, who had sensed, if not seen, the smile. 'I want you to go to China and find out just how matters stand. Why Chiang can't balance his books. How big the Communist threat really is. What the Japanese are up to. Will they stay in Manchuria – what do they call it now – Manchukuo? – now that their invasion has been internationally sanctioned by those damned fools at the League of Nations? Or will they try to extend their influence farther south into China? Those are the questions I want answered before we go ahead with this loan, and they're pressing for it already, so you must move as fast as you can. Say three months – all right?'

April, May, June . . . thought Stephen. The best months at Longmarsh. Three months away from Romy. Will absence make the heart grow fonder? He enjoyed these missions Sir Charles had the habit of flinging at him: like balls off a slip-catcher, he never knew what their angle of trajectory would be until they arrived. They broke the routine of office life, put him on his mettle, got the adrenalin running.

Sir Charles was already sketching out an itinerary, suggesting contacts, promising the full cooperation of his business networks.

'We'll make your visit semi-official, of course. The Chinese set a lot of store by ceremony, face . . . That way we'll ensure that you can go where you like, see what you like, ask the relevant questions. You'll be preparing a report for me to give to Sir Frederick Leith-Ross when he visits China later in the year. Doing some of the groundwork. All right? Let me know when you're ready to leave.' He added, watching Stephen carefully, 'I assume you'll take your wife, of course.'

Rumour spoke of a widening rift between Russell and his pretty young wife; hinted that he scolded her for her racing debts and made her show him all her bills. She had been seen at Wimbledon and Henley escorted by men of rather dubious reputation. There were other tales of wild parties at Longmarsh Park when Stephen was not present, and stories suggested that young Mrs Russell had been publicly cut by some of the stuffier Cotswold dowagers. Now Stephen's fractional hesitation before he answered suggested that some, at least, of this malicious gossip might be true.

'If you think it's advisable, sir.'

'I do, indeed,' said Sir Charles heartily. 'Three months is far too long to leave a pretty girl like that on her own.' He ignored Stephen's frown and signalled to a passing waiter. 'Two more brandies, please. Any idea what's going to win the Gold Cup, my boy?'

They talked racing until it was time to leave.

CHAPTER TWO

'Good morning, madam. Here's your tea.'

'Thank you, Edith.'

The print-clad maid's brisk footsteps tapped over to the window and as she pulled back the heavy velvet curtains light flooded into the high-ceilinged bedroom.

'A beautiful morning, madam.' There was a pause, then she added in an awed whisper, 'My, but it don't arf look strange out there. Whatever's the master going to say when 'e sees it?'

Rosemary Russell opened her eyes and lay for a moment wondering what she meant. Wondering, also, at the unaccustomed brightness of the sun on the ceiling. Then she remembered. Throwing back the covers she swung her legs out of bed and pattered across to stare, in her turn, out of the window.

Yes, the double hedge was gone. The dark, ancient yews which had cast their gloomy shade over this side of the house lay neatly chopped, ready for burning; their stumps like the twisted roots of wisdom teeth jumbled into a great heap to one side of the lawn, with only the scarred turf to show where the hedge had been. How different it looked without it! How magically improved the view across the park, the broodmares grazing amid stately oaks, chestnuts just coming into leaf, and the Guernsey herd like yellow toys, placidly chewing the cud against a backdrop of misty, undulating hills. Romy gave a sigh of satisfaction which was only faintly marred by a tingle of apprehension. '*Whatever's the master going to say when he sees it?*'

He'll be pleased, of course, she told herself stoutly. He's sure to be pleased to find me taking an interest in the home he loves so much, and trying to improve the garden which has been neglected since his father's death. Sir James had been an enthusiastic gardener, but since his death old Carson and his underlings had been allowed to carry on in their old-fashioned ways – which was all very well as far as the glasshouses and vegetable garden were concerned, but sadly lacking in imagination when it came to the flower-beds.

Romy had disliked the yew hedge ever since she first set eyes on it, but it was only a few days ago when Josephine, the cook's four-year-old daughter, had made herself seriously ill by eating the attractive scarlet berries, that her determination to have it removed suddenly crystallized. In her mind's eye she saw how beautiful it could be: the dark old trees rooted out and replaced with massed roses; a lilypond full of fat goldfish; a sun-dial . . . Impulsively, she had given the orders, overridden Carson's loudly-expressed disapproval and supervised the work herself even though it meant cancelling a luncheon party.

Perhaps, she thought belatedly, she should have waited for Stephen's approval. He had been away in Frankfurt and Paris and was not expected home for another three days. By then the matter would have seemed less urgent, her vision would have become stale and tarnished, the impetus lost. Besides, if her roses were to bloom this year there was no time to waste. She had called in men from the village, who were always glad of a few extra shillings in these days of depressed agricultural prices, and set them to dig the lily-pond. Once they understood what she wanted, they had worked with a will. When Stephen returned the bones of the scheme would be visible. He would not – could not – disapprove . . .

All the same, apprehension would not entirely leave her despite her reasoning, and when she heard the scrunch of wheels on gravel, just as she finished dressing, she felt a lurch of the heart which was far from being the joyful anticipation of a bride about to greet her returning husband. Oh no! she thought. Not before I'm ready and the mess is cleared away. He's so often late, why did he have to choose today of all days to turn up early?

She hurried to the landing and looked out over the gravel sweep. Sure enough, Stephen's dark green Lagonda stood before the front door and Baynes, the butler, was taking suitcases from the boot. Romy hastily smoothed her hair and went down the handsome, polished, staircase, wondering how she could prevent him from seeing the hedge before she had judged his mood. He must have left London at cock-crow to get here before nine o'clock.

'Darling! What a lovely surprise. We weren't expecting you until Saturday.'

At the sound of her voice he swung round, dropping the coat he was carrying over a chair, and his long-featured face, solemn to the point of severity when in repose, broke into its charming smile. He crossed the hall quickly, the stiffness in his left knee slightly more pronounced than usual after his long car journey. He kissed her lightly on the mouth.

'Good morning, my sweet. Nice to find you're up already. I would have telephoned to warn you I was on my way if I'd had any hope that Mrs Honeyball would be manning the exchange before dawn. As it was, I drove down without stopping.'

'Heavens, you'll be starving! Come and have something to eat.' She tried to deflect him into the breakfast room where the parlourmaids were placing covered silver dishes of bacon, grilled kidneys, and scrambled eggs on the hotplate; but he turned aside towards the library whose windows overlooked the lawn.

'One minute – I'll just put these papers on my desk. My God! Those can't *all* be bills. I thought I told you not to . . .' His voice died away and she heard a gasp, followed by nerve-tingling silence. Her heart sank. He'd seen it. All her apprehension rushed back. She should have waited . . . She should have asked him first . . .

'Come here a moment, Romy.'

Reluctantly she crossed into the library. Stephen was standing by the window, his face very pale. There was an ominous bulge of muscle in his jaw and his fists were clenched tight as if he was restraining some inner violence with difficulty.

'Would you mind explaining,' he said in a hard, controlled tone she'd never heard him use before, 'what has happened to the yew walk?'

'Oh . . . The hedge. I – I had it cut down.' Try as she might to speak confidently, the tremor in her voice betrayed her. He looked so angry. The grey eyes which a moment before had smiled into hers had turned to cold steel, bleak as a December sky. She knew she'd made a terrible mistake.

'I can see that. And what were your reasons for this act of vandalism?'

'It used to make the house so dark.' Even to her own ears the explanation sounded woefully inadequate. 'I wanted to plant a rose garden there. It was going to be a surprise for you,' she faltered, wishing her voice wouldn't shake so. She wasn't afraid of him. It was her garden as well as his. Why shouldn't she shape it as she liked?

'A surprise? Then I congratulate you on your success,' he said bitingly. 'You've succeeded admirably. I'm more than surprised. I'm astonished – *astounded* that you could destroy something that's survived for hundreds of years for the sake of a passing whim. Don't you realize those yews were famous? That they were older than the house itself? I suppose it doesn't interest you that they're mentioned in William de Clifford's *Curiosities of Gloster*, which was written years before Longmarsh Park was built? And you – you've gone and pulled them up like a row of nettles because you imagine they make the house dark!'

Guiltily she remembered Carson's protest when she told him to cut them down: 'They do be powerful old, them yews be, so they do say,' and her own quick rejoinder, 'Being old doesn't make them beautiful, Carson, and remember they nearly killed little Josephine. I'd like the job finished before tonight.'

With relief she remembered Josephine's narrow escape. Surely Stephen would understand why the yews had to go?

'Stephen, will you listen to me?' she said urgently. 'It wasn't only because they were dark. That hedge was dangerous. Little Josephine ate some of the berries on Wednesday and she very nearly died.'

He looked at her blankly. 'Josephine? Who's she?'

'You know – Mrs Cook's little girl. The one with curly hair. She picked a bowl of the berries and ate them. It might have happened again. You weren't there to ask, so I decided to get rid of it right away before there was a tragedy.'

'What nonsense,' said Stephen harshly. 'You're simply using that as an excuse. The cook's child had no business to be playing in front of the house anyway.'

'I can't help that,' Romy flared, suddenly angry in her turn. 'Children aren't machines, you know, to be parked where you want them. Besides, it could have been any other child. Sybil's, for instance – your own nephews and nieces.'

'At least it couldn't be one of ours,' said Stephen flatly.

Romy flushed. 'I'm thankful we had no child of our own to play there while that evil growth was in the garden. All right! I'm sorry I didn't ask you first, but I'm not sorry it's gone.'

'It'll have to be replanted, of course.'

She stared at him but his face was unyielding. 'What about my rose garden?'

'What's wrong with the existing rose garden? Why do you want to change everything? When I come home I don't know what new outrage I'm going to find, just because of your mania for alteration. Why can't you leave things alone?'

So all her efforts to beautify Longmarsh had been in vain. Stephen would prefer her to leave it exactly as she had found it, ensuring that no trace of her personality would linger in the old rooms that had housed so many generations of Russells. Tears welled up in Romy's eyes.

'Because this is your home, not mine,' she cried. 'I don't belong here in this great gloomy house and you won't let me make any bit of it my own, not even the garden. How do you think I like living in your family museum and being told I can't shift a chair or a stick of furniture from where they stood in your grandmother's day? I hate Longmarsh and I hate England, and I wish I'd never married you.'

She spun on her heel and ran from the room, blinded by tears, oblivious to the curious glances of the parlourmaids. Slamming the door of her bedroom, she flung herself down on the unmade bed and buried her face in the pillow. The toils and anticipation of the last few days had been wasted – worse than wasted. Instead of being surprised and pleased by her endeavours, Stephen had been coldly furious. He was a heartless, hidebound, double-faced Englishman, just as Mairead had warned her. Oh, why hadn't she listened to Mairead?

Romy now remembered her sister's warning more clearly than her mother's fulsome delight over the announcement of Romy's engagement to the brilliant young banker Stephen Russell, who had come to Ireland to buy horses and remained to court her younger daughter.

'You know nothing of the man,' Mairead had said slowly, putting her hand against the small of her back as if it ached. 'Oh, he's a fine handsome fellow, I won't deny, and he's the money to give you all you want, but what do you know of him when he's home by the fire? Will you really be happy to leave your home for a man who's a stranger to you?'

'Ah, he loves me. What more do you want?' said Romy impatiently. Poor Mairead, with three children at her skirts and another on the way, you'd think she'd be glad to have her sister marry a man who could give them all a helping hand from time to time. But no, it was Mairead's nature to look for troubles even when they weren't there.

'There's plenty others that love you nearer at hand,' urged her sister. 'Take Jamesy Corcoran, now. He's a good lad and set to inherit his uncle's land at Ballyhinch. Why won't you settle for him?'

'Jamesy Corcoran!' laughed Romy. The idea of turning down her glamorous Englishman for a red-faced hobbledehoy with no interest beyond the price of cattle and the racing results was quite absurd.

'Then Cathal O'Reilly?' persisted Mairead. 'If it's brains you're looking for, Cathal's your man. You know he'd come running were you just to snap your fingers. He'd make you happy, I know. Haven't the English done Ireland enough harm without stealing you from us as well?'

'Is that your grudge against Stephen?' said Romy, her face clearing.

'It is, of course.'

'That he's English? Isn't your own mother English? Aren't you half English yourself?'

'It is my sorrow,' said Mairead, and Romy couldn't help laughing. Mairead was forever singing of Ireland's past glories and imagining herself the fiercest of Republicans, when the truth was she was much too timid to harm a fly.

'You can laugh now,' said her sister, 'but wait till you find I'm right. Haven't you heard how her English family tormented the life out of Mother when she told them she was to marry Father?'

'Their tormenting didn't stop Mother and yours won't stop me,' said Romy, still laughing. 'Come now, Mairead, won't you wish me happy instead of croaking disaster like an old crow?'

'I will, of course.' Mairead still sounded doubtful.

'Then I shall be! I'll marry Stephen and live happy ever after, and you shall come to stay in my great house and have servants to wait on you hand and foot,' cried Romy extravagantly, trying to bring a smile to her sister's solemn face. 'I shall wear dresses of silk and satin and eat off gold plate. What's more,' she added with a glance at Mairead's enlarged waistline, 'I'll take good care I don't have a single child before I'm thirty years old. The London doctors are wonderful, so they say.'

At that Mairead had clapped her hands over her ears, begging the saints not to listen to such wickedness; and Romy went blithely on her way, her head full of dreams . . .

Now, lying on the bed in silent misery as her sobs died away, she wondered if her sister was gifted with second sight. Far from living happy ever after, she was acutely aware that as mistress of Longmarsh Park and wife to Stephen she was a failure. Only in bed – and not always even there – could she satisfy or understand her husband. The daytime Stephen – formal, remote, immersed in business matters – was a stranger, utterly different from the laughing debonair sportsman to whom she had given her heart. What had gone wrong between them to make him change so?

She painfully remembered those carefree gold-and-silver days when Stephen had courted her. Sun-dappled days walking on Slievekimalta, with the fertile Shannon valley spread like exquisite patchwork below them; silver nights on quiet Lough Derg, when they'd slipped away from the midnight boating party. Days in the rain at sales and fairs, frosty days following hounds when the banks looked big and black between the horse's pricked ears. She was overwhelmed by a sharp sense of loss; a longing for home so acute that it made her physically sick.

She came to a sudden decision. She would go home to Tipperary. She didn't belong here and never would. Stephen didn't love her. He would be angry at first, no doubt, but eventually he'd see that she had done the right thing. She would pack and go quickly, before she was tempted to change her mind, before anyone tried to talk her out of it.

She hastily dragged a suitcase from the cupboard and pulled open drawers. Heavens, what a lot of clothes! She would have to take what she needed most and wait for the rest to follow.

But before the suitcase was half-filled, misery overwhelmed her again and she lay down in the comforting dark of the curtained four-poster bed, silently crying for the wreck of all her dreams.

Stephen, who heartily disliked displays of temperament, calculated that his wife would need twenty minutes in which to run through her repertoire of emotion – anger, self-pity, remorse – and reach a frame of mind in which they could converse like reasonable beings. He filled in the time by munching his way doggedly through a selection of the contents of the covered silver dishes on the hotplate, more in the manner of a man stoking a fire than of one enjoying an excellent breakfast. He realized that a sleepless night and empty stomach must have contributed to his uncharacteristic loss of self-control over the despoliation of the yew walk. Rarely did he allow himself to express his anger so openly. Ever since he had half-strangled a bully at school and seen him carried off, white and limp, to the sanatorium, he had been wary of allowing his feelings to get the upper hand, no matter how severe the provocation. Instead he fought with tongue and brain; few people ever guessed at the depth of emotion beneath his carefully controlled facade.

As he munched, he considered the problem of Romy. It was no good telling himself now that he'd been a fool to marry her. He had allowed his all too susceptible heart to rule his head – with the usual unfortunate consequences. He knew he should never have attempted to prolong the romantic idyll which began when he asked Jonjo O'Halloran, Romy's brother, to find him a horse that would jump round Aintree. He ought to have realized that a wild flower which flourished on the Tipperary mountains would not transplant successfully into a formal herbaceous border. But from his first glimpse of Romy in the pouring rain at Ballinasloe Horse Fair, flying over brush-filled dykes on a wild-eyed leggy three-year-old watched by a knot of gaitered horse-dealers – tangled curls streaming down her back, improbable oaths punctuated by bursts of laughter on her lips, her whole vivid, pointed face alight with the sheer physical pleasure of the struggle – he had fallen helplessly under her spell.

In the dark of the bedroom the spell persisted, but he knew now that he shouldn't have hoped to force her into a mould she could not fit. Ordering the life of a big country house, directing servants, calling on neighbours, organizing charity dances were activities that bored and stifled her, and she had not hesitated to show her distaste for them. When he held her warm, lithe body in his arms he could forget her deficiencies as mistress of Longmarsh. One could not, he reasoned, have everything. One could not expect one's wife to be a wanton at night and a bluestocking by day. Romy was beautiful, warm-hearted, generous: the fact that she was also extravagant, thoughtless and emotional was simply the other side of the coin.

But dared he leave someone so extravagant and reckless in sole charge of his ancestral home for three long months? Despite Sir Charles' veiled instruction to take her with him, Stephen would have preferred to go to China alone. He could undoubtedly concentrate better without Romy's distracting presence. But if he did, what might he not find on his return? Stephen thought of the yew walk and shuddered.

Resignedly, he fetched the week's harvest of bills from the library and whistled softly as he totted them up. The dressmaker's account alone would have kept four families in meat for a month. His wife appeared to have had a successful race-meeting at Cheltenham, but her winnings there did not cover her dramatic losses at Towcester the previous week, when one of her brother's slowest horses had made its first appearance on a racecourse.

The twenty minutes were up. Stephen shoved the bills aside, folded his napkin and pushed back his chair. He went upstairs to the bedroom.

'Go away,' said Romy in a muffled voice from within the four-poster's drawn curtains.

Stephen stood his ground. 'I want to talk to you.'

'Well, I don't want to talk to *you*. Please go away,' she said, her voice still unsteady.

Evidently he had underestimated the time element. He considered returning for a last slice of toast and marmalade but decided there was no real point in delaying the confrontation any longer. Things could not go on like this. Something had to be done before he left for China. He surveyed the disordered room. A large leather suitcase lay open at the foot of the bed, half-full of clothes and cosmetics, flung in higgledy-piggledy with no respect for shape or texture. Every flat surface was piled with dresses, coats, underclothes and shoes which she had evidently dragged from their cupboards in her first burst of indignation. His tidy mind was offended.

Automatically he began to sort the jumbled contents of the case, putting trees into the shoes before laying them neatly heel-to-toe in the bottom, folding jackets and coats inside-out, sleeves crossed, smoothing skirts so that the pleats lay flat.

'What are you doing?' demanded Romy. He glanced up from his work. Her disembodied head peered through a gap in the curtains like a trophy displayed on a gunroom wall. A very pretty trophy, he thought, with the catch in his breath that her beauty always produced. It was his weakness, his Achilles heel. Short dark curls, cut by a master hand, clustered round her face with its wide cheekbones and pointed chin. Her amber eyes, now somewhat pink and puffy about the lids, were fringed with thick curling lashes and set beneath dramatically slanted brows. They regarded him with suspicion.

'As you can see, I'm sorting out your packing. By the way, this is my favourite suitcase. I hope you're not planning to run off with it, because I'm going to need it myself.'

'You can have it back,' she said, sniffing and searching her pockets in vain. Silently, he handed her a clean handkerchief.

'Are you planning to be away for long?' he asked politely.

Romy gulped. 'I'm going away for ever. I'm leaving you. I can't stand it here any longer. I'm going back home where I belong.'

'You mean you're running away just because I was angry about the yew walk? Isn't that rather excessive?'

She caught the mockery in his tone and reddened. Trust Stephen to strip all the drama from her gesture and make it seem silly and trivial.

'It's not only because of the yew hedge – you know it as well as I do,' she muttered.

'Then what is it? Stop peering through those curtains like a Cheshire cat and tell me all about it.'

Invited to put her grievances into words, she found it almost impossible. 'Oh, it's everything! Don't pretend you don't know it too. Nothing I ever do is right. I try to please you and you accuse me of ruining your home. I don't belong here and never shall so it's no good trying any longer. I can't even give a party without every busybody in the county telling me it's not the kind of entertainment they're used to at Longmarsh. This house stifles me, Stephen. Everything I do is watched and criticized – by you, by the servants, by all those nosy interfering neighbours, and you're never here when I need your help. When I thought you loved me I didn't mind people talking about me behind my back, but now I know you don't . . .' Her voice broke and she scrubbed fiercely at her eyes. 'Damn you, go away. Leave my clothes alone. Can't I have even a moment's peace?'

'Stop it, Romy,' he said sharply. 'Stop making a scene out of nothing.'

'Oh, it's nothing to you, of course. You don't care if I'm miserable. You don't love me.'

However absurd her accusations and inappropriate the hour, he was touched by her genuine unhappiness. There was only one sure way to comfort her; talking would merely exacerbate the situation. Pulling back the curtains he took her in his arms, but to his surprise she resisted him. When he tried to kiss her she turned her head away.

'Romy, look at me,' he said wearily. 'You know you don't mean it. Of course I love you, my darling.'

She continued to struggle, refusing to meet his eyes, and in an effort to calm her, he gripped her shoulders rather harder than he had intended.

She gave a gasp of pain, twisted violently from his grasp, and reached for the bell-push. The bedside lamp went over with a crash.

'Stop it, Stephen! I'm not in the mood. You needn't think you can make me change my mind just by . . . Oh!'

'You rang for me, madam?' said Edith, who must have been very near at hand. Her sharp dark eyes took in the scene with avidity. The master and mistress struggling on the unmade bed in broad daylight! Whatever were things coming to? She could hardly wait to relay the news to the servants' hall.

Stephen cursed under his breath and hastily released his wife.

'Yes, I did. I want you to pack my clothes,' said Romy with a defiant glance at him. '*All* my clothes.'

'Now, madam?' Edith's curiosity was almost palpable.

'Good idea,' said Stephen, quickly recovering his self-control. 'But you'll hardly need all those thick tweeds, darling. Shanghai's pretty hot, you know, even in April.'

Romy and the maid stared at him in complete bewilderment.

'*Shanghai?* What on earth are you talking about?'

'Didn't I explain? I thought when I found you busy packing that you must have anticipated my news in some mysterious way,' he said coolly.

'What news?'

Stephen said deliberately, 'Sir Charles is sending me to China for a few months. It's a business trip, but he was anxious that you should have the chance to come too – that is, if you can spare the time.' His eyes met hers with a definite challenge. 'Will you come? Or would you rather pay a nice long visit to your family in Ireland while I'm away?'

He was offering her a choice, she realized confusedly. Come to China with me and forget this nonsense about leaving. Or go home and admit that your marriage is a failure. It's up to you.

This time she must make the right decision. Silence stretched out between them as she struggled to gauge what Stephen really wanted. His expression remained polite, attentive, unreadable; his grey eyes as blank as a poker player's.

'It's entirely up to you,' he said aloud.

'Then I'd like to come to China,' said Romy slowly.

He did not move, but she felt the tension in him ease, as if every muscle held rigidly at attention had been allowed to relax. With relief, or disappointment? She couldn't tell.

'Good,' said Stephen briskly. 'At least that's settled then.'

But he did not smile and as he left the room she realized that she still had no idea if she'd made the right decision.

CHAPTER THREE

Romy watched the American couple whirling like moths on the moonlit afterdeck and wished that Stephen enjoyed dancing. It was their last evening aboard the battered old *Empire Queen* and the band was playing with an air of determined gaiety. In deference to the occasion, Stephen had risen twice since dinner, to trundle her briefly on a few circuits of the small square of polished boards before returning with ill-concealed relief to their table where stout Mr Sanyato, flown with fizzy lemonade, was discoursing endlessly on the benefits to China of the Japanese occupation of Manchuria.

'Never before these poor mens have justice, security, full employment!' he cried, crescents of brown eye gleaming behind his gold-rimmed glasses.

'How very interesting. Tell me, how have you managed it?' encouraged Stephen. Romy couldn't really believe that he was interested in Mr Sanyato's monotonous staccato explanations; no doubt, she thought ruefully, he was using it as an excuse not to dance again. The *Empire Queen*, now in her twentieth year of plying across the Pacific from Shanghai to San Francisco and back again, had smoke-blackened funnels and evil-smelling bilges; she was a very different ship from the splendid *Aquitania* in which they had crossed the Atlantic, and was moreover, half-empty. There always seemed to be more stewards than passengers in the dingy saloon. Apart from Mr Sanyato and his colleagues, sallow bespectacled businessmen who held sheafs of papers in their neat brown paws as they ate silent, solitary meals, there were a few elderly American missionaries, clinging together in woeful anticipation of the lonely years ahead of them; Daisy Cummings, a self-possessed English nine-year-old, travelling to Shanghai to join her parents, and a fistful of old China Hands with yellow faces and loud voices, who commandeered the canvas chairs on the sun-deck and waited like spiders to ensnare newcomers with their interminable stories.

'Now, even, they have their own Manchu emperor,' announced Mr Sanyato.

'Amazing,' murmured Stephen.

Romy closed her ears to their talk. She propped her chin on her hand and concentrated on the American couple. At least they were worth watching.

They had boarded the *Empire Queen* at Yokohama and gone straight below to their cabin. Although she had not yet had a chance to scrape an acquaintance with either of them, the omniscient steward had provided Romy with a certain amount of information.

They were Mr and Mrs Eugene Lyon, recently married in San Francisco. They had spent their honeymoon in Japan and were now returning to Shanghai where Mr Lyon worked as a reporter for a West Coast news agency. Mrs

Lyon, added the steward in awed tones, was the only daughter of a millionaire.

'Are you sure? I thought they'd all vanished in the Wall Street crash.'

'Oh no, madam. Mrs Lyon's father is in the automobile business, I understand. Nothing to do with Wall Street.'

'That must be a relief . . .'

Millionaire's daughter or not, the girl was certainly beautiful: a long-legged, slender, ash-blonde whose shining shoulder-length hair, cut straight in a fringe across her forehead, swung out behind her like a silver bell as she whirled and spun on impossibly high thin heels. Her dress was a drift of pale chiffon, cut daringly low in front to display tanned shoulders, and cinched with a wide belt of half-pearls which gleamed softly in the moonlight. Her pale, luminous face was raised towards her partner, eyes half-closed and lips parted in an expression of rapture. Romy, searching for flaws, decided she was wearing too dark a shade of lipstick. It over-emphasized her rather thin mouth, with its slightly petulant droop. Her hands, too, looked predatory, their painted nails dark against her husband's linen jacket.

Romy turned her attention to Mr Lyon. Viewed from the back he was broad-shouldered and narrow-hipped, graceful and quick-moving in a way that hinted at Latin blood. His thick dark hair was an inch or two longer than fashion dictated, nearly meeting his collar, and his method of holding his partner clamped against him, with one hand pressed to her breast and the other low on her spine would not, thought Romy with an inward chuckle, have found favour with the Cotswold dowagers.

Indeed, she was even a little shocked herself. There was something disturbingly sensual in his attitude and the couple's complete absorption in one another. She felt obscurely that such obvious physical pleasure belonged behind closed doors; but despite her uneasiness on this score she found it hard to take her eyes from them. The man's face was shadowed as he bent over his partner, but as they turned again she had a clear glimpse of a hard dark profile, olive-skinned, with a strong curved nose, a lean jaw, and eyebrows so straight and black they were like a pencil-stroke ruled across his forehead, guarding the shadowed eyes beneath. Idly, she wondered what colour his eyes would be.

As if aware of her scrutiny, Lyon glanced up swiftly and caught her fascinated stare. At once he smiled, his teeth white and even against the olive skin. Romy blushed and quickly looked away, as if surprised in some faintly dishonourable act. Though why I shouldn't watch them I don't know, she thought, ruffled. There's nothing else to look at.

She bent to pick up her bag from beneath the table and touched Stephen's arm.

'I think I'll go to bed now, darling. We dock at nine tomorrow and I haven't even begun to pack.'

'All right. I won't be long.'

'Good night, Mr Sanyato.'

The Japanese rose and bowed. 'It has been a pleasure to talk with you,' he said earnestly, though she had not addressed more than two remarks to him all evening.

'Just a moment,' said Stephen, staring over her shoulder. 'I think someone wants a word with you.'

She turned. The American couple had left the floor and were approaching their table. The blonde girl held out her hand in an easy, impulsive gesture.

'You must be Mr and Mrs Russell,' she said in a bright, sociable voice. 'We saw your names on the passenger list and came over to make your acquaintance. You don't mind, I hope? I'm Linda Lyon, and this is my husband, Eugene.'

They shook hands all round.

'Will you join us for a drink, Mrs Lyon?' Stephen skilfully caught the eye of a passing waiter.

'Why, that's very kind of you,' said Mrs Lyon, promptly seating herself between Stephen and Mr Sanyato. More slowly, her husband took the empty chair opposite Romy, with his back to the dancefloor lights. She could not see the expression on his face, but the set of his shoulders suggested a certain reluctance to contribute to a cosy foursome. She guessed that his wife had dragged him over against his will.

Seen at close quarters, Mrs Lyon was even more striking

in appearance than Romy had supposed. She had fine grey eyes and regular Nordic features marred only by the slightly receding chin and a mouth whose lower lip curved downward with a suggestion of petulance. Her manner was effusive; her conversation directed specifically at Stephen.

'Are you staying long in Shanghai, Mr Russell? Is it your first visit? Then we're all in the same boat . . .' they laughed politely, 'except for Gene. He was born in China, so this is kind of a homecoming for him, strange as it seems. Tell me, is it business or pleasure that brings you out East?'

It was impossible not to admire Stephen's skill in deflecting her questions without giving offence or arousing further unwelcome curiosity, thought Romy. He and Mrs Lyon settled down to sound one another out, but she was no match for Stephen. Within a few minutes he had extracted from her all the information the steward had given Romy, and added an intriguing new slant. Linda Lyon, the millionaire's daughter, was not at all pleased that her brand new husband had been assigned to the agency's Shanghai office.

'I hoped we'd be given Paris,' she complained. 'I just love Paris – and your country, too. Europe is so exciting and I have so many friends in England. All those quaint old houses are just adorable. Architecture is a very special interest of mine. Are you a Londoner, Mr Russell?'

Mention of Longmarsh Park introduced a new dimension to their conversation. Mrs Lyon had seen photographs of the house and gardens in her book on Georgian architecture. She became respectfully rapturous, plainly angling for an invitation to visit what she described as 'that lovely, gracious dwelling' some time in the future. Despite her hectic manner, her interest seemed perfectly genuine and she clearly knew what she was talking about. *She* wouldn't have hacked down the famous yew walk, thought Romy with a small pang. She's just the kind of woman Stephen should have married: knowledgeable, with instinctive taste, someone who would appreciate Longmarsh instead of wanting to put a match to it.

Listening with half an ear, she was acutely aware of Mr Lyon's brooding presence opposite. He, too, was watching his wife, gripped by some strong emotion Romy could not identify. Bafflement, anger, reluctant admiration – or a blend of all three? From time to time Linda Lyon darted him a glance as if to say, 'You see? This is my world, not yours. Now it's your turn to watch and admire.'

To Romy's surprise, she realized that Stephen was deliberately abetting the performance, putting in a question here and a comment there in order to provoke further flights of cultural virtuosity. Romy felt oddly uncomfortable, as if the Lyons had chosen to sit with them in order to have neutral witnesses to their private battle.

'Do you share your wife's interest, Mr Lyon?' she asked in an effort to include him in the conversation.

He switched his attention to her with a look as surprised as if a doll had spoken. 'Do I . . . ? Excuse me! No, I can't say I do. I've led kind of a wandering life and old houses don't mean much to me. I guess I've always preferred people to objects.'

'I quite understand. I feel the same. Where do you come from, then?'

'Oh, my family always moved around. I spent most of my childhood in China before my parents bought a ranch in Colorado.'

'Oh, how lovely! I've always wanted to live on a ranch.'

'You have?'

She sensed a tinge of mockery in his tone and added quickly, 'It must be such a wonderful place to bring up a family.'

'My mother didn't think so. She claimed the ranch cost the lives of her two daughters,' he said sombrely. 'She was glad when Pa decided to move back into town.'

If he's going to disagree with everything I say, this conversation is doomed, thought Romy. How could I have known about his unfortunate sisters? The band was playing again, and once more Mr Lyon looked down the table to where his wife sat absorbed – or pretending to be absorbed – in what Stephen had to say. Something in the tilt of her head and the pitch of her voice gave Romy the distinct impression that she was intent on baiting her husband.

'May I have the pleasure?' he asked Romy unexpectedly.

She hesitated. Although she'd longed all evening for an

invitation to dance, she found herself curiously reluctant to leave the safe, if dull, haven of the supper table for the uncharted sea of the tiny dancefloor. She remembered the way he had held his wife: sensual, dominating, unaccountably disturbing.

'Come on,' he urged.

Across the table Stephen gave an almost imperceptible nod of encouragement without appearing to divert his attention from Mrs Lyon for a single instant.

'Take Nôtre Dame,' she was saying earnestly. 'The apotheosis of the perpendicular . . .'

Romy wondered if she might have a drop taken – or more than a drop – but her speech was clear enough and you wouldn't choose words like 'apotheosis', whatever that meant, if you weren't sure of getting them out in one piece.

Mr Lyon was still waiting. 'Thank you,' said Romy, 'I'd love to dance,' and tried not to flinch as his hard brown hand closed over her bare elbow to steer her towards the band.

'What did you make of that chap?' Stephen asked later as they prepared for bed. 'He looks a pretty tough customer.'

'Oh, he was all right. Quiet. We didn't talk much,' said Romy carefully. It was true as far as it went. There was no need for her to confess to the purely physical thrill of those moments in his arms, when all her pent-up energy and frustration found expression in one glorious burst of rhythm and speed that left her as breathless and relaxed as after making love. Stephen wouldn't understand. He might even feel there was something faintly disloyal in her enthusiasm.

'Quiet! You couldn't say the same for his wife,' exclaimed Stephen with unusual asperity. 'I felt all the time that she was putting on an act just to annoy him.'

'How strange – so did I.'

He said rather apologetically, 'I thought it would be best to give her her head to see if I couldn't defuse the situation. I'm not sure now that I was right. She wasn't at all pleased when he took you off to dance, and began telling me things she ought to have kept to herself.'

Romy was intrigued. 'What kind of things?' she said, turning away from the dressing-table mirror.

'Oh, she talked a lot of rot about how her husband hadn't any ambition and shouldn't have let himself be fobbed off with a posting to Shanghai, when there was a plum job in Paris he could have had for the asking. How she was getting her father to use his influence to have their posting changed. All rather embarrassing, but once she'd got the bit between her teeth I couldn't stop her.'

Romy smiled. 'You shouldn't be such a good listener! People always want to tell you their secrets.'

'Oh, rubbish! She kept saying she had to *drive* him if he was to get anywhere. The odd thing is, he doesn't look a chap who'd take kindly to being driven.'

'No,' she agreed. 'He doesn't.' She wished Stephen would stop discussing the Lyons. She didn't want to be reminded of that dark, intense gaze holding her spellbound as they spun and reversed, nor the immediate understanding she'd felt for his hard, muscular body.

'I must say, when you watch him you realize there's a good deal more to dancing than simply shuffling from one foot to the other as so many of us do,' said Stephen. Although he spoke casually, even admiringly, her senses were instantly alert. He knew. He had been watching every move she made, and his uncanny instinct had told him what she wouldn't admit even to herself – that she found the big dark American disturbingly attractive.

It didn't matter, though. The voyage was almost over. Once they docked in Shanghai there was no reason for her to have any further contact with Mr or Mrs Eugene Lyon.

'Good night, darling,' she said, snuggling under the bedclothes and turning out the light, and wondered at her sense of relief when he kissed her briefly and rolled into his own bunk without another word.

CHAPTER FOUR

Shanghai

Ugly girls often improve with age, and Abigail Bentley was living proof of this axiom. Plain and raw-boned as a girl, gawky in her 'teens, she'd been a lantern-jawed woman of thirty, whose parents had long given up hope of seeing her marry, when a chance meeting on the Welsh hills with Alexander Bentley, a silver-haired executive of the Standard Oil Company in China – twice married, twice widowed, and more than twice her age – seemed to offer a glimpse of glamour and adventure.

She seized her chance without hesitating. She accepted Mr Bentley's proposal of marriage, somewhat to the chagrin of her sisters, who thought the services of a maiden aunt were theirs for life, and travelled with him to China. They settled in Shanghai and she soon very happily adapted to living in his airy Chinese house, with its four courtyards and willow-fringed lilypools on the edge of the International Settlement.

When Alexander Bentley died seven years later, leaving her the house and a comfortable income, Abigail rejected suggestions that she should return to England and spend her declining years as dogsbody to her sisters and their children.

'My home is in China, and that is where I am going to stay,' she told them firmly, and no protests could make her change her mind.

She was now in her early fifties. The formidable hook nose and long, narrow jaw which had intimidated so many young men who might otherwise have kissed her had been subtly softened by the years and now looked distinguished, rather than forbidding. Her black hair was thickly streaked with grey, but her large lustrous eyes, always her best feature, still sparkled with the enthusiasm of a schoolgirl.

Her restless energy and passion for fast walking, despite the heavy humidity of Shanghai's climate, ensured that her tall, bony body suffered no hint of middle-aged spread. Since the death of her husband, her interest in Chinese affairs had begun to take a more political turn. When British troops were ordered to break the seamen's strike in Shanghai she unhesitatingly chose the side of the underdog, and several noted Chinese trade union leaders on whom the police of the International Settlement would have liked to lay their hands slipped instead through their fingers.

From that day on, Abigail Bentley's rambling home on Nanking Road became known as a safe house for political refugees. The International police suspected as much, but had never managed to prove their suspicions. During the bloody days and nights of Chiang Kai-shek's bid to exterminate the Shanghai Communists, more and more desperate men and women, fleeing for their lives before the right wing troops, scratched softly on the side door in the courtyard, where one-eyed Li Ping, Abigail's trusted 'boy' kept vigil – and were admitted to safety. Even the Generalissimo's police had no right to enter the International Settlement and question a lady with so many distinguished friends as the widowed Mrs Bentley.

Smuggling political refugees out of the city, and setting them on their way to join other survivors of Chiang Kai-shek's purges in the remote mountainous area round Chingkangshan, provided Abigail with the spice of excitement her life had previously lacked. Her dusty little black Ford car was a familiar sight as it bumped through villages on the outskirts of the city, on her way to intercept the Yangtze ferries at minor staging posts upriver, where fewer questions were likely to be asked. Abigail's well-known enthusiasm for archaeology stood her in good stead, and no one in authority ever suspected how often the tools of her hobby – old-fashioned cone-shaped baskets, camera cases, picks, shovels and boxes of photographic plates – were superimposed on the huddled figure of a refugee as the laden car chugged slowly along the dusty roads. Li Ping was adept at developing and printing the large, old-fashioned plates which were welcomed by reputable periodicals such as the *Illustrated London News* and the *National Geographical*; and if he sometimes printed copies of Red propaganda leaflets as well as archaeological curiosities, no one except his mistress was any the wiser.

Mrs Bentley's clandestine political activities (of which he was perfectly unaware) were not, of course, mentioned by Michael Holmes, the deferential young area manager from the Hong Kong and Shanghai Banking Corporation who had been detailed to greet Mr and Mrs Russell off their ship.

As his black, chauffeur-driven car crawled along the noisy crowded *Bund* beside the Pearl River estuary, he sat between them on the luxuriously padded, dark-curtained back seat and explained why it had been decided to lodge them with Mrs Bentley instead of booking rooms in one of the big hotels.

'We've had bad reports of hotel service lately, I'm afraid,' he said apologetically. 'There's still a good deal of resentment against foreigners, especially since the Japanese invasion of Manchuria, and the Bolshy element in Shanghai exploits this for all it's worth. I'm told that some of the room-boys are very surly and insolent nowadays, as well as being bone-idle. We didn't want you to experience that kind of unpleasantness, so we asked Mrs Bentley if she could take you, and she was delighted. I'm sure you'll be very comfortable. She's been here so long she's almost an institution in Shanghai. Knows everyone, speaks the lingo . . . She's got a lovely old Chinese house with several courtyards, pools, terraces, lots of flowers. Most attractive and ideal for the climate, you know. She says it's far too big for a woman on her own – did I tell you she's a widow? – so she occasionally takes in lodgers, more for the company than the cash, if you ask me. She's quite an expert on Chinese archaeology, too, though not in the same class as her late husband.'

'Alexander Bentley – of course!' Stephen snapped his fingers. 'I thought I knew the name.'

'Have you read any of his work? It's a bit dry for me,' confessed young Mr Holmes. 'I can work up an interest in the Ming and the Song, all right, but when you get back to the Han dynasty, over two thousand years ago, I'm afraid I go a bit blank.'

Romy stared out of the window, listening with half an ear. All she knew about the Ming, the Song and the Han dynasties could be written on a postage stamp and she felt little inclination to extend her knowledge. Night had fallen an hour before they docked, but the swarming streets of the International Settlement were brilliant with colour and bright as day. Flaring torches, paper lanterns and modern neon signs flickered and glowed. It was raining, a heavy warm enervating drizzle more like a vapour bath than real rain, and the slick black tarmac reflected pinpoints of dazzle from the winking shop windows and silver-gilt Chinese characters on flapping banners hung over the steets.

Hot oil and garlic mingled with petrol fumes and excrement in a throat-catching, entirely alien blend of smells; and the shrill chatter of Chinese shoppers combined with bells, gongs, rattles, blaring car horns and the strident cries of rickshaw coolies to assault the ears. Romy wound down the car window and stared at the crowd, half-frightened, half-exhilarated by the strangeness of it all. Here and there, the broad shoulders and white linen suit of a European stood out of the throng, but these were rare. Chinese faces flowed past the car like a river: neat old ladies with high-piled grey hair swaying along on tiny bound feet, their servants staggering behind under huge bundles of purchases; husky young peasants in blue cotton jackets and trousers tucked up to the knee; scrawny, parchment-faced coolies with deep-set, desperate eyes, pulling laden carts; silk-clad girls, businessmen in European-style suits; old men in long flowing robes . . . She felt dazed, almost smothered, by the colour and bustle and noise. She hadn't imagined there could be so many people in the whole wide world. Christmas shopping in O'Connell Street was nothing to this. How can they stand the pushing and jostling? she thought numbly. How can they even move, let alone go where they're going? I'd go mad if I had to live in such a turmoil.

She tried to pick out individuals as the car honked and

nudged its slow way through the crowds which seemed bent on suicide beneath its wheels; but the yellow skins, black hair and slanted eyes blurred before her gaze. They all look alike, she thought. No matter what they wear, they've all got the same face.

'Better shut that window. We're coming to the dried fish quarter,' advised Michael Holmes, leaning across her to wind it up. Romy saw that the open-fronted shops opposite were festooned with row upon row, tier upon tier, of contorted whitish-yellow shapes, swaying in the damp breeze like weird futuristic necklaces.

'Fish? It looks more like sponges to me,' she said; then gasped, for the next breath she drew into her lungs was so foul that she feared she might suffocate. The ammoniac stench of decay brought stinging tears to her eyes. With a stifled cry she fumbled for a handkerchief and clapped it over her mouth.

'Sorry, should have warned you sooner. I didn't realize the window was open,' muttered Michael Holmes. 'Don't worry, you'll soon get used to it.'

'Whew! Is that what they spread on the fields?' Stephen, renowned in the family for being both nose-blind and tone-deaf, had for once realized that the atmosphere was less than pure.

'Oh no, it's considered a delicacy,' said Holmes with perfect gravity. 'Mrs Bentley's cook is famous for his way with dried fish.'

Romy had to laugh at Stephen's expression of distaste. 'Is it true they eat dogs and slugs and seaweed as well?' she asked.

'Quite true. You have to realize that a Chinese really can't look at any living substance without immediately wondering what it tastes like. He isn't usually curious about how things grow or what they're made of, but he is intensely curious to know how things taste. It's one of the reasons I'd never put myself in the hands of a Chinese surgeon,' he added. 'I'd be scared he'd forget all about the operation and start fancying a taste of my liver or kidneys . . . Ah, here we are at last.'

The car had stopped before black-lacquered double doors

set in a high, blank wall. At the sound of the horn, a Chinese gatekeeper in neat blue jacket and baggy trousers hurried to fling wide the doors and shout to another servant within. The news of their arrival was shouted from courtyard to courtyard, and white-jacketed Li Ping, the Number One boy, came hurrying to escort them to their hostess.

'Leave all the luggage – they'll know what to do with it. Come this way,' said Holmes as he helped Romy from the car. 'Here you have the traditional "spirit wall," built to prevent demons coming into the house,' he added, ushering her past a kind of brick screen.

'Why don't they go round it, like us?'

'Fortunately evil spirits can only move in straight lines,' he told her solemnly, 'so they're baffled when they find this in their path. They'd also slide down the eaves if they could and get in that way, but the wily Chinese make a practice of giving their roofs an upward flick, which leaves the poor old devil suspended in mid-air.'

'Devilish unfair!' said Stephen, smiling.

'Oh, you mustn't make the mistake of feeling sorry for evil spirits. They have all sorts of nasty little tricks up their sleeves. Mrs Bentley will be able to tell you all about them. She knows more of their wicked ways than I do.'

He led them across two courtyards linked by a covered walk weighed down with a mass of wisteria, its long purple racemes swaying gently in the breeze. They entered an enchanting garden, its pools and flower-bright terraces framed by gracefully drooping willows. Mrs Bentley's own quarters were on the far side of the garden; the two outer courts being given over to the servants and their families and the innermost court to guests.

'Welcome to Shanghai!' said Mrs Bentley with a warm smile, coming forward to greet them with outstretched hands. She stood framed in the doorway of the drawing-room, a tall, serene woman with greying hair coiled in a chignon at the nape of her neck. There was nothing in her manner to betray the frenzied activity of the past hour, when the six Chinese women who had begged her for refuge the night before had been transferred with their pathetic bundles of belongings to the back of the Happy-Time

Laundry van, and driven away by Li Ping's brother to the point upriver where they might slip aboard a ferryboat unobserved, on the first stage of their journey to a new life in the Communist bases.

'Would you like me to show you round the museum this morning?' asked Mrs Bentley when Stephen had left for an appointment at the Hong Kong and Shanghai Bank the following day. She had taken an immediate liking to young Mrs Russell and wanted to make her visit to China as agreeable as possible. She was, moreover, anxious that her guest should not have the opportunity to become too familiar with the faces of the servants and their families, in case she should be struck by the curiously shifting population of the two outer courtyards. It was better to direct her interest away from the house.

'The museum?' Romy put down her delicate teacup with care, searching for an excuse which would be both polite and truthful. With relief she remembered Eugene Lyon's formula and adapted it to her needs.

'I'm afraid I'm not very interested in museums,' she said apologetically. 'I know so little about Chinese history that it really wouldn't mean much to me. What I'd like best – if it's not too much trouble for you – would be to see how the Chinese live nowadays. I prefer people to things, if you know what I mean.'

Mrs Bentley regarded her with approval. 'Of course I do. I think that's an excellent plan. It's most unusual for any newcomer to want to learn about the Chinese people, you know. They're generally so overwhelmed by China's glorious past that they tend to disregard the present. I'll show you what I can of Shanghai, Mrs Russell. Of course, it's no more typical of the rest of China than New York is typical of America, but personally I've always thought that the two cities have a lot in common. Things *happen* in Shanghai – just as they do in New York. It's like a barometer – or weathervane, if you like. You see both the best and the worst of the country here.'

She picked up her spectacles and rang the bell with an air

of purpose. 'Just as soon as you're ready I'll ask Li to call two rickshaws, and we'll begin our tour.'

She was as good as her word. In the days that followed, Romy saw a very different Shanghai from the one presented to Stephen. His business was with China's rulers: generals, financiers, mandarins. He flew back and forth to the seat of government at Nanking. He juggled figures with bankers and businessmen, and often ate in their luxurious homes, waited on hand and foot. And while he sipped rare tea with ministers or conferred with mandarins, Romy and her hostess were out in the streets, prying into many different aspects of Chinese life. Mrs Bentley's energy was amazing, and so was the breadth of her acquaintance. She introduced Romy to Manchu princesses and the expensively-dressed wives of Japanese millionaires. She avoided only one section of her friends: she could not quite trust Romy's discretion when it came to meeting trade union activists. Almost daily, new refugees begged her to shelter them from the police. She could not forbid Romy the run of the grounds for ever, and was careful to warn her clandestine visitors to stay out of sight.

Romy very soon succumbed to the lure of glowing silks and brocades, jade and ivory. In a tiny shop near the Garden of the Purple Clouds of Autumn she found the perfect present for Stephen's birthday: an ivory dragon some twelve inches long, spiked and spined, with a rolling eye and long scaly tail. The inside had been hollowed out so that all the people and animals the dragon had consumed during his wicked career could be seen between his latticed ribs. Tiny mandarins, peasants in baggy trousers, shaven-headed *bonzes*, warlords and their baby-faced concubines, donkeys, ducks and lion-shaped dogs, perfect in every minute detail.

'It costs so little!' she marvelled under her breath. 'How can he make a living?'

The grey-gowned merchant, whose head was as smooth and polished as an amber egg, watched benignly from hooded eyes.

'It took him more than a year to make this,' he replied in answer to Abigail's question.

'Oh! Does he know the man who made it?'

The merchant spoke again, bowing over folded hands. 'He's inviting us to tour his workshop,' said Abigail. 'Do you want to? If we do, it'll more or less commit you to buying that piece.'

'Oh, but I want to,' said Romy gaily. 'I can't possibly go home without him. I've fallen in love with my dragon. Do let's see the workshop.'

'It may not be quite what you expect,' warned Abigail.

Even so, Romy was unprepared for the hideous din which burst on their ears when, after crossing a number of yards, the merchant unlocked a door and ushered them inside. It was very hot, and the smell of human sweat mingled with scorched bone as the screaming treadle drills cut into chunks of ivory. The air was full of a fine, white, suffocating dust, which powdered the workers' hair and skin and made it difficult to breathe. The windows were high up and apparently hermetically sealed; coils of unprotected wires snaked about the floor.

The workers were crowded together at narrow work-benches, two to a drill. By the dim flickering light of naked electric bulbs they worked at feverish speed, cutting and shaping the ivory before it was passed to the craftsmen.

The noise seared through her head; the fetid air choked and sickened her. She couldn't imagine how anyone could work in such conditions, let alone create the beautiful toy she still carried. How could a work of art so full of wit and vitality, delicacy and intricacy, have emerged from this stinking, frenetic hellhole?

The merchant was moving ahead of them down the rows of benches; he stopped and tapped a thin, cotton-clad shoulder.

'This is the man who carved that dragon,' said Abigail.

The craftsman raised dull, pink-rimmed eyes with grotesquely swollen lids and glanced briefly at the strangers before returning to his work. He was quite young, no more than twenty Romy guessed, but very thin and frail, with hollow cheeks and a high, knobbly forehead. He coughed monotonously without shifting his attention from the little tiger he was chiselling: the sound was lost in the general din.

Romy smiled and tried to show that she thought the dragon was beautiful, but he stared at her uncomprehendingly and she knew his suffering face would haunt her every time she looked at the ivory souvenir.

Back in the shop she paid for it, though her pleasure in the lovely toy was gone.

'Are all the workshops like that?' she asked in a shaken voice as they climbed into rickshaws to drive home.

'Some are much worse. The silk filatures, for instance, and the match factories. Those are really terrible.'

Romy was silent for a long time, her eyes on the muscles in the rickshaw coolie's back, which slid in rhythm to his trot. What a life, she thought. What a horrible hell of a life. And I imagined I was unhappy at Longmarsh! Her head ached from the noise and stale air.

Abigail cast an assessing glance at her pale profile. Yes, young Mrs Russell might be pretty, frivolous and indulged, but she was getting the message, all right. She was beginning to realize, unlike some Westerners who lived their working lives in Shanghai without realizing, that beneath the glamour and glitter of this most cosmopolitan city lay unplumbed depths of human misery and exploitation. Abigail was deeply interested to see how she would react. After this morning's experience, would she determinedly close her eyes to the social evils and avoid contact with the ugly reality of Chinese life? Or did she really want to get to know the people, as she'd claimed? This was evidently the turning point.

They were nearly home before Romy said quietly, 'Will you take me to see a match factory too, Mrs Bentley? I think I ought to know what they're like.'

'Oh, my dear child, do call me Abigail! Surely we know one another well enough to dispense with formality? And yes, of course, I'm certain that Mr Yoritomo would be delighted to let us visit his factory. He was telling me how proud he was of it the other evening.'

The match factory was in the suburbs beyond the Northern District, a group of corrugated iron sheds surrounded by a high wire fence.

Mr Tamako, the fat, jovial Japanese manager, displayed his workforce of skeletal children aged from four to eight with the pride of a ringmaster, and appeared oblivious to Romy's shocked looks. He bawled details of their working lives to Abigail above the clatter of machinery, and she translated.

'He says they work twelve-hour shifts. They get two meals of rice soup every day. After they are eight years old he has to turn them out because their fingers become too clumsy to pick up matchsticks fast enough.'

Romy could hardly bear to look at the small pinched faces, eyes dull with apathy. Tiny fingers filled matchboxes at frenzied speed as the conveyor belts bore them past. A squat, heavy-browed overseer with an expression of malignant brutality strolled up and down between the rows of workers, carrying a short thick baton and glancing alertly to right and left in search of slackers.

Mr Tamako said something to Abigail and waited with a self-satisfied, expectant air.

'He wants to know your opinion of his modern factory.'

'I think it's horrible. Quite unspeakably horrible,' said Romy under her breath.

'I don't think he'd be very pleased to hear that . . . It's no worse than England during the Industrial Revolution, you know,' said Abigail, watching her carefully.

'Ireland's never had an Industrial Revolution, praise be,' Romy retorted. 'Whoever owns this torture-house ought to be shot.'

'Oh, but you've met him! You said he was so charming. Mr Yoritomo was the Japanese gentleman who sat next to you at Mr Grayburn's party – don't you remember? He owns several of these factories. He's looked on as a public benefactor,' said Abigail. 'Make no mistake, Rosemary, *these* children are the lucky ones. At least they aren't starving to death on the streets, like all the poor mites who can't get work. There have been terrible famines in the North-West for the last three years, and thousands of peasants have left the land and come south to beg for food. They sell their children to anyone who'll buy them.'

'Sell them?' said Romy, sickened.

'Oh yes, indeed. The girls go for "child daughters-in-law" – that's to say, household slaves, or child prostitutes; and the boys mostly become coolies or get work in the factories so long as their health holds out. *That*'s why Chinese goods are so cheap – they're made by slave labour.'

Romy was silent and thoughtful on the way back to Nanking Road. She was beginning to see the slant of Abigail's own political convictions, and wondered what Stephen would say if he knew that their hostess was a Communist at heart.

A few days later they were seated side by side in rickshaws, bowling smartly along to take tea with a Manchu princess, when the hollow-cheeked coolie pulling Abigail's conveyance began to wheeze alarmingly. Romy was just about to comment that he sounded like a broken-winded horse when the man gave a cavernous groan and collapsed between the shafts. His triangular hat tilted over his face as he knelt in the road, his chest and shoulders heaving convulsively. His rickshaw began to run backwards and Abigail hastily scrambled out. Before they could summon help or persuade the swiftly-gathering crowd to do more than stare, the rickshaw coolie keeled over sideways. His whole frame shuddered. He made a last effort to rise and then lay still.

In stunned silence, Romy stayed beside the body while Abigail summoned the International Police. An English sergeant was in charge. 'A nasty shock for you ladies,' he commented sympathetically. 'You could have had a bad bump. Sure you're all right?'

The rickshaw coolie's body was scooped unceremoniously from the gutter by the two Sikhs under his command, and dumped in the back of a cart.

'Will I get you another rickshaw, ma'am?' enquired the sergeant.

Though he had spoken quietly, a dozen coolies crowded round them at once.

'Rickshaw, missee!'

'Velly strong, velly cheap!'

'Take you home chop-chop!'

'Get away, you rascals,' exclaimed the sergeant. 'Give the ladies room.'

Romy and Abigail looked at one another and shook their heads.

'I'd rather walk,' said Romy.

'Come on, then. We haven't far to go. It's all right, Sergeant. We'll go on foot, thank you. I'm sorry, my dear,' she added when they were clear of the crowd, picking their way through the refuse on the pavement, peanut-shells crunching underfoot, 'that was my fault.'

Romy stared at her. 'You couldn't know he was going to die.'

'I could have guessed. It's not the first time it has happened to me. I make a habit of hiring the oldest coolies, because they're the ones who are desperate for work. I should have realized that man was too ill to be working at all.'

Romy felt a sudden hatred for this crowded, heartless city with its constant din, its shoddy skyscrapers festooned with washing, its air of cheap Americanization. 'Can't anything be done for these people?' she demanded.

'That's the question quite a lot of people are asking nowadays,' said Abigail.

CHAPTER FIVE

'Missee Lusser! Missee Lusser!'

Romy paused in her leisurely examination of the basket-maker's wares and looked about her. The Chinese crowd milled and jostled past the stall, beneath the flapping overhead banner. A moment ago she'd been enjoying a sensation of complete anonymity. Now it appeared that someone, at least, knew her name.

The soft, urgent whisper had come from an unexpected angle, low down, about knee-level, where a stack of large laundry hampers was displayed. She moved a pace or two to her left, and the voice immediately spoke again with a note of frantic pleading.

'Do not go, missee! I am in trouble. I beg your help.'

She stared ahead of her as if fascinated by a set of picnic baskets. 'Who are you?' she said quietly to the air. 'What do you want?'

'I am Mr San. I was on the boat.'

She remembered him at once, a fat, friendly, talkative young Chinese who wore shiny pointed shoes and a creased Western suit. Stephen had talked with him several times and formed the opinion that he was a political activist, possibly a trades union official or a member of the banned Chinese Communist party.

'I follow you today and hide in this basket to ask your help.'

'What's the trouble, Mr San?'

She had to bend down to catch the strained whisper from the laundry hamper. 'I am wanted by police. The Blueshirts . . .'

Despite the heat she felt suddenly chilled and her heart lurched disconcertingly. You couldn't live in Shanghai for long without hearing stories of police brutality. If poor Mr San was wanted by Chiang Kai-shek's dreaded secret police, he was indeed in trouble.

'What can I do? Tell me quickly – people are watching,' she said in a low voice, trying to move her lips as little as possible. She picked up a basket from the heap and held it up to the light as if trying to decide whether to buy it. The idle group of watchers drifted chattering on their way.

From within the hamper Mr San spoke in gasps, as if on the point of suffocation. She couldn't imagine how he had managed to squeeze into it. 'Find Mr Lyon, the American. He was on the boat too. Tell him – my sister has been betrayed. She must not go home tonight when she finishes her work. The Blueshirts will be waiting. Tell her to hide . . .' His voice died away.

'Does he know her?' she asked urgently. 'What's her name? Where does she live?'

'At six o'clock she will cross the Pearl Bridge to go home,' gasped Mr San. 'He must meet with her there.'

Romy's heart sank. How could anyone find a single girl

among the thousands of Chinese streaming homeward across the bridge? It would be like finding a needle in a haystack. 'But what does she look like? What's she wearing?'

'Her name – is Kuang-mei . . . San Kuang-mei. Go now! Go quickly! I can not . . . talk . . . any more.'

To her dismay she saw a dark stain seeping through the bottom of the wicker hamper, spreading across the pavement in a glistening puddle. 'You're hurt!'

'Go!' he insisted.

She had to obey. As she turned and pushed through the crowd his last words echoed in her ears like the sad thin whisper of a ghost. 'She wears red shoes, missee. Fine red shoes and a red bag . . .'

The girl with red leather shoes crossed the Pearl Bridge with a light, carefree step, humming softly as she threaded her way through the hurrying crowd. A matching handbag of red leather swung from her shoulder.

'That's her,' said Romy, touching Gene Lyon's arm.

'It must be.' Broad-shouldered and confident, he moved forward swiftly to intercept her.

Romy felt a profound sense of relief. He'll know what to say to her, she thought thankfully. Now we've found her I can leave the rest to him. I've done my bit.

It had been a surprisingly simple matter to find the office where Gene worked. For some reason Romy preferred not to analyze, the address she had glimpsed on the *Empire Queen*'s passenger list had stuck in her memory. After sending a message to tell Abigail that she was taking tea with a friend, Romy summoned a rickshaw and had herself taken straight to Gene's office. At first she thought his manner a trifle reserved, but when he heard her story the dark brooding look left his face.

'Poor San!' he exclaimed. 'He must have been in a bad state to choose such a roundabout way to send a message. You say he was wounded, as well?'

'There was blood trickling out of the hamper,' said Romy slowly, 'and his voice sounded very peculiar. Weak, and scared. He wouldn't let me go any closer. He was too afraid of attracting attention. That's probably why he didn't come to you himself.'

'Maybe you're right.' He sat for a moment deep in thought, staring abstractedly out of the window at the forest of masts lining the nearby jetty. Romy had time to consider the handsome clearcut profile under the thick thatch of dark hair and felt a sense of relief at having transferred the responsibility for Mr San and his sister into such capable hands.

'Will you come with me to look for her? Two of us stand a better chance of spotting her coming over that bridge.' After an instant's pause he added, 'Don't if you'd rather not, but frankly I need help and I'm reluctant to involve anyone else.'

I've no business to involve her, either, but poor San hasn't left me much choice, he thought. Of course she can always say no . . .

'I'll come,' said Romy, and was rewarded by the flashing upward smile that totally transformed his dark face.

'Then what are we waiting for?' he exclaimed.

And now they had, indeed, found Miss San. To see her standing before them in her splendid red leather shoes, a look of polite enquiry on her pretty painted face, made Romy shiver. They might so easily have missed her.

'San Kuang-mei?' asked Gene.

The girl nodded. She had shoulder-length black hair pulled smoothly back from a centre parting, and a round moon face with high-arched, plucked brows. Her eyes looked wary.

As Gene spoke, Romy watched the pretty face slowly transform into a white, scared mask. She glanced from side to side like a trapped animal and gave a little moan. 'I must go home!' she cried in English.

Gene caught her arm as she tried to dodge past. 'No, Miss San. You have been betrayed. You must hide.'

She looked from one to the other, seeking reassurance, unsure how far to trust the strange foreigners. Her small hands twisted. 'I must go home. There is something I cannot leave . . .'

'Are you afraid the police will search your home and find something incriminating?'

She nodded and gave a little sob. 'Papers, documents . . . the names of our members. They must not find them.'

'That is a problem,' Gene agreed. 'Now, what shall we do? You can't go and fetch them yourself. Tell me, Miss San, do you by any chance work for Europeans? Is that where you learnt to speak such good English?'

'Yes, I am a typist for the Stanway Steam Company. I am working there two years already,' she said with a timid smile.

'Good, then I tell you what we'll do. Mrs Russell and I can pretend to be colleagues of yours on a social call.' Romy gave him a startled look. She hadn't bargained for quite such a positive role in the affair, but the American seemed to take her acquiescence for granted. He went on, 'Now you tell me exactly what you want us to fetch and where to find it. The police won't bother us and I doubt if they'll have searched your home already for fear of scaring away more of your friends. They usually wait till everyone they want is boxed up neatly in one place – then they pounce.'

Romy shivered, but Miss San had regained a measure of her self-possession. 'You are most kind, Mr . . . ?'

'Eugene Lyon. I met your brother in Tokyo, Miss San. He's a brave man.'

She acknowledged the introduction with a little bow, but her eyes filled with tears. 'Ah, my poor brother! Where is he now? What will become of us? The group of our friends was to meet tonight at my house to distribute our leaflets, but now –'

'You don't mean you want me to fetch out a printing press?'

'No, no. The press is in a ruined temple, some miles outside the city.'

'Thank heaven for small mercies! Now tell me, where do we find the leaflets – and other documents?'

She told them, her directions interspersed with soft moans and lamentations. Sorry as she felt for the girl, Romy was also conscious of irritation. Surely Miss San must have realized the possibility that her home would be raided, and made some provision against such an emergency? It appeared she had not. Was there any means of communicating with her friends, warning them of danger? Another shake of the long black hair, another sorrowful exclamation. Miss San seemed to have embarked on her perilous game as heedlessly as a child. Really, thought Romy, even I would have known how to go about conspiracy more discreetly. And I would certainly have prepared myself a hiding place. What on earth are we going to do with her now?

She was uneasily aware how conspicuous they were, standing arguing on the bridge. Every moment's delay made it more likely that Miss San's unsuspecting friends would blunder into the police trap.

She said urgently, 'Let's go now, at once. Miss San can take a rickshaw back to your house, Mr Lyon, and wait for us there.'

'Make it Gene,' he said mechanically. His black brows drew together. He looked doubtfully at Miss San and lowered his voice. 'I wouldn't be too happy to land her on Linda without warning. She's new here. She doesn't understand the political situation too well yet.'

She's been here as long as I have, thought Romy. I suppose I've been lucky in having Abigail to explain things. Aloud she said, 'Perhaps you could write her a note? Or . . .' she was struck by a better idea, 'why don't *I* send a note asking Abigail Bentley to take care of Miss San? I'm sure she would.'

'That's the ticket,' said Gene, obviously relieved. 'Then we'll go along to her apartment together and see if we can't clean it up before the cops arrive.'

The Chinese girl seemed thankful to have matters taken out of her hands. They packed her into a rickshaw with a scribbled message to Mrs Bentley, and promised to join her as soon as possible. Then they set off on foot for her home.

Miss San lived in a dark, rather sleazy apartment house above a dress shop. If the Blueshirts were keeping the building under observation they were doing so discreetly, and Romy and Gene made their way up to the second floor unchallenged. The smells of hot oil, garlic and ammonia hung about the scuffed staircase and solemn-eyed children drew back into dark doorways with whimpers of alarm as the 'foreign devils' passed them. The air was thick and stifling.

'Here we are,' said Gene, studying the dog-eared card pinned beside a door. He pressed the bell and waited.

Romy leaned limply against the wall and searched for a handkerchief. It was a mistake to hurry in Shanghai, no matter how urgent the errand. Her light cotton dress clung stickily to her spine and her heart pounded as much from exertion as apprehension. She fought against gathering waves of nausea as the heavy stale air seemed to press in on her. 'Gene,' she said faintly, 'I'm afraid I'm going to . . .'

He cast her a worried glance. 'Hang on, honey. Someone's coming.'

Slow, uncertain footsteps approached the door from the other side. It opened and an old *amah* with an apron tied over her baggy trousers stood swaying before them on tiny bound feet. At the sight of their strange white faces her mouth opened slowly, as if she would scream, but Gene spoke swiftly to reassure her.

'We are friends of Miss San. She has sent us to take away her documents before the Blueshirts come looking for them.'

'The Blueshirts!' Her wizened face took on the same frightened, trapped look as Miss San's. 'Enter, enter, gracious and honourable ones,' she quavered, holding the door wide and bowing. When she tried to move Romy felt her knees buckle and she clutched at the wall for support. There was a roaring sound in her ears and black mist clouded her vision. She felt as if she might suffocate.

Gene's arm was instantly round her waist, holding her upright; when the mist cleared a moment or two later she found herself seated with her head between her knees in a dark, cluttered room with bamboo furniture and curtains of coarse yellow lace. Gene's hand was pressed firmly on her back.

'Let me up. I'm all right again,' she said, struggling upright, ashamed of her weakness.

'It's the heat. I shouldn't have let you hurry. I guess you have a touch of the sun. Are you sure you're all right now?'

'Quite all right,' said Romy firmly. She pushed away the temptation to lean against him just a little longer. The old *amah* was standing before them, offering tea, and Romy had a curious sense of unreality, as if she'd strayed into a dream. She sipped the pale scalding liquid gratefully, feeling her strength return and with it the need for haste. Her foolish attack of giddiness was costing them precious time. At any moment the Blueshirt watchers might grow suspicious of the presence of foreigners in the building and decide to investigate.

'Don't worry about me,' she said, forcing a smile. 'You go and look for those papers – I wouldn't know them if I saw them. I'm sure we're being watched. The sooner we get out of here the better.'

He nodded and went behind the bamboo screen where the old woman hovered anxiously. Romy waited with mounting impatience for what seemed an age, but at last he reappeared carrying a stack of notebooks, a few textbooks and a sheaf of muzzily-inked leaflets. Moaning softly, the *amah* helped him cram them into wicker baskets which she covered with squares of cotton.

'That's the lot, I think,' said Gene, looking round. 'There's nothing else the Kuomintang could object to. Now the apartment's clean Miss San may even be able to come home and brazen it out. Ready, then? Let's make tracks.'

She was only too glad to do so. They thanked the old woman and left her, her broad face still creased with worry.

Outside it was drizzling. The damp, noisy bustle of the street suddenly seemed both safe and familiar. Romy drew in great lungfuls of the warm wet air, glad to be out of the claustrophobic apartment with its dark corners and frightened, scurrying inmates.

'We'll get home just as fast as we can,' said Gene, switching both baskets to his left hand and putting his right arm round Romy.

'Let me take one of those,' she said to cover her embarrassment. She tried to take the nearest basket but he wouldn't let go.

'They're not heavy. I can manage.'

'Don't you trust me with them?' She smiled and at the

same time pulled gently away from his encircling arm. 'You shouldn't put all your eggs in one basket, you know.'

'These are pretty explosive eggs. I'm not sure I want you burdened with them,' he said seriously.

'Oh, don't worry. I'll be safe enough in a rickshaw. Let me take this one.' Again she tugged at the handle and this time he relinquished it.

'All right . . . be careful, though.'

They stood at the junction of two streets and looked about for rickshaws. Usually a European, particularly if he was encumbered with parcels, had only to pause for an instant before he was besieged by coolies eager for a fare, but in this maze of mean alleys there was a curious absence of conveyances. The warm damp drizzle began to fall more thickly, and Romy's dark curls clung round her face.

'You're getting soaked. Will you have my jacket?' he offered.

She shook her head. 'I'm warm enough. It's really rather refreshing . . . ah . . . there's a rickshaw!'

'Where?'

'Right down at the end of the street.'

'*Lai*!'

Astonishingly, the coolie heard Gene's shout through the general hubbub. He came directly towards them – a sturdy, square-built fellow, his well-muscled chest naked above the usual loose blue cotton trousers. He looked stronger and better nourished than most coolies.

'What luck! I thought he'd never hear you at that distance.'

Romy hopped nimbly into the light carriage, tucking the basket down by her feet and pulling the hood over her. 'We'll be home in no time now. This chap looks as if he can go like the wind,' she said gaily.

Gene stood with his hand on the shaft, reluctant to let her go. Something nagged at the edge of his consciousness, a suspicion that all was not well. The coolie glanced round impatiently.

'Take care. I'll be right behind you,' said Gene.

She waved. 'We're off!' and was borne away into the stream of traffic.

He stared after her, gripped by apprehension. Should he have let her go alone with those damned incriminating papers? She hadn't felt well. What if the faintness overcame her again before she reached Mrs Bentley's house? There'd been something odd – something faintly disturbing about that coolie. In an area where rickshaws were rare, hadn't his sudden appearance been just a little too pat?

It's no good standing here worrying, thought Gene. If I can't find a rickshaw of my own I'd better follow on foot. He began to push through the crowd in the wake of Romy's conveyance, keeping it in sight. Holy smoke, he thought after half a mile, she was right about one thing: the fellow certainly can run. He was weaving in and out of the slow-moving traffic as if the devil was at his heels, but where the hell was he going? That wasn't the way back to the International Settlement.

Gene glanced swiftly round to check his own bearings and plunged in pursuit, certain now that his instinct was right. Romy was in danger. They crossed two main thoroughfares, crowded and brightly lit, then dived into a rabbit-warren of narrow alleys where there was little traffic and Gene, fit as he was, could hardly keep pace with the swiftly-moving rickshaw. Chinese children stared after him, open-mouthed at the strange sight of a white man running through the streets.

Gene's heart pounded and cramp threatened his calf muscles as sweat streamed from him. He hadn't the breath to shout, and time and again he thought he'd lost the rickshaw completely before catching another glimpse of it half a block ahead, the coolie still running doggedly between the shafts as if he could keep up the pace for ever.

They were fast approaching the old Chinese town. Were Romy to vanish into that maze of dark streets she might never be seen again. Gene cursed and began to run even harder, the basket swinging and bumping at his side. He must catch up with her. He must. Gathering his strength he put on a final spurt and as he drew level grabbed the back of the rickshaw.

'Jump, Romy! Jump out!' he shouted.

He had a fleeting glimpse of her white face huddled back

beneath the vehicle's hood; then the coolie, realizing what was happening, swung down an alley barely wider than the rickshaw itself. Gene was knocked sideways by the wheel. He stumbled over a pile of refuse and fell to his knees. By the time he had picked himself up, the alley ahead was empty. Romy and her abductor had vanished.

He stood with hands hanging limply at his sides, chest heaving, wondering what to do next. Faintly, away to his right, he heard a woman's screams.

Romy had travelled some distance in the swift-moving rickshaw before it struck her that something was amiss. At first she leaned comfortably against the backrest, enjoying the damp breeze on her face as they bowled along; enjoying too, though with a slight feeling of guilt, the memory of Gene's arm round her waist and her own impulse to lean against it even when it was no longer strictly necessary. Why, then, she wondered, had she felt it necessary to break that easy, agreeable contact as soon as she saw the opportunity? Was it because it seemed faintly disloyal to Stephen to take such pleasure in the touch of another man? Stephen had an almost cat-like distaste for casual physical contact. Not for him the meaningless bumping of cheekbones – 'nun's kisses' as Romy and her sister used to call them – that signified a little more pleasure in meeting a friend than a mere handshake. The slap on the back and the bear hug were equally foreign to his nature.

Suddenly Romy realized how much she missed that warm, easy contact which her own family and friends offered without thought, but Stephen's circle regarded with raised eyebrows. I've changed, she thought. A year or so ago I wouldn't have given it a second thought if a man put his arm round my waist; now I shy away like a frightened virgin in case Stephen reads something in the gesture which isn't there. Yet there was no disguising from herself that she found Gene's touch more exciting than mere friendship warranted: probably because I'm not used to it any more, she reflected.

Deep in thought, she had paid little heed to where they

were going relying, as one did here, on her rickshaw coolie to bring her safe to her destination by the shortest route. Presently, however, her subconscious sense of direction began to insist that, improbable as it seemed, this man wasn't taking her towards the International Settlement as Gene had told him to, but directly away from it. She sat up straighter, looking for landmarks. The streets were narrow here, and it was difficult to see any distance between the tall buildings, but occasionally at street junctions she got a glimpse of something she recognized. There, for instance, was the river, while far away to her left twinkled the high window-lights along the *Bund*. She was undoubtedly being carried towards the old Chinese town.

She felt a certain indignation as this fact sank in. He's taking me for a ride! she thought. Does he imagine he'll be able to charge extra for going the long way round?

'Stop!' she called. 'You're going the wrong way.'

To her consternation, the coolie took no notice but continued swiftly on his chosen route.

'Hey! Stop!' she shouted more loudly.

Far from obeying, the man increased his speed, the knotted muscles in his legs sliding up and down like pistons. Suddenly she was afraid. She knew she was being abducted – there was even a local word for it: *Shanghaied*. Stories of recent kidnappings, murders, mutilations – the kind of gossip the comfortable European ladies scared one another with while waiting after dinner for the gentlemen to join them – flooded her mind. Listening to such stories, she'd always thought the ladies must be overdramatizing. Now she realized that such things actually happened – were about to happen to her unless she acted swiftly.

Her brain felt frozen; she couldn't think clearly. She huddled beneath the hood of the bumping, swaying rickshaw, wondering if she dared risk a jump. Even if she managed it without breaking a leg, which seemed unlikely, she would still face the problem of getting back to the main thoroughfare without being recaptured. The rickshaw coolie ran fast enough encumbered by his vehicle. Without it he'd be capable of catching her in a few strides. And then what would he do? She shivered, clutching the sides.

At that moment she heard pounding footsteps close behind, and suddenly the rickshaw jolted violently as a hand grabbed the back of it.

'Jump, Romy!' she heard Gene shout. 'Jump out!'

It was impossible to obey. The vehicle swung sharply left, scraping against the wall. For an instant it balanced on a single wheel, threatening to turn over, then righted itself and bowled on down the dark alley, with Romy still clinging to the sides.

Gene was left behind, but the sight of him had given her fresh courage and jolted her mind into action. The reason for her abduction was suddenly plain. Of course, it was the papers they wanted. This must be a Blueshirt plot to seize Miss San's incriminating documents.

Well, they shouldn't have them. Romy took the basket from between her feet, lowered it gently over the back of the rickshaw and then, with her eyes still staring ahead at the running coolie, she dropped it behind her. For a moment she held her breath, wondering if a white cascade of papers would catch his eye, but he ran on unnoticing. She felt a rush of triumph. The papers were safe – the next thing was to save her own skin.

She waited until the rickshaw was forced to slow down to negotiate a sharp corner out of the alleyway, then stood up in the swaying carriage and took a leap into the blackness. It was an awkward take-off. Her foot slipped, her skirt caught in a wheel, and for an agonizing moment she was dragged bumping along behind the rickshaw, knees and elbows scraping on a gritty surface, before the coolie halted abruptly. He dropped the shafts and whirled round on her.

She couldn't move. The breath had been knocked out of her and she lay perfectly still, expecting at any moment to feel a knife between her ribs. Nothing happened. She was turned over roughly, as her abductor sought the missing basket; she heard his grunt of disappointment. Then the wheels scrunched round in a tight turn. He was going back to look for the papers. She prayed that Gene was still following and would find them first.

Dim shadowy figures were emerging from the huts on either side of the alley, closing in on her like hungry vultures.

She filled her lungs with all the air she could and began to scream.

When he found her she was silent, lying face-down in the alley, and for a heart-stopping moment he feared she was dead. As he approached, a group of tattered figures who had been crouching round her rose and fled. Whether their intention had been to rob or to help her, he could not tell. They might simply have been curious to know how a foreign devil dies.

He knelt beside her. 'Romy!'

To his relief he saw a flash of white as her eyes opened. 'Oh, Gene, I thought you'd never hear me,' she whispered. 'I was so frightened.'

'Does this hurt? Or this?' Swiftly he checked for broken bones. As far as he could tell, she had suffered only cuts and bruises. He said, 'Do you think you can walk? My house is the nearest – we'll go there. Mrs Bentley'd have a fit if she saw you in such a state.'

So would the husband, he thought guiltily. I should never have involved her in a business like this. I've plenty of reason to know the Kuomintang plays rough. He imagined Stephen Russell's cold fury if he were to see his pretty young wife now, covered in blood, her dress in tatters, all because he – Eugene Lyon – hadn't sent her straight home after hearing poor San's story.

He helped her to her feet. 'Can you walk or shall I carry you?' He hoped she'd ask to be carried, but instead she laughed shakily.

'No need for that. I've had plenty of worse falls from horses. It was just . . . being alone . . . and not knowing which way to go . . .' Her voice died away. He tucked her arm firmly through his, ignoring her half-hearted attempt to pull away.

'Come on then, let's go.'

'Gene – the papers!'

'It's all right – I found the basket you dropped. They're safe enough but I'm not putting them – or you – in any more rickshaws tonight. They're staying right here with me until I get the chance to burn the lot of them.'

At the sound of her husband's key turning in the door of their modern house on a tree-lined avenue to the north of the river, Linda Lyon trailed out to meet him. Her grey eyes were stormy, her cheeks unusually pink.

'So you finally decided to put in an appearance! Just where the hell have you been? Did you forget you'd invited guests? *Your* friends, not mine. I had to start the meal. We couldn't sit there staring at one another a moment longer. You're just so inconsiderate I could scream. I could kill you for landing me in a situation like that.'

'Linda, I'm sorry. I'll explain how it happened. Listen, honey, I've brought Rosemary Russell home with me. She had an . . .'

'*Another* goddam guest!' Linda looked ready to explode.

Embarrassed, Romy got down stiffly from the carriage. She went straight up to Linda, hand outstretched. 'I'm so sorry to land myself on you at an inconvenient moment,' she said with a smile. 'I had a silly accident in a rickshaw and your husband kindly said I could come back to your house to make myself presentable before seeing Mrs Bentley. I don't want to alarm her.'

Linda forced her features into a more agreeable expression with all too obvious effort.

'Why, Rosemary! I'm sorry to hear that. My God, your dress . . . whatever happened to you?'

'My coolie turned a corner too fast and I fell out. I believe it happens quite frequently. I wonder, could I come in and wash?'

Linda made no effort to invite her in. Her grey eyes narrowed. 'And did Gene just happen to find you lying there?'

Romy flushed. It hadn't occurred to her that she might need a cover story. She'd been worried about Stephen's reaction; now that anxiety faded. Clearly it was going to be

Gene who paid most heavily for their adventure. Afraid of making matters worse by telling the truth, she looked at him for help.

'Come on in, we can't stand on the doorstep all night,' he said promptly, catching the appeal. 'I'm really sorry I forgot I'd asked Chang and Lin Yu-tang to dine, Linda; it went clean out of my head. I had a busy day . . .'

'*You* had a busy day!'

'And I'm late because there was some work that wouldn't wait,' he went on imperturbably, ignoring her sarcastic tone.

'But you weren't in your office. I rang your secretary and she told me you'd left early.'

'That's right, honey. Rosemary was kind enough to bring me a message about a business matter, and I had to go out and deal with it right away.'

'A message from your husband?' She swung round on Romy. 'But I heard he's gone to Nanking.'

Seen in electric light, Linda's skin had lost its glowing ship-board tan and now appeared sallow, faintly greasy. The pale hair had greenish lights and her jawline looked blurred, as if she was putting on weight. She needs exercise, thought Romy; or perhaps she's having a baby. For some reason she found the idea distasteful. But pregnant women were prone to bouts of irritability. It could account for Linda's jealousy and suspicion. Romy felt suddenly sorry for her. It must be hell not to trust your husband alone with another woman.

She said soothingly, 'I had two messages, actually, and I had to take them to the AmCanCo office because I didn't know your home address. One was about the – the business matter; and the other was to ask if you would both dine with us next week. It's Stephen's birthday on Wednesday and I want to arrange a little surprise for him.'

To her own ears it sounded unconvincing, but this time to her relief Linda decided to accept the olive branch.

'That's next Wednesday?'

'Yes.' Romy couldn't help hoping the date would already be filled, but after Linda had pretended to consider whether her crowded social life would allow her to accept this invitation, she gave a sharp, decisive nod.

'I think we'd enjoy that very much, Rosemary. I'll have to confirm it with my engagement diary, of course, but I think we could arrange to be free that night . . . Now, Gene,' her voice took on a discernible snap, 'you go straight on to the dining-room and keep those poor guests of yours happy. They'll think they've come to a madhouse. And don't stay up talking too long, either. If you don't turn them out at midnight they'll still be here at breakfast time. I'm going to look out a skirt for Rosemary and get those cuts cleaned up. My, but you certainly have some nasty bruises. You'll be black and blue tomorrow.'

She didn't sound as if she found that prospect altogether displeasing. She added mournfully, 'And to think I was looking forward to an early night! What's that in those baskets, Gene? Something for me?' She eyed the wicker panniers with the acquisitive glance of a magpie.

Expressionless, Gene shook his head. 'I'm sorry, dear. I had no time to look around the shops today. These are just papers I brought home.'

She took them, nevertheless, and peered inside. 'Chinese papers! Why ever do you want to bring that trash home with you?' Without waiting for an answer she stalked away down the hall, gesturing for Romy to follow. As she did so, Gene gave her an encouraging, conspiratorial wink; stiff and sore as she was, her spirits lifted. Wednesday didn't seem so far away after all.

CHAPTER SIX

Romy's instinct had been correct. Faced with the problem of hiding Miss San from the Shanghai police, Mrs Bentley showed an unexpected familiarity with the needs of refugees. In no time at all she had the Chinese girl snugly ensconced in a secluded pavilion behind the flowering rockery, equipped with new clothes, papers, and a new identity. She had also set in motion mysterious machinery which would spirit her out of the country to join her mother's Third Uncle who lived in Tokyo.

Romy was very surprised.

'Oh, it's not the first time I've had to shelter these poor people,' said Abigail diffidently, 'one gets to know the ropes . . . They often ask me for help – in fact we've got quite a little organization now for getting them away to safety.'

This from Mrs Bentley, the respectable doyenne of Shanghai society! Romy's astonishment grew. Questions jostled one another.

'But – but isn't it dangerous? What would happen if they caught you? Why do you do it? Are *you* a Communist, too?'

'Certainly not!' Abigail sounded shocked by the suggestion. 'I believe in individual freedom – the very opposite of Communism.'

'Then – why?'

'I suppose it's a question of humanity. I find myself unable to stand by and see these poor people – children, most of them – tortured and imprisoned just for trying to improve their wretched lives. So I do what I can for them. Besides –' Her mouth twitched and behind the gold-rimmed spectacles her dark eyes held a distinctly naughty twinkle.

'You enjoy it!' exclaimed Romy.

'I'm afraid I do. It adds such a spice to life here. The Kuomintang are really very unpleasant characters; it gives me the greatest satisfaction to outwit them.'

She might have been a village schoolmistress explaining her methods for frustrating fourth-form bullies. Romy imagined how surprised Stephen would be to see his hostess in this new light, but almost as if reading her thought, Abigail added gently, 'There's just one thing . . . I wonder if you'd be so kind as to keep my little secret? You see if anyone in authority knew of my involvement, my usefulness would vanish. I don't like to have to ask this, but I'd rather you didn't mention the matter – even to your husband. He's here on government business; knowing his hostess is engaged in anti-government activity might be professionally embarrassing for him.'

She was right, of course. Reluctantly Romy nodded. 'So you don't want me to tell Eugene Lyon, either?'

'Mr Lyon?' Abigail gave her a sharp, assessing glance. She said, 'Journalists are seldom noted for their discretion, my dear, but in this case the young man seems to have acted with a good deal of sense . . . Why don't you just tell him Miss San is safe, and leave it at that? I'm sure he'll understand.'

'Oh! What about poor Mr San? Is there any hope of rescuing him, too?'

Abigail shook her head. 'I'm afraid his chances are very slim, poor fellow. All the same, I'll send Li to find out what he can.'

Li was quickly despatched on his errand, but as soon as he returned they could see from his expression that the news was bad. Very soon after entrusting Romy with his message, it appeared that Mr San's uncomfortable hiding place had been discovered. Alerted, no doubt, by some informer in the crowd, a posse of Blueshirts had stamped into the *hutung* and surrounded the basket-maker's stall. When demands for Mr San to show himself met with no response, the police flung back the lid of the hamper. Inside they found their quarry, limp and lifeless. Mr San had died from his wounds.

Cheated and furious, the Blueshirts revenged themselves by wrecking the basket-maker's stall and kicking the hapless proprietor until he squealed for mercy. But Mr San was already beyond their clutches: after a time the Blueshirts had gone away.

Two days later, Abigail and Romy were drinking tea on the shaded terrace, watching the darting orioles encouraging their brood to fly among the heavy-scented lilacs, when Stephen returned from his visit to Nanking. After greeting them he sank wearily into a wicker armchair and Romy noticed a network of new lines about his mouth and eyes. He's been working too hard in this heat, she thought. He's run up much too light. Indeed, there was something of the tense, strained look of the over-trained racehorse about her husband's lean, rangy figure.

He gulped his tea and reached for a cigarette. 'Do you mind?'

'Of course not. I'll join you, if I may,' said Abigail. 'How did you get on with the Generalissimo?'

'I never set eyes on him.' Stephen sighed, and launched into an account of the delays and frustrations of his visit to the seat of government. Everyone he wanted to interview 'happened' to be out of town. All the figures relevant to his enquiry were being 'revised'. Every question he asked was politely blocked. Like many another European before him, he was discovering how difficult it was to pin the Chinese down to facts, or disentangle reality from fantasy about the country's economy.

'It's beginning to seem as if you only get what you want by bribing the right people,' he finished ruefully. 'But if you're prevented from meeting the right people in the first place, how can you get a chance to bribe them? It's a vicious circle.'

Abigail drew thoughtfully on her cigarette, supporting it between puffs in a manner of the inexperienced smoker. Romy guessed she had only asked for one to put Stephen at ease.

'I'm afraid that's broadly true,' she said. 'All the same, I may be able to help you. If you and Rosemary will come with me to the opera tomorrow night, I should be able to give you some introductions that may prove useful. Once you've met the men who wield power on a social level, you'll find it's much easier to talk business with them. Not that it's ever *very* easy,' she added, 'but at least an introduction from me may break the ice.'

'I'd be very grateful,' said Stephen. 'At the moment I seem to be getting nowhere, and I'm sure it's all a question of breaking into the right circle. What I really need now is a trip down south to take a look at the Kuomintang army in action.'

'Or inaction,' said Abigail sardonically.

'Will you be able to talk about that kind of thing at the opera?' said Romy. She had visions of Stephen trying to discuss money matters in competition with a soaring soprano.

Abigail laughed. 'You'd be surprised. More business gets done in restaurants and opera houses than in any office here. The Shanghai opera's the great place to see and be seen. Tomorrow is billed as a gala performance in honour of the Young Marshal, the Manchurian warlord, so anyone who's anyone is bound to be there.'

'Can you get tickets?' asked Stephen eagerly.

She smiled. 'My cook's wife has a cousin whose nephew by marriage sells hot towels at the opera. I expect he'll be able to arrange something.'

As they took their seats in the covered central courtyard of the tall galleried opera house on Yan An street the following evening, Romy's eye was caught by a commotion near the entrance.

'Ah, here he comes,' murmured Abigail with satisfaction.

Romy craned round. Like a flock of gorgeously feathered humming birds, a tight-packed group of Chinese officers in colourful uniform, swords clanking, medals a-glitter, lanyards and white gloves gleaming, jostled into the middle aisle, which cleared as if by magic for their passage.

A pace or so behind them strode a heavily-built, red-haired European, a head taller than his companions, whose plain dark dinner jacket and black tie stood out in stark contrast to the rest of the gaudy throng.

'Who is it?' Romy was standing on tiptoe, trying to spot the central figure, round whom the officers clustered as tightly as bees around their queen. 'Is it Chiang Kai-shek?'

'No, the Generalissimo doesn't often come to the opera. That's the Young Marshal of Manchuria, Chang Hsueh-liang, and some of his officers.'

For a moment the heads in front of them swayed apart, and Romy glimpsed the Marshal. He was a fine, intelligent-looking man in his thirties, with a high forehead and strong, resolute chin. He was very thin, with parchment-coloured skin drawn tight over prominent cheekbones, and deep-set, elongated eyes. He moved constantly, laughing and talking with a kind of determined gaiety; gesturing with quick, nervous movements of the cigarette held between finger and thumb. He gave an impression of intense energy.

'He doesn't look so very young,' she commented.

'No.' Abigail lowered her voice. 'In China, you know, "young" is hardly a term of respect, either. Poor fellow! I'm afraid he's rather a playboy. He used to have an expensive weakness for opium mixed with powdered pearls – so they say – but last year he went to Europe in search of a cure. All the same, I doubt if he'll ever be the warrior his father, the Old Marshal, was. Now *he* was a real character – even his enemies had to respect Chang Tso-lin. He was nearly as broad as he was high, fierce as a Manchurian tiger, and a real thorn in the flesh of the Japanese. They murdered him in the end by blowing up his train, and now they've driven the Young Marshal and his army out of Manchuria altogether. He's been dancing attendance on Chiang Kai-shek for the last three years, waiting for an opportunity to win back his homeland, but instead the Generalissimo has sent him to subdue the Communists in Kiangsi province.'

She paused and turned to Stephen, who was listening with interest. 'If you want to visit the front line, Chang Hsueh-liang's the man you ought to talk to. I'll see if I can't introduce you during the interval.'

'Who's the tall man in the Marshal's party?' asked Romy. 'I thought he was waving at Stephen.'

'It's a chap called Harvey Lombard,' said Stephen briefly. 'I knew him at school, but haven't seen him since.'

Lombard, H, he remembered suddenly, had left under some sort of cloud, though whether of the moral, financial, or purely academic variety he couldn't recall. It didn't seem necessary to mention this to Romy.

'How strange to see him here.' Her eyes were still on the black dinner jacket.

'Dr Lombard is the Young Marshal's personal physician,' explained Abigail. 'He goes everywhere with him.'

'Oh, so you know him too.'

'I know of him,' corrected Abigail gently. 'It's not quite the same thing . . . Now, listen. I must give you some idea of the plot before the opera begins, or you'll be completely at sea. I'm so glad we came tonight – it's a real treat for me. This is one of my favourite operas – *The Three Generals of Kiangsi*. They must have chosen it in honour of Marshal Chang.'

Romy found it hard to concentrate on Abigail's synopsis of the plot. Moths and mosquitoes, attracted by the lights, blundered against her, tickling her bare arms and tangling in her curls. She felt sticky and itchy and plied her paper fan vigorously.

'There are three brothers who are generals,' said Abigail, 'and two of them quarrel. Oh, it doesn't matter what they quarrel about – I won't go into all that – the point is that the third brother tells the first that the second one is dead. The second dresses up as the first and escorts the third one's two brides to the first brother's city. The third brother – who by this time is pretending to be the second, refuses to let them in . . . Am I making this clear? Then there's a woman general as well . . .'

Romy was thoroughly confused. 'Is it *all* about these generals? Isn't there a love interest?'

'Not tonight, I'm afraid. Hush now, it's going to begin.'

A ferocious rattling and banging of gongs reduced the audience noise by about a third, and the first of the generals, gorgeously apparelled in scarlet with an immense head-dress of plumes which trailed down to his heels, glided onstage, uttering a weird high-pitched wail. His face was totally masked in paint. The audience gasped in admiration and the gongs beat frenziedly, on and on.

Another, identically dressed general entered, and then a third. They circled the stage and one another with little darting runs which reminded Romy of cock pheasants displaying in the spring. The deafening din continued unbroken.

Could this be *opera*? Bewildered, Romy stole a sideways look at Abigail and saw that she was totally absorbed, her lips slightly curved in a smile of pure rapture. Together with the rest of the audience, she had entered a new world where Romy could not possibly follow.

Three hours of this! The chair which had seemed comfortable enough when she first sat on it now began to dig into Romy's seat bones and shoulderblades. The midges and moths redoubled their attacks. She wriggled and scratched surreptitiously, and looked forward to the interval when Abigail would introduce them to the Manchurian warlord. If it wasn't for that, she thought, I could hardly endure this a moment longer.

As it happened, Abigail's promised introduction proved unnecessary. Hardly had the stage lights dimmed and the audience's subdued chatter – which had continued throughout the act – risen to its normal volume, than the black-jacketed figure of Dr Lombard rose from his front row seat and shouldered purposefully towards them.

'Stephen Russell, isn't it?' he asked, towering over their seats. 'Do you remember me? Harvey Lombard. Nice to see you again. I was told that someone called Russell was coming to sort out this financial mess for us, but I'd no idea it would be you.' He looked with open curiosity at Romy.

'This is Dr Lombard, darling. My wife, Rosemary.'

'How do you do?' He took her hand in a firm, warm grip, smiling into her eyes. 'It's a pleasure to see you here. Ah, good evening, Mrs Bentley.'

Abigail's nod to him was barely civil, Romy thought, but Harvey Lombard remained unruffled.

'I must explain I'm here as the Marshal's errandboy,' he went on. 'He's in a holiday mood tonight, and he wasn't at all pleased to see important official guests seated so far back.'

'Oh, we're not here in an official capacity,' protested Stephen.

'That doesn't matter. He asks if you'd do him the honour of moving forward to join his party, and then coming on to dine with him. What do you say?'

'That's very kind of him.' Stephen hesitated. 'Does the invitation include my wife?'

'The Marshal would never forgive me for excluding her,' said Lombard easily. 'And Mrs Bentley too, if you'd care to come.'

Abigail shook her head. 'I'm afraid late nights no longer agree with me. I'll gladly pay my respects to the Marshal, but he must excuse me from the supper party.'

As they left their seats to move forward, three young Chinese girls, giggling excitedly, ran down the aisle and slipped into the vacant places. Observing them, Abigail smiled. 'It's an ill wind that blows nobody any good,' she murmured.

If the Young Marshal spoke English, he didn't mean to display the accomplishment in public. He regarded Romy with an alert, connoisseur's eye as Dr Lombard performed the introductions, and bowed gravely over his own joined hands. We shake other people's hands, but the Chinese shake their own, thought Romy, amused. Much more hygienic. She remained respectfully silent while, through the medium of Dr Lombard, the Marshal made polite enquiries about Stephen's family, age, and state of health. Jasmine-scented tea was offered, and steaming towels with which to wipe their faces. All too soon the rattling trays and banging gongs signalled the start of the second act.

Was it because she knew what to expect, or was it the presence of Dr Lombard at her side, explaining the plot in his deep, agreeable whisper, that made the second part of the programme so much easier to tolerate than the first? Perhaps, thought Romy, it was simply because the front row seats were luxuriously cushioned that she was conscious of neither boredom nor stiffness as the final general uttered his final wail and the lights went up again.

With the rest of the audience staring open-mouthed and affording it a respectful passage, the Marshal's party swaggered out to the brightly lit street where a fleet of curtained limousines with uniformed chauffeurs waited. A moment later, it seemed, their car was speeding down the narrow street at a reckless pace, horn blaring, in the wake of the Marshal's flag-flying procession.

'Hold your hats,' called Harvey Lombard from the front seat. 'The more important his passengers, the faster a Chinese chauffeur feels obliged to drive. It's a matter of face.'

'What happens if he runs over someone?' said Romy breathlessly.

'I doubt if he'd stop. It doesn't often happen; they usually jump in time,' he said indifferently. From the obscurity of the back seat, Romy had the opportunity to look at him in profile.

She guessed he was a year or so older than Stephen, and built for strength rather than speed. He had a thick-shouldered, powerful frame, and a square-jawed face whose contours were just beginning to blur with good living. His features were blunt, forceful rather than distinguished; thick coppery hair waved strongly back from a centre parting above his broad low forehead, and his natural high colour had tanned instead of yellowing in China's heat, giving him a healthy, open-air complexion. He had a pleasant deep voice with a hint of gravel in it and an easy, assured manner. He looked solid, confident, and dependable. Nevertheless, from the slight stiffness in Stephen's attitude and tone, she could tell that he did not like Dr Lombard. She wondered why.

The limousine screeched to a halt outside a brightly lit restaurant, gaudy with coloured bulbs and paper lanterns. Heads turned and conversation faltered at nearby tables as they were ushered into a private dining-room, then broke out with renewed vigour the moment the door closed.

There were three tables, discreetly sheltered by handsome lacquered screens, and each table setting was a work of art. The white cloths were decorated with a triple border of magenta rice laid out in a meticulous key pattern, not a grain out of alignment, and the individual place-settings were in turn surrounded by fresh flower petals and tinsel.

The middle of the table was filled with a profusion of dishes so colourful and exotic, so harmoniously pleasing to the eye, that it seemed a crime to alter the position of a single plate. These, and the short-handled spoons, were of delicate eggshell porcelain; the chopsticks of smooth carved ivory.

Dr Lombard took Romy's arm. 'Come along, you're at my table over here. I'm officially in charge of all the foreign guests, while the Marshal entertains his own officers.'

'It's very kind of him to ask us.' She wished he would let go of her arm.

He shrugged away her thanks. 'Oh, he enjoys it, when he's in the mood. He's quite the cosmopolitan since his trip to Europe last year. There's one thing I ought to mention, though . . .' he bent his head confidentially. 'I take it you won't mind if I ask you to slip out when the party gets rowdy? Some of these old Manchurian warhorses are a little . . . er . . . lacking in polish. Their ideas of fun date back to the warlord era; sooner or later they get drunk and start shooting, and things tend to get broken. Plates, and so on. We're bringing them into the modern world gradually, but at times, believe me, it's uphill work! They're not used to women eating with them, for instance – except for sing-song girls, of course.' He laughed, showing square white teeth, 'Don't look so worried. It's all quite harmless. You sit here, Mrs Russell, next to me. The Marshal has particularly asked your husband to sit at his table. Over here, Stephen . . .'

Romy took the place he indicated and tried not to feel abandoned as he led Stephen away. She was lucky to be here at all, she reflected; if Stephen had realized she'd be the only woman present he might well have made some excuse to send her home with Abigail. She saw him cast a slightly anxious glance over his shoulder at her, and smiled reassuringly. If Dr Lombard thought it was all right for her to join the party, there was surely no need to worry.

All the same, she could not ignore the stir her presence was causing among the Marshal's officers. She could feel eyes on her all the time, and whole groups would turn and stare openly at her; almost, she thought, as if she was a piece of merchandise on display. It made her uneasy. There was much laughter and staccato chatter but no one came over to speak to her. She felt uncomfortable seated alone at the table while the other guests milled about; she wished Dr Lombard would come to her rescue. She could see him on the other side of the room, engaged in a three-cornered conversation with Stephen and a short, stout, balding European encased in tight mess kit.

'What on earth are you doing here?'

She swung round, smiling. She'd have known that slow drawl anywhere. 'Oh, Gene! I'm so glad to see you,' she said thankfully. 'Do come and sit beside me and tell me who everyone is.'

To her surprise his dark face broke into no answering smile. His expression was stern, almost grim. 'Why are you here?' he said again. 'Who invited you to this place?'

'The Young Marshal, of course. Surely you don't take me for a gatecrasher?' Although she tried to speak lightly something in his expression warned her of trouble.

He shook his head disbelievingly. 'You mean he actually invited you here?'

Romy hesitated. 'Well . . . not exactly.'

'Then who did?'

The snap in his voice made her hackles rise. The way she was being alternately stared at and ignored had made her edgy; this inquisition from Gene seemed the last straw. 'Dr Lombard asked us to come – not that it's any business of yours,' she said sharply.

'Lombard!' he said disgustedly. 'I might have guessed he'd be at the bottom of it.'

'The bottom of *what*? Why shouldn't I be here?' she demanded.

'Because, my dear Rosemary,' he said patiently, as if explaining something any idiot understood, 'no respectable woman would ever accept an invitation to The Happy Dragon restaurant. I'd have thought you'd have realized the kind of place it is the moment you stepped through the door.'

Her cheeks felt hot. 'What ridiculous rubbish!' she said loudly. 'Stephen asked if it was all right for me to come, and Dr Lombard insisted I did. This is a perfectly ordinary restaurant.'

'Your confidence does you credit. I suppose you've known the doctor long enough to trust him?' said Gene dryly.

She stared at him, trying to fathom his meaning. 'I haven't – but Stephen has. They're old friends. They were at school together.'

'So that makes them friends?' He raised one dark eyebrow. 'Would you believe me if I said that Lombard has enticed you here precisely because he wants to discredit your husband in the eyes of China's rulers? A man who lets his wife attend an all-male banquet could hardly be well regarded in official circles, you know. As far as women are concerned, the Generalissimo's a strong believer in the ancient virtues.'

'Ancient nonsense!' she said furiously. 'I won't listen to such a ridiculous suggestion.'

'All the same, I'm going to have a word with your husband. I doubt if he realizes quite what he's let you in for,' said Gene, rising with a purposeful air as Dr Lombard at last returned to the table. ''Evening, Harvey. I gather you're responsible for Mrs Russell's presence this evening. Do you really think it's well advised to bring her here?'

Romy was still seething. How dare he try to spoil my fun? she thought indignantly. With Dr Lombard there to give her confidence, all the uncertainty raised by Gene's hateful insinuations melted away. People were taking their seats, and as the tables filled up an army of waiters carried in the first 'great dish' and its accompaniments. The appetizing scents of garlic and ginger, roast meat and rich sauces filled the air and Romy realized how hungry she was. She wouldn't dream of leaving the party now.

'Oh, Dr Lombard,' she said, ignoring Gene's frown, 'Mr Lyon has been trying to scare me away by telling me a woman has no business here.'

She felt antagonism crackle like static electricity between the two men. 'Believe me,' said Lombard, addressing her while never taking his eyes off Gene, 'your presence here is every bit as welcome as Mr Lyon's.' He seated himself deliberately and picked up his chopsticks. 'The Marshal is honoured that you have consented to attend his poor entertainment. Now, if you'll excuse us, Lyon . . .'

Gene had no choice but to withdraw. He bent swiftly towards Romy and said in a low voice, 'Watch out for the wine. It's stronger than you'd think. And leave the spirits alone.' He turned on his heel and withdrew to his own place between two bemedalled officers, leaving her torn between indignation and amusement.

'Take no notice of our American friend,' said Dr Lombard, helping her deftly with his own chopsticks. 'Just because he happened to live in China as a child he imagines himself the world's greatest authority on things Chinese. What he fails to realize is that all his information is years out of date. What was his parting gem of advice?'

'He said the wine's stronger than it looks,' said Romy, eyeing her glass doubtfully.

'Only if you've been reared by total abstainers,' said Gene, smiling again. 'Try it. I'm sure you'll agree that it's a very tolerable drink.' He raised his own glass, toasting her with warm, admiring eyes.

Defiantly, aware of Gene's dark, intent gaze across the room, Romy did the same. The deep red wine tasted uncommonly like cough linctus, she decided, swallowing it with difficulty, but the colourless liquid in a smaller glass was clean and refreshing. She drained it, unable to resist a challenging glance at Gene.

'Delicious!' she declared, loud enough for him to hear. Did he take her for some country wench who'd start giggling after a glass of cider? He was shaking his head warningly, but she drained a second glass. Instantly the waiter refilled it.

'That's the spirit!' said Dr Lombard approvingly. . .

Course followed course in bewildering variety, and little by little the noise level rose. At the Marshal's table a word-game was in progress; sharp syllables were shouted back and forth across the tablecloth, punctuated by bursts of laughter and applause. She could see, even at this distance, that Stephen was enjoying the fun.

Then Romy's right-hand neighbour called out a challenge and several voices took it up. They began to play a simple guessing-game, shaking fists in rhythm and shouting numbers as they took turns to shoot out one or more fingers. Every time a player guessed right, his opponent rose to his feet and drank off a thimbleful of the colourless liquid, as a forfeit.

The broad-faced Chinese officer next to Romy, who had the high cheekbones of a Northerner and elongated eyes which crinkled into inverted sickle moons as he smiled, nudged her and asked a question.

'He wants to know if you'll play.' Lombard had to shout the words in her ear to make himself heard.

'Oh . . . yes.' She was pleased by this sign of acceptance. She nodded and began to shake her fist like the others.

'One – two – three . . . *seven*!'

She shot out four fingers: her opponent chose to display three. By pure chance she had guessed the correct total and the table roared its applause. Moon-eyes rose and bowed from the waist; then he tossed off his glass of liquor with a practised flick of the wrist.

'Again!' called Dr Lombard.

Romy won five times in succession, and Moon-eyes began to sway as he drank his forfeits. The noise at the table was deafening. Musicians had joined the party, scraping away piercingly at three-stringed instruments or thumping drums. Here and there a slender girl, her face a painted mask below smoothly-piled black hair, waited demurely for some merrymaker's attention. Romy felt lighter than air, borne up on a cloud of laughter and goodwill. This was her lucky night: she couldn't lose. She had only to smile, and shoot out her fingers once more, calling: 'One, two, three . . . *nine*!'

Wrong. What did it matter? She drank her forfeit in two searing gulps and played again.

Wrong once more. This time as she tried to stand the room spun alarmingly and she caught at the chairback just in time to stop herself falling.

That's enough, she thought muzzily. I'd better stop. That's more than enough. She tried to say so to Dr Lombard, to ask him to stop the game, but a waiter was whispering to him and she couldn't attract his attention.

She caught at his arm – at least, she tried to catch his arm but her wavering hand misjudged the distance and knocked a plate off the table instead. Divine Praises! she thought in sudden panic. I'm jarred! How did it happen? Just two or three of those tiny glasses and I don't know if I'm on my head or my heels. If only Stephen would come! I'll never get across the room as far as his table . . .

'Doctor Lombard . . .' she said painfully, 'h – help me.'

Then she realized that his chair was empty. He had gone, abandoned her, left her alone with this crowd of grinning yellow faces, which advanced and receded as she looked at them, shouting incomprehensibly, urging her to play again, to drink again . . .

At that moment she felt her shoulders gripped and she was lifted almost bodily from her chair.

'Time to go home, Cinderella,' said Gene in a voice that allowed for no argument. Not that she felt inclined to argue. Her head was spinning and the floor seemed to tilt under her feet. She was vaguely aware of a roar of disappointment at her departure – disappointment that turned to delighted laughter when Gene responded with a rapid-fire burst of Chinese. She was too relieved even to feel humiliation as she stumbled towards the door on legs that seemed to be stuffed with cottonwool.

Like runners in a weird three-legged race, they passed down a few steps and along a dark corridor, and suddenly they were out in the fresh damp evening air of a courtyard. Beyond the gate the Marshal's fleet of curtained limousines waited like a school of sleek dark porpoises. At Gene's crisp order, the uniformed chauffeur of the leading vehicle sprang to open the door and help Romy into the softly cushioned interior, then leapt back into the driving seat. The limousine purred smoothly away down the black, glistening street.

'What about Stephen?' She spoke slowly, pronouncing each word with enormous care.

'What about . . . ? Oh, your husband. Don't worry, I've left him a message,' said Gene. His voice was amused. 'He isn't in very good shape himself just now, but Otto'll see him safe home. You just relax and we'll be back before you know where you are.'

I hardly know where I am now, thought Romy. She felt his eyes on her and sat up straighter, smoothing her hair, making an effort to regain her dignity. Her mind was clearing, although she felt an alarming lack of muscular coordination and found it hard to stay awake. She longed to lay her head on the strong, inviting shoulder beside her and drift off effortlessly into the whirling vortex of blackness that hovered at the edge of her vision.

'Who's Otto?'

'He's a German pilot. He used to fly reconnaissance

planes for Chiang Kai-shek, and now the Young Marshal's taken him on.' He was silent a moment then asked abruptly, 'How do you feel?'

'Much better, thank you,' she lied. She surreptitiously pinched the skin of her forearm until tears stung her eyes, but she couldn't shift the heavy weight of drowsiness. 'It was the heat and the noise that made me dizzy,' she said, challenging him to deny it.

In the gloom she saw his teeth flash white as he laughed. 'Much more likely the *mao t'ai*. That stuff kicks like a mule. I tried to warn you but you kept on knocking it back like lemonade. Still, you won't make that mistake twice. Do you think you'll be able to walk straight across the courtyard, or shall I carry you?'

No one with a grain of tact would have asked such a question. Romy ground her teeth. 'Of course I can,' she said hotly.

'Good. Here we are, then.'

The chauffeur sprang to open the door and Romy tried to step gracefully out of the vehicle, but to her dismay she found that her legs wouldn't obey her. They buckled like spaghetti and she clutched hastily at the car door to prevent herself collapsing in a heap. Clinging to the rags of her dignity she said shakily, 'I'm – I'm sorry, but I seem to have got cramp. My legs won't move. Please will you call the servants and tell them to bring a chair?'

She dreaded his laughter, but he said gravely, 'If you ask me, it would be a mistake to disturb the servants. They are always so curious, and you know how they talk . . . Mrs Bentley would know all about it before breakfast. Wouldn't it be simpler if I gave you a hand, just as far as your room?'

She felt helpless and ridiculous, propped against the car door, not daring to move a muscle in case it betrayed her. She said reluctantly, 'Well, if you're sure it wouldn't be too much trouble . . .'

'No trouble at all. A pleasure.' With an easy movement he put one arm round her shoulders and the other behind her knees and scooped her off her feet. 'There's really no need to wake up the servants,' he said, carrying her across the paved court.

'Of course not. They need all the sleep they can get.' Eagerly she grasped the excuse, relieved that no one else was about to witness her discomfiture. I'll never touch strong drink again, she vowed, silently, I'll never ignore well-meant advice. I'll never think I know best. She reeled off these resolutions in an effort to ignore the pounding of her heart as the animal warmth of his body touched hers. His face was very near, his breath warm against her cheek, and she kept her eyes steadfastly on the line of his jaw, fearing that if she looked up and met his gaze her inner excitement would be all too plain to him. Through her thin silk blouse she could feel the hard muscles in his arms moving as he held her against his chest. The fingers of his right hand were only inches away from her breast and she resisted with difficulty the temptation to move just a fraction within the circle of his arms and let them touch. I'm mad, she thought. I've no right to feel like this. He's married. I'm married . . . and I love Stephen. What's happening to me? She knew the answer to that question all too well, and every instinct she possessed told her that if Gene was given so much as an inkling of her feelings he wouldn't scruple to exploit them. She must at all costs conceal the truth and avoid any opportunity of being alone with him in future. This terrible, overwhelming attraction must be strangled before its hold on her became too strong.

'Here we are.' He set her carefully on the dressing-table stool in her own bedroom; she wondered how he knew so unerringly in which room she slept.

'Thank you, that was very kind. I can manage now. Good night.' She sat there rigidly, waiting for him to go.

'I'd better help you undress.'

'No, you will not!' The hurried refusal betrayed her agitation. Gene smiled.

'You'll never manage all those buttons.'

He moved towards her purposefully, and she shrank back, hissing through clenched teeth, 'Mr Lyon, if you don't go away *this minute*, I'll . . . I'll scream!'

'Surely you wouldn't deprive the servants of their sleep, Mrs Russell?'

The grin which accompanied the words disarmed her,

and she reluctantly smiled back. 'Well, perhaps the ones I can't reach . . .' Before she could move his fingers were deftly at work, unbuttoning her blouse, unzipping her skirt, unfastening suspenders with practised speed. The flesh seemed to glow and tingle where his hands brushed against her skin, as if a trail of fire was moving here and there, and hot blood mounted to her face and neck.

'No, really, that's enough. I can manage.'

'Stop fidgeting, you're as bad as Linda,' he said with a trace of impatience. 'Don't worry, you're not the first girl I've helped out of her clothes . . .'

'That,' said Romy with unexpected dryness, 'is precisely what's bothering me.'

His busy hands slowed; he gave a choke of laughter. 'Oh, gee, not what you're thinking! All in the line of duty, I assure you.'

'What a strange kind of duty.' She found it helped to talk. It kept her mind off the embarrassingly intimate things he was doing to her. She tried to remember the last time other hands than her own had removed her clothes, but the memory was lost in childhood mists. Since her long braids were cut she had never needed a maid to assist with her hair, and it took considerable persuasion to get Stephen even to unfasten the safety-chain on her pearl necklace; he would have been deeply reluctant to undo zips and buttons as Gene was now doing with such expertise.

'I used to cover fashion shows now and then,' he was saying. 'Those poor mannequins needed every hand they could beg, borrow, or steal to get them in and out of some of Mr Victor's creations. They were always glad of my help.'

I bet, thought Romy. She wondered whether to believe him. The thought that Stephen might appear any moment made it almost impossible to submit calmly to Gene's ministrations, but her present physical incapacity made independent movement equally impossible. She flexed her hands experimentally and thought that the motor nerves were at last beginning to respond normally. Across the room her bed looked cool and inviting. It was only two steps away and she was determined to cover them without assistance. Aware that he was watching every move she made, she managed it without a stumble and lay back, relaxed and triumphant, against the welcoming pillow.

'Good night, Gene, and thanks again,' she said and closed her eyes. A moment later she heard the door click shut.

Why had he left the light on? she wondered drowsily, but hadn't the strength to get out and switch it off. When the door opened again she kept her eyes closed thinking it must be Stephen, a supposition that was rudely dispelled a moment later when something warm and damp, like a huge soft tongue, licked unexpectedly across her forehead.

'Wh . . . what the *hell*. . . ?' she demanded, considerably startled.

Sponge in hand, Gene met her gaze. 'You're not going to sleep with all that muck on your face,' he said firmly.

It wasn't a question, it was a statement of intent. Romy's temper flared. 'Oh yes I am! It's none of your business and anyway it's not muck but very expensive make-up,' she said hotly. 'I don't need you to tell me what I can and can't do. Go away and leave me in peace.'

'Quickest way there is to spoil your complexion,' he murmured, working away with sponge and soap as if she hadn't spoken. 'Now keep still or you'll upset water all over the bed. You didn't imagine I'd let you go to sleep without *washing*?' She couldn't make out if his shocked tone was genuine or if he was laughing at her.

'What if Stephen comes in?' she said in an agonized whisper as he wiped rouge from her cheeks and mascara from her eyelashes. 'He'll have fifty fits. Why won't you do as I ask?'

'Because I care for you too much to let you go to hell in your own way,' he said lightly. 'I thought you realized that by now. All right, I'll just dry you off and we'll call it a day.'

She was glad that the muffling towel hid her expression and the racing of her heart was concealed beneath the sheet. He shouldn't *say* such things – not to a casual acquaintance, another man's wife, she thought with a mixture of anger and guilt because her own feelings towards him would not bear examination. He shouldn't behave like this. Had he no sense of decorum? Had he no sense at all?

'There, now you're all clean and beautiful.' He leaned down and kissed her on the lips, lightly at first and then with increasing passion. Her head began to whirl. Faintly, outside, she heard people approaching.

'Gene!' she gasped, twisting away from him. 'Stop! They're coming. Can't you hear them?'

Lights flickered against the drawn curtains; there was a shuffle of footsteps and a loud laugh, quickly hushed.

'There's time for one more kiss,' he whispered. Again his hard, demanding lips touched hers and against her will her whole body responded to him. She pushed him away with desperate strength.

'Quick. You must go.'

As light on his feet as a huge cat he crossed quickly to the door. 'Sleep well, darling,' he murmured and stepped unhurriedly on to the veranda.

Tense with fear, she strained her ears to listen. He was bound to encounter Stephen. There was no way of avoiding a meeting.

'Who's that?' Stephen's voice was sharp. 'Ah, it's you, Lyon. Is everything all right?'

Romy began to tremble violently. The idiot – he must have walked straight into the returning reveller. Now how could he explain his presence?

'I'm glad you're back, Mr Russell,' said Gene coolly. 'Your wife wasn't feeling too well so I saw her home. I think she'll be all right now.'

'Very decent of you to look after her. I'm much obliged. I hope it didn't spoil your evening.' She tried to detect the faintest note of irony in Stephen's voice but there was none; he was genuinely grateful to the friendly young American for taking care of his wife.

If he only *knew*, she thought; and then, immediately, thank heavens he doesn't know! Whether she liked it or not, the guilty knowledge of the evening's activities would have to remain her own secret because there was no possible way to explain them to Stephen. He simply wouldn't understand.

She dreaded meeting Gene again; but she dreaded not meeting him even more. It was with as much surprise as relief that she heard Stephen announce the next morning that he had arranged a three-day flying visit to the front line with Otto Liebermann, the Young Marshal's personal pilot, and if she liked, Romy could accompany him.

CHAPTER SEVEN

Frowning in concentration, his thick black hair flopping forward over his temples, Mao Tse-tung, newly-elected leader of the Revolutionary Military Council of the Chinese Communist Party, squatted on his lean haunches in a luxuriously-furnished room belonging to a former landlord, and pored over the captured map which he had spread out on the polished floorboards.

There must, he told himself, be a way out of the trap into which the Red Army had been manoeuvred. If he looked long enough and hard enough he would find it.

He carelessly shoved aside an elegant ebony chair inlaid with mother-of-pearl and left it where it fell while he stood up to consider the map from a different angle, one foot kicking absently at the corner of a brass-bound lacquered cabinet as he did so. Why, he wondered, couldn't capitalist exploiters put a proper table in a room, instead of cluttering it up with cabinets and pottery stools? They had too many possessions, that was the root of the trouble. Now if he lived here, he'd have all this junk cleared out and burnt and a few good solid country-built chests brought in: a table, some sturdy chairs, a bed . . . Sighing, the Chairman scratched at the angry insect bites that spread across his abdomen like a sprinkling of red pepper. He returned to his hunkered position again. There must be a way out of this mess.

It was nearly four months since Mao Tse-tung, the young peasant with the hooded, brooding eyes and relentless will, had called a party conference at Tsunyi, and managed to bludgeon his way into the leadership. He had chosen his moment carefully, taking advantage of the absence of most members of the Politburo. He then forced the remaining few to accept his Fourteen Resolutions, and agree that the whole civil war had been hopelessly mismanaged by the existing leadership. Mao had brought his allies among the military men into the conference, and it had ended triumphantly with Po Ku ousted and himself firmly in power for as long as the Red Army remained on the march. He had his gruff old ally Chu Teh to back him up on the military side; and wily soft-tongued Chou En-lai, bending gracefully with the wind of change, had promised his allegiance as well.

So far, so good. Mao had no doubts concerning his own ability to lead. He looked back on Tsunyi with pleasure as the moment when the Red Army in humiliating flight had been transformed into the Red Army on the march. Nevertheless it had to be recognized that the tactical position in which the army now found itself was very far from satisfactory. They had been marching westwards for months, but Generalissimo Chiang Kai-shek, chief among their enemies, continued to pursue both on the ground and in the air. National minorities who had suffered for so long at Chinese hands took their revenge by launching lightning attacks on the straggling columns of Red marchers, then faded wraithlike into their sheltering hills. Their clothes and bedding were constantly damp and much of the heavy equipment with which they had started out from Chingkangshan had already been jettisoned. Coughs and bronchitis further weakened the marchers. Food was scarce and tobacco a forgotten luxury. But the enemy which now trapped the Red Army was not a human one. Struggling westwards through territory unknown to them, misled by inaccurate and inadequate maps, the marchers had reached the huge barrier of the Tibetan foothills and, as they swung north to skirt this unscalable rampart, found themselves trapped in a triangle formed by the least relenting of foes, China's deep and dangerous rivers.

They had conquered the mighty Chinsha, the River of Golden Sand, which, despite its charming name, was as treacherous a dragon-headed spate as any man might fear to drown in. For five miserable weeks they had dodged and feinted, evading Chiang Kai-shek's troops on the borders of Kweichow and Szechuan, before making a desperate forced march to seize the only feasible ferry. That had been a triumph which resulted in the capture of the Chou P'ing fort, together with a great bonus of ammunition, stores, and much-needed maps – a powerful boost to the Red fighters' morale which gained them a welcome respite as Chiang Kai-shek's forces detoured to find another crossing.

Fierce flows the Golden River . . . Fiercely the Golden River flows . . . No, *flows* was wrong. The River of Golden Sand didn't flow; it tumbled, gushed, spewed, cascaded . . . Mao's tired mind played with words for a moment or two, then he brought himself back to the business in hand. Poems could be written later. First he must find a way out of this new trap. For the crossing of the Chinsha had been a short-lived triumph. Ahead of them lay an even more menacing obstacle, the savage Tatu river where, within living memory, another rebel army had met its fate. Better not to think of that. Better to concentrate on the future than brood on the past. Once more he bent over the map. The Tatu river must be crossed, and there were only three possible crossing-points.

There was a shuffle of feet outside and the low murmur of voices. Chen Chang-feng, Mao's bodyguard, put his bedraggled head round the door and announced that the other leaders had arrived.

'Come in, come in,' said Mao abruptly, flinging wide the door. 'Don't hang about outside in the rain. We've work to do tonight.'

They stamped in, shaking raindrops from their hair and clothing, their faces uniformly solemn. Blunt-featured, blunt-mannered Chu Teh, the grizzled ex-warlord whose change of heart had brought him to Mao's side in the early days at Chingkangshan, and now commanded the First Front Army, slapped a dripping parcel wrapped in banana leaves down on a marble table. A pinkish tinge spread across the creamy veined surface.

'We liberated a pig!' His wide grin showed strong yellow teeth.

'I hope you paid for it.'

'What d'you take me for?' snorted Chu Teh. 'Of course we paid, and I've brought the liver for your supper. Have you eaten?'

Mao tried to remember. Certainly Chen Chang-feng had told him food was ready, but had he eaten it? A glance at the servant's reproachful face as he hurried to serve hot water to the newcomers was enough to tell him he'd forgotten all about it – not for the first time.

'I'll eat later,' he said tersely. 'We've work to do first. Take a look at this map. Here's the river – here's the Luting bridge; this is our position now. Our latest information puts the enemy about *here*. Now, the question is, can we reach the Luting bridge and capture it before the enemy brings up reinforcements, or should we detour again?'

'You'll be no help to the Red Army if you starve yourself to death,' grumbled Chu Teh, solicitous as any *amah*. He beckoned the servant. 'Here, comrade, take this for the Chairman's supper and see that he eats it before he sleeps or you'll answer to me. It's good pig's liver, just what he needs to build up his strength. Now then, show me the map.'

Sharp-featured Lin Piao, the young strategist, was already down on hands and knees, his supple fingers spanning the distance between Anshunchang, where they were encamped, and the Luting bridge. 'Over three hundred *li*, I should guess,' he said in the gentle, precise voice that gave little clue to the quicksilver brain it articulated. 'You say that the Kuomintang are already on their way to Luting, travelling by the east bank of the river. Now if we could send a flying column to fall on them from the rear . . .'

'That would mean keeping the rest of the army waiting here, at the ferry,' objected Chu Teh heavily. 'I don't like it. It's an unlucky place for rebels.'

'Who's calling us rebels? We're the Red Army! Just because Prince Shih Ta-kai's luck ran out here, it doesn't mean the same will happen to us. Look how lucky we've been already! If a ferryboat hadn't been left here on the south bank, against the orders of Chiang Kai-shek himself . . .'

'Just because the KMT commander wanted to sleep with his new wife!' put in stocky little Peng Teh-huai with a grin.

'. . . we'd have had a bitter struggle to cross here. Now we must make the most of our opportunities and forget old superstitions.'

'All the same, it's haunted,' said Chu Teh doggedly. 'I remember the Old Weaver telling me how the spirits of Shih Ta-kai's dead soldiers still wail here on moonless nights. I don't want to join their number. I vote we cross back to the western bank of the Tatu.'

Chou En-lai stroked his beard, his clever black eyes darting from one to another, content to let them fight it out. He was no military strategist. He would leave it to the army men to decide what they should do. His great talent was diplomacy, smoothing ruffled feelings and persuading opposing factions to act in harmony.

He had thought deeply before transferring his own allegiance to Mao Tse-tung back in Tsunyi, and when he had done so, it had been with some reluctance. Not that it was difficult to recognize Mao's authority: poor peasant he might be by breeding, but he was also a born leader, a big man with big ideas to match his physique; possessing, moreover, a leader's charisma, a certain air of remote aloofness that seemed to mark him out as a man of destiny. It went some way towards compensating for his lack of social grace. Chou En-lai's own mandarin blood might deplore the new Chairman's natural coarseness, the way he scratched and spat and received visitors in any old clothes he happened to be wearing – or not wearing, as the case might be – but defects of that kind went no more than skin-deep. What worried him more was Mao's tendency to oversimplify: to see affairs in terms of black and white – or more precisely of Red and White – without the subtle shadings of colour that Chou instinctively recognized.

A peasant himself, Mao was inclined to idealize peasants, seeing them as all good and wholly good: brave, industrious, virtuous, honest, capable of learning or doing anything. Well, it was posible that some peasants were like that, but Chou had not been fortunate enough to meet them. In his view, peasants had no more claim to natural virtue than the rest of mankind. Some were more good than bad; more were more bad than good. Chinese peasants had been shamefully oppressed in the past and deserved a better life, but it would serve no good purpose to set them above the professional classes, trained for generations to use their brains instead of their hands. Equality was one thing, setting the peasant on a pedestal too high for him quite another. It would only make his inevitable fall the harder. For hand in hand with Mao's idealization of peasants went a compensating suspicion of intellectuals.

Po Ku, who had been ousted from the leadership, ranked as an intellectual in this company. He came from a family of magistrates and had served his apprenticeship in Moscow with the Twenty-eight Bolsheviks. Well, Moscow men were out of favour and out of power these days. It would be interesting to see if the peasant-worshippers could make a better hand of matters than their predecessors.

The discussion was getting heated. Chu Teh's weathered face had darkened and his voice rose as he repeated his opposition to keeping the army at Anshunchang. Lin Piao and Peng Teh-huai had united in their desire to push forward with a single column and capture the bridge. Gaunt and remote, Mao was brooding, his thick, straight eyebrows drawn together over hooded eyes. It was time to intervene.

'Gentlemen . . . Honoured comrades,' said Chou En-lai gently, agreeably, 'we seem to be getting nowhere.' His warm smile embraced them all and took any sting from his words. 'Allow me to suggest a compromise . . .'

He was rudely interrupted. There was the patter and splash of quick feet running in the mud, a shake at the door and a guttural explosion from the sleepy young guard on sentry-go. Then they all heard the unmistakable sound of a ringing slap. It was followed by howls of amazingly piercing intensity; attention-attracting howls which went on and on. Sunk in his abstraction, Mao Tse-tung ignored them but the other leaders, glad of a diversion, cast curious glances towards the door.

It opened, and the flustered face of Chen Chang-feng appeared, beckoning to Chu Teh. 'Comrade general, one moment, if you please . . .'

Chu Teh stumped out, shoulders hunched in embarrassment. Gleefully the others awaited his return.

'The little devil,' said Peng Teh-huai, half-admiringly. 'He's overstepped the mark this time, anyway. It's high time our brave Chu gave him the hiding he deserves.'

Hysterical high-pitched phrases seeped through the wall. '. . . woke up and you weren't there. You promised! The devils are going to eat me. They say they'll slice me in little pieces . . . screaming and wailing. I can't! I won't let you go. No, no, no! You promised . . .'

Rumble, rumble went Chu Teh's gruff voice, soothing, placating.

'It doesn't sound much like a hiding to me,' smiled Chou En-lai.

He was right. When the grizzled veteran rejoined them he was followed by a small, grubby boy, fragile as a sparrow beneath his absurdly large, red-starred cap; his brows arched high above eyes puffed with crying. 'It's these nightmares again. They won't leave him alone. What can one do?' apologized Chu Teh gruffly, resuming his seat. 'He's all right so long as he's with me. Lie down over there and go to sleep,' he added, shoving the child on to the heated *k'ang*. 'You can stay so long as you don't make a single sound. I'm very busy. Now then,' he turned to Chou En-lai, 'you were saying . . .'

The others politely hid their smiles. What could one do, indeed! There was nothing wrong with that little monster that a good beating wouldn't cure, but it was useless to say so to the comrade general. Equally useless to enquire why the boy was with the Red Army at all, since he was clearly too young to be a Young Pioneer and should by rights have been left with the rest of the women and small children in Chingkangshan. No, on this one subject Chu Teh was deaf to reason. He had found the boy in some desecrated temple out in the wilds with his slaughtered family lying all around, and instead of despatching him to join his ancestors as any sensible man would have done, what must old Chu Teh do but take the child under his own protection! Well, this was his reward. The boy never gave the general a moment's peace. If he wasn't having nightmares he was fighting with the other Little Red Devils, or inciting them to steal fruit, tease slow-witted peasants, and break every rule by which a Red marcher's life was governed. He was impatient of discipline, bored by political discussion, out for his own good rather than the good of the masses.

No wonder he was having nightmares here at Anshunchang, where his people had so cruelly slaughtered the Taiping rebels! For it was plain to see that Celestial Sparrow, as he was known (quite absurdly, since there was nothing in the least celestial about him) was a Manchu and possessed in full measure all a Manchu's failings. Yet Chu Teh obstinately turned a blind eye to his misdemeanours and treated him as a lucky mascot. While the comrade general stood high in the Chairman's favour, there was little anyone could do to shake Celestial Sparrow from his exalted perch, and the whole of the First Front Army had grown accustomed to the sight of their redoubtable commander pursued by this fragile but apparently tireless child, and the sound of his imperious high-pitched voice. 'Don't go so fast, Comrade General. Don't go without me. I want to come with you!'

Otto Liebermann was a first-rate pilot, but he was not a happy man. In addition to thirty pounds of surplus flesh, he carried a burden of worry.

He had lost his job as test-pilot for Messerschmitt aeroplanes soon after Hitler's National Socialist party grabbed power in Germany, and it had not taken him long to realize that in the new political climate his Jewish blood was going to prove a barrier to promotion in either civil or military aviation.

Leaving his wife and three children in Augsburg, he had come to seek his fortune in China, flying reconnaissance planes on contract for Chiang Kai-shek and, lately, for Manchuria's Young Marshal, Chang Hsueh-liang. The pay was good, the work suited his skills, but the climate disagreed with him and he worried perpetually over news from home, where anti-Semitic laws proliferated, and harrassment increased daily.

'If my contract shall be renewed, I am bringing Ilse and the boys to join me in the next year,' he told Stephen gloomily when they met to discuss details of Stephen's flying visit to the Kuomintang front line. 'It is bad for their educations, but what can one do? Hansi has two more years of school only, and my little twins must learn where they can. Ilse does not wish to leave Germany, but every week there is more trouble for Jews and one day, perhaps, we wake to find the door is shut and she may not leave.' He sighed.

'It might happen,' agreed Stephen. 'I was in Hamburg last summer, and none of my banking colleagues liked the way things were shaping.'

Otto brightened. 'Ha, you are financier? You try to make Chiang Kai-shek balance his books? You wonder why he must spend so much of your money to fight the Communists?' he enquired with sudden animation. 'Ho, ho, my friend. You must know that the Generalissimo must buy weapons for the Red Army as well as the Kuomintang!'

'Oh, surely not. There's been no suggestion of collusion . . .'

'Collusion, no; but still he buys weapons for the Reds. Quite sure,' said Otto emphatically. 'I ask you, when the Red Army catches the soldiers of Chiang Kai-shek, what do they do?'

Stephen shrugged. 'Shoot them?'

'Only officers they shoot. From the rest they take all weapons and give one silver dollar. Then they send them home. So you see, all the Reds' weapons are paid for by Chiang Kai-shek,' said Otto triumphantly.

Stephen smiled and raised the question of Romy. Could he bring his wife on the trip?

'*Kein Problem*,' said Otto promptly. Indeed, he seemed pleased. 'There is no danger and she will be happy to leave Shanghai for some days, I think.' He ran his fingers through the black hair curling low on his collar and made an effort to transpose his disgraceful beer belly into the position of a martial chest. He looked like a rather tattered farmyard rooster preparing to crow. 'Come to the flying field near the racecourse tomorrow morning at seven, and we will make a nice journey together,' he announced.

They departed with the minimum of formality on a hot,

still muggy morning. The little white four-seater plane had squared-off wingtips and, Romy thought, a disturbing air of fragility. Otto showed her to her seat and demonstrated the use of the intercom.

'Now fasten your seatbelts,' he called, and a few minutes later the engine burst into life with a spluttering roar.

The cabin walls trembled. Romy gripped the arms of her seat and kept her face impassive, trying to appear calm although her heart had made an unscheduled ascent into the base of her throat and she had to keep swallowing to stop it choking her. She had never flown before. Louder and louder grew the engines, and at last when she felt she could endure it no longer, the note changed and they began to taxi down the tarmac, swaying and bouncing over potholes. Through the window she caught glimpses of lorries, carts, the blurred faces of coolies turning to stare . . .

In a moment, thought Romy, torn between terror and delight, in a moment I shall be *flying*! She could hardly believe her luck. Even the nagging suspicion that Stephen was already regretting the moment of weakness when he agreed to let her come on this trip could not spoil her pleasure. She stared at the back of his head adorned with the monstrous earphones, willing him to turn and smile, to reassure her he was glad she was with him; but he was too busy studying a map spread out on his knees to take any notice of her. As usual when he was at work, she had ceased to exist for him. She knew that any attempt she made to attract his attention, so that she could share her excitement in this new sensation of being airborne, would be acknowledged by a puzzled frown, the briefest of answers, before he turned back with ill-concealed relief to something that mattered, the business she had interrupted. He never understood her impulse to share her thoughts and feelings, because he never felt the least desire to make anyone party to his own.

She wondered if he even remembered, now, that he had nearly forgotten his work and his duty long enough to make love to her yesterday morning. *Nearly*. She had analyzed the incident a hundred times already, trying to see where she had failed; but she guessed that Stephen would have jettisoned the memory immediately, as he disposed of all unwanted or unprofitable impediments, mental or physical. His brain would have labelled the incident, *Not Wanted On Voyage: Throw Overboard*, and it would have slid like a weighted coffin into the bottomless depths of his subconscious, where it would lie quiet and never bother him again.

Romy sighed. She wished she could do the same. Memories like that were uncomfortable companions, and she had collected too many of them in the past year.

Something punched her sharply in the small of the back. The engine note rose and she realized they were already above the ground; the brilliant green rice paddies spreading out below them like a chessboard, with geometrically neat irrigation channels like ruled silver lines intersecting them. Toy donkeys and long lines of miniscule coolies with miniature loads slung on poles as fine as needles plodded along the white roads. In the fields, peasants in wide conical hats turned pale faces upward. It was a new and delightful angle from which to survey the land.

'All is well?' enquired Otto over the intercom.

'Yes, thanks,' responded Stephen.

Romy pressed her switch. 'How far are we going?' she yelled into the airy static.

She saw Otto flinch. 'It is not necessary to shout,' he reproved her. 'We go for two hours only, then down. Then up, and two more hours. Tomorrow we reach the river.'

So quickly! It had taken the Red Army nearly seven months to march into Szechuan – the plane would be there tomorrow.

They rose higher. Soon the rice paddies and fields of corn were only a blur of light and dark green. Romy's neck began to ache. She stopped peering through the window and leaned back, surprised to find herself so sleepy. The strange swaying – almost dancing – movement of the plane might account for it, together with the earsplitting drone of the engines. Wisps of cloud as fine and soft as thistledown drifted past the windows.

Stephen seemed to have forgotten that she was there – or perhaps he was deliberately shutting her out of his mind.

She tried to recapture the elation she'd felt when they left the ground, but isolated as she was in the rear seat, she found excitement impossible to sustain for long. The cabin was stuffy and the headset pressed into her temples. She could see Stephen's lips moving as he talked to the pilot, his expression alert and interested. She couldn't be bothered to switch on the intercom to hear what they were saying, but a moment later her husband at last twisted in his seat, gesturing.

'What?' She pressed the switch.

'Please make sure your seatbelt is fastened,' came Otto's voice. 'This may become bumpy. We're running into a storm.'

CHAPTER EIGHT

It was the first of many storms. By the time the sun began to redden over the Tatu gorge late the following afternoon, Romy had had enough of flying. She was sick of the bumping and roaring, the sudden lurches that left her stomach suspended in mid-air, the ache of congested eardrums whenever they lost height. She longed to stretch her legs. The well-padded seat that had seemed so comfortable yesterday had become a hated straitjacket.

It was, moreover, galling to discover that neither Stephen nor their pilot seemed aware of these discomforts. Whenever they landed to refuel or collect information at some farflung outpost of Chiang Kai-shek's front line, Romy needed at least an hour to recover from the rigours of the last flight, but Stephen climbed out of the plane ready to interview anyone or take an interest in anything.

Ashamed of her weakness, Romy was careful not to complain for fear of being told she should have stayed at home. Her reluctance to re-enter the hot little cabin grew at each staging post on their journey.

At the second camp they visited, the reality of the war was

brought home to her by the sight of three shaven-headed prisoners, who drooped in their bonds as they stood lashed to stout poles in the unshaded courtyard of General Ho's headquarters. Communist bandits, captured in the general's latest raid, explained Otto in a whisper. As they sat drinking tea and exchanging compliments with the suave, smiling general in the building's cool interior, Romy's eyes were continually drawn back to the dejected, immobile figures. There was no glamour or heroism about them. They were dirty, ugly, and doomed.

One was squat and pockmarked, his stupid, brutal thick-featured face set in sullen apathy. The others were boys in their teens, their scrawny arms and legs bare, their clothes a collection of rags. Flies swarmed round their eyes and from time to time one would pass a dry tongue over cracked, blackened lips. Otherwise they never stirred.

'Ah, now you are looking at our prisoners,' said the general indulgently, catching her staring out of the window. 'You find it interesting to see Communist bandits, eh?'

'No, I think it's horrible,' burst out Romy. 'Why can't you put the poor things in the shade? They must be dying of thirst.'

'They will die soon, anyway,' said the general, smiling pleasantly. 'Tomorrow we shall cut off their heads. Then other peasants shall know what happens to Communist bandits.'

'It's inhuman . . .' began Romy, but a sharp nudge from Stephen warned her not to continue.

General Ho was not in the least put out. 'When you see what Communist bandits do to landlords' families, you do not think this punishment is excessive,' he said gently. 'I have seen women buried alive because they would not tell where their treasure is hidden, and little children still living with sharp sticks driven the length of their bodies.'

Romy's tea suddenly tasted bitter. She said no more and was glad when the interview came to an end. As they walked back across the courtyard she averted her eyes from the drooping figures lashed to their poles.

Two more long hops brought them to Fulin, and now

they could see the silver thread of the Tatu river far below, its dark cliffs frowning on either side.

'Hallo – what's that?' Stephen's binoculars picked up a thin line of grey-clad ants plodding along the eastern bank.

'You want I go lower?' Otto dived and Romy leant back in her seat, eyes closed, until her stomach caught up with her.

'Ha, it is the KMT, bringing reinforcements to Luting,' said Otto, after a careful scrutiny. He flew low over the column, waggling his wings, then headed upriver again. After a few moments he gave a guttural grunt of surprise.

'What's up?'

'Look across the river and tell me what you see.'

'It's the Red Army, by God!' exclaimed Stephen excitedly. 'Or a bit of it, at any rate.'

'Where? Where? Show me!' Once again Romy had forgotten to press the 'send' button, and neither of the men responded; before she could repeat her question she saw them for herself.

No more than a mile ahead of their enemy, on the opposite bank of the river, another column was marching, and this time when Otto flew low over the water Romy could clearly see the red star decorating their caps.

'It looks like a race to the bridge,' commented Stephen. 'D'you suppose the Kuomintang know about this? It's going to be a close-run thing.'

'They must know.' Otto was positive. 'They are too close not to know.'

'Don't forget we've got a bird's-eye view. They may well be hidden from one another and a river like that must make a hell of a din. They probably can't hear a thing above it.'

Romy was struggling to get her box camera out of her suitcase. Turbulent air currents above the rushing water made the plane bob about like a cork on a string, but she was too excited to feel sick. Here was the famous Red Army on the march, and she was determined to get some photographs to show Abigail.

'Please will you fly over them again, as low as you can,' she begged. 'I want to take pictures through the window.'

'We're going too fast, darling. They'll be all blurred,' said Stephen; but Otto, with a daredevil smile over his shoulder, rose to the challenge. Not for nothing had he test-flown planes for Messerschmitt. He prepared to obey her request to the letter. Taking the plane down to a mere fifty-odd feet above the marchers, he roared over the column, with Romy clicking away at the terrified faces turned up towards them.

'Ha!' shouted Otto exultantly. 'That is good, yes?'

'Marvellous!' cried Romy.

A string of pack animals at the back of the column bolted; some of the marchers flung themselves flat on the path, others raised their rifles to fire at the aerial aggressor.

'Again!' cried Romy. 'That was wonderful – I got some beauties that time. Just once more – *please*!'

'This time I go more low,' promised Otto, delighted with the chance to show his prowess. He made a long loop round the next bend in the river and returned to zoom low over the column again.

'Look out!' called Stephen sharply.

The Red soldiers had scattered as far as they were able on the narrow path, but the drivers of pack animals could not leave their charges and still stood in plain view, fighting to control the plunging, wild-eyed beasts to prevent them from stampeding over the cliffs into the river. Others had speedily unlimbered weapons, and it was the skyward-pointing muzzle of a gun that Stephen spotted as Otto roared in for his final run.

Romy was craning downward, directing her lens at the pack animals, when a sudden violent buffet shook the plane, knocking the camera from her hands. She looked up in alarm. Otto was slumped forward in his seat, one hand clutching his opposite shoulder, hauling desperately at the joystick with the other. The little plane yawed upward in a crazy spiral, smoke pouring from the tail.

'We're shot!' screamed Romy in mindless terror, forgetting to press the button again.

Sky and river spun in a blur of blue and silver as Otto fought to regain control. The plane slipped sideways, levelled out, slipped sideways again and began to glide. Romy could see the wingtip on her side drooping exactly like the wing of a shot bird. Alone in the back seat, skimming great boulders and scrubby trees, she jacknifed into a foetal position, hugging her knees and whimpering like a lost puppy as the ground rushed up to meet them.

Celestial Sparrow scuffed his straw sandals as he dawdled along the cliff path in the gathering gloom of late afternoon, rehearsing the injurious words he would hurl at treacherous old Ah Song when he and the column of pack animals caught up with him. The left sandal was coming to pieces already, and the right had started to fray between the straw sole and cloth upper. It was the second pair he had worn out in a week; it would be necessary – later – to forgive Ah Song and cajole him into plaiting yet another pair. He'd have to go though the time-honoured ritual of pretending to watch closely, and saying: 'Oh yes, *now* I see how you do it. Next time I'm *sure* I can make them myself'; although both he and Ah Song would know all the time that this was the purest fiction. Celestial Sparrow had no intention of ever trying to plait his own sandals, nor did Ah Song mean to lose this one hold he had over the General's demanding young protegé. If Kang Ke-ching, Chu Teh's formidable wife, had known how Celestial Sparrow employed the General's orderly for his own purposes, there would have been great trouble; but since the arrangement suited them both, the culprits took care that she remained unaware of it. Occasionally Ah Song would use her name as a lever and a threat, but Celestial Sparrow was a gambler by nature and relied on calling his bluff.

The matter of the sandals, however, would have to wait. If he walked carefully they would last a day or two yet. First Ah Song must be punished for his treachery. It was nothing short of treachery to have promised to wake his young master (which was how Celestial Sparrow regarded himself, in regrettable defiance of Communist dogma) before the vanguard of the Fourth Regiment left the hamlet where they'd spent the night – and then failed to do so.

'I tried to wake you but you would not stir,' the old man had said unconvincingly when Celestial Sparrow finally opened his eyes and found the advance party had gone. 'In the night Commander Wang got the order to press on with the utmost speed to capture the bridge. You couldn't have kept up with them. Two hundred and forty *li* to march in a day and a night! Impossible. You're better off with me and the pack animals. Don't fret, youngest brother. We'll get to the bridge soon enough.'

But Celestial Sparrow was too angry at the way he'd been tricked to listen to reason. He wanted to reach the Luting bridge with Commander Wang's vanguard – it was a matter of pride. He'd boasted to half a dozen other boys that he would, and if he failed they'd surely mock him. Celestial Sparrow detested mockery if it was directed at him, though he had no qualms about doling it out to others. He had rushed off without another word to Ah Song, leaving him to make ready the pack animals unaided. All day he'd toiled after the leading three companies of the Fourth Regiment, following their muddy tracks along the river path through blinding electric storms, and over the rough sides of Wild Tiger Mountain, short legs aching, heart pounding, stomach grumbling.

At last, as the sun began to sink in a glory of purple storm clouds, he admitted defeat. He wasn't going to be able to catch up with the vanguard; they'd got too big a start. His steps slowed, meandered, finally stopped. Now all he could do was wait for the plodding pack animals to catch up. He didn't want to spend the night alone, not on Wild Tiger Mountain. He knew that Ah Song wouldn't be very far behind. Some time earlier one of Chiang Kai-shek's reconnaissance planes had flown over him, and he'd heard a burst of gunfire. The plane had sheered off with smoke from its tail trailing across the sunset. Good riddance, thought Celestial Sparrow, making a rude gesture after it. That was the way the Red Army treated spies from above.

The gorge ahead of him was very dark, and even the roar of the river seemed muffled. He remembered the spirits of the Taiping army who were supposed to wail on moonless nights; he wished very much that Ah Song would make haste. To keep up his own spirits he began to chant aloud the epithets he would fling at the General's orderly. 'Mother-abusing son of a black pig! Defiler of ancestral graves! Dragon-excrement! Lying son of a Shanghai whore!' He shook his head, dissatisfied. It all sounded a little conventional – a little *tame*. What he really needed was a phrase Ah Song wouldn't understand, something that smacked of magic. That would scare him out of his wits.

A moment's thought and he came up with the perfect answer. He would frighten Ah Song by scolding him in the foreign devils' tongue he had learnt long ago in Tientsin.

'You are a naughtee boy. You shall go to bed without your supper,' he said carefully, twisting his tongue round the unaccustomed syllables. That was what his English *amah* – he had been taught to call her 'Nanny' – used to say when he rode his little bicycle over the flowerbeds of the palace, or threw his rice at the servants. Nanny . . . it was a long time since he had thought of her. When his mother's secret was discovered by those sister-defiling Japanese dwarfs who had taken away his father, and she'd sent Celestial Sparrow into hiding with his Third Aunt, he'd said goodbye for ever to Nanny, and his mother. It had been a long road from Tientsin to Kiangsi, and on the way he had lost most of the things she'd given him to remind him of his exalted birth. Not that such matters bothered him: who would wish to be a Son of Heaven when he could be a Red marcher? Two things remained: a tiny gold key, now tucked snugly into the cloth pouch round his neck, and his knowledge of the foreign devils' tongue.

The loss of his black jade elephant had been Third Aunt's fault, and he still blamed her bitterly. Desperate for money when they reached Shanghai and Celestial Sparrow fell ill, she had given it in payment to a foreign doctor. Ill as he was, Celestial Sparrow had protested loudly.

'There are other ways to obtain money!'

'Do you wish me to sell myself on the streets?' she said bitterly.

Truth to tell, he would have preferred it, but realized in time that if he said so it would jeopardize relations with Third Aunt without saving his treasure. But he still mourned his lost elephant.

'Naughtee boy! Naughtee boy!' he shouted, imagining Ah Song's shocked face. Nanny used to call him many other vile names: 'little monkey', 'Mr Sharp', and 'Young limb', had been her favourites. But 'naughtee boy' was the one she used most. He shouted it over the muffled roar of the river, enjoying the sound of his own voice.

'You are naughtee boy! You go to bed at once. You have no tea today!'

Crouching behind a rock a dozen yards away, Romy listened in blank amazement. Was she dreaming? Had the crash addled her wits? This dirty little boy in the absurdly long tunic and trousers was *speaking English* – he must be an angel sent from heaven to help her.

But wait, what about that red-starred cap and the old-fashioned but obviously serviceable gun lying beside him? Perhaps he was part of the Red Army. But if so, why was he alone? Another possibility struck her: perhaps he had *stolen* the gun and the cap from some dead Communist bandit and was taking them home as trophies. Was that why he was calling himself a naughty boy? Perhaps – oh, blissful thought! – there was a mission station somewhere near which would take them in and dress their wounds.

Whoever the boy was, she would have to ask him for help. There was clearly no alternative. Stephen and Otto lay unconscious up on the rocky hillside half a mile away. She had dragged them from the wreckage but that was as much as she could do. Stephen had a huge purple swelling on his forehead and might have internal injuries as well. He was groaning horribly. Otto's face had a curious leaden tinge and his breath came in loud, slow snorts. Since they crashed, a cloudburst had soaked both unconscious men to the skin. She knew that if she didn't get help they might die of shock and exposure, quite apart from any other injuries.

Taking a deep, steadying breath, Romy stood up. She walked towards the boy, speaking slowly and clearly. 'Please will you help me? Do you speak English? My plane has crashed and two men are hurt.' She flapped her arms, miming a plane, then held up fingers to show the number of injured. The boy watched blankly. At her approach he had sprung to his feet and snatched up his weapon, levelling it at her stomach. It was an uncomfortable feeling to see the gun pointed straight at her, but she persevered. 'I need help.'

There was a long tense silence. Then, slowly, the boy lowered the gun. 'Help?' he echoed. 'You are English ladee?' He paused again, staring at her assessingly while she held her breath and prayed. Then he said simply, 'I help you.'

Romy felt dizzy with relief. The odds against running into someone who spoke English in the wilds of Szechuan must have been truly astronomical – yet the miracle had happened. She breathed a prayer of thankfulness and beckoned to the boy. 'I'll show you where they are.'

'I come.' Bursting with self-importance, Celestial Sparrow shouldered his gun and followed her up the hill.

She had scrambled down the slope in such haste that she'd forgotten to take any bearings, and now as they climbed upward in the gathering gloom, she felt a sudden panic that she wouldn't be able to find the crashed plane. Subconsciously, however, she must have noted land-marks, because after only a moment of indecision she spotted the over-hanging rock which had torn the plane's wing to bits, and almost immediately heard men's voices. She stopped short, unable to believe her ears.

'Stephen?' she called.

There was a startled silence, then Stephen replied:

'Where are you? We're over here.'

She broke into a run, the boy following slowly, warily. 'Oh, thank God you're all right!' she exclaimed. In the dim light Stephen's bruise showed livid against his pale face, but he smiled and pulled her close against him.

'I'll echo that,' he said jerkily. 'We thought you must have been thrown out – when the wing broke off. I was terribly afraid –'

Stephen, afraid? She shook her head to clear it and said quickly, 'Don't worry, I fell soft. You and Otto had the worst of it. I pulled you from the plane, but you were both unconscious, so I went to get help . . . Where *is* Otto?'

The stocky figure of the pilot loomed up from behind the engine cowling. 'I, too, have escaped injury, but the plane is *kaput*,' he announced gloomily. 'I can do nothing. We must stay here hidden till daylight and then make contact with the Kuomintang. There are many Communist bandits near. Why did you go away? We were searching. We have been anxious.'

'I told you – I went to get help. I thought you might be dying.' With the air of a conjurer pulling a rabbit from his hat, she urged Celestial Sparrow forward. 'Look who I've found! This boy can speak English . . .'

'You found a boy? What boy?' interrupted Otto. '*Gott in Himmel!* He is a Communist, little fool!' he exclaimed violently, staring at the telltale red star. 'Quickly – catch him! Don't let him go. He must not tell what he has seen . . .'

He fumbled at his belt for his revolver, but Celestial Sparrow summed up the situation in a flash. Before Otto or Stephen could lay hands on him, he slipped like an eel behind the nearest rock and faded into the shadows. Otto's gun spat flame after him: too late. They heard the boy's pelting footsteps slipping and sliding down the steep hillside; then silence broken only by the muffled drone of the river.

'Now you've done it,' said Romy flatly.

Otto turned on her in a fury. '*I* have done it? Oh no, it is *you* who have done it, *Dummkopf*! You have brought a nest of hornets on us. Could you not see that boy is our enemy? Could you not wait until someone of sense told you what to do? No, no! Like a stupid woman you must rush off and stir up trouble for all of us. You know what Communist bandits do to their prisoners? They cut off their ears and rip up their stomachs. Then they bury them alive. Now we shall all be killed and it is completely your fault!'

The attack was so sudden, so unfair, that Romy gasped. This – after she had struggled to save him! 'Of all the ingratitude!' she burst out. 'Would you rather I'd left you to fry in the wreckage? I wish I had, you German pig!'

'There was never a question of frying. The plane is not on fire. All we must do is wait quietly here until the KMT soldiers come up the river; but you – you have to lead our enemies to this very spot.'

'Cut it out, you two,' said Stephen fiercely. 'This is no time for a slanging match. If that boy's gone to fetch his pals, as Otto thinks, we'll have to make ourselves scarce, and the sooner the better. Come on, up the hill and find somewhere to hide.'

'Already it is too late.' Otto pointed to bobbing lights on the path below.

'Rot. Grab what you need from the plane and come on.'

'But, Stephen –' Romy protested.

'Don't argue. Get going.'

Still muttering and glaring at one another, Romy and Otto did as he said, and followed him up the steep bank behind the plane. In a few moments they found themselves looking down on the cliff path, and Romy's heart gave an uncomfortable lurch. Evidently the boy had lost no time in summoning his friends: a long chain of flaring torches was already winding up the hillside in pursuit. She scrambled after Stephen with renewed energy, leaving Otto grumbling and cursing in the rear.

Tangled bushes tore at their clothes; their feet slipped on loose rocks as the sky grew darker. Soon it became impossible to see more than a few yards ahead and eventually Stephen, who was leading with his hands stretched out like a sleepwalker, was brought up short by a sheer wall of rock. He began to sidle round the obstacle, but his foot went over an edge into space, and he stepped back hastily.

'Sorry, darling. This looks like the end of this particular road,' he said quietly. 'There's some kind of chasm ahead. I daren't go on in the dark.'

They crouched beneath a rock, holding their breath, listening to the jabber of excited voices drawing steadily nearer.

'Sounds as if they've found the plane,' said Stephen after a while. 'Where's Otto got to?'

'I don't know. He must have found a hiding place lower down. He's too fat for climbing.' Romy shivered. 'D'you think they'll come up here?'

'I hope not. One simply can't tell. They may be satisfied with the stuff they find in the plane.' He put his arm round her. 'Are you cold? Have my jacket.'

'Not cold, just frightened. Oh God, they *are* coming up . . .'

The procession of torches was winding upward once more; the voices were suddenly much nearer.

'Keep still,' whispered Stephen. 'They may go straight past . . .'

Now I know what it feels like to be hunted, thought Romy. Like a fox or hare or deer, or a man on the run. Waiting, watching, hoping I won't be found. Her heart thudded painfully, high up in her throat, and she had an absurd longing to break cover shouting: 'I'm here!' Anything – even capture – would be better than the suspense of waiting passively to be discovered.

All at once there was a burst of shouting close beneath them. Footsteps scrabbled frantically over loose stones; there was a despairing grunt: '*Mein Gott* . . .' Tensely they waited for the next sound – a blow, a scream, a shot? Instead there was a torrent of Chinese: high-pitched commands from Otto's captors and the pilot's deeper tones replying, protesting, arguing.

'Will he tell them we're here?' she breathed in Stephen's ear.

'Of course not.'

There was no of course about it, thought Romy. She felt instinctively that Otto would do anything that promised to save his well-filled skin. Her fears were confirmed a moment later as the light of a dozen torches shone into their inadequate refuge. Otto had betrayed them.

Many hands hustled them down the hillside they had climbed so painfully. Their captors were jubilant, teeth flashing in the torchlight. Another party was busily engaged in stripping the aeroplane, taking the luggage, radio, food, medical supplies, and maps from the cabin, dismantling usable pieces from the engine, and finally shoving the stripped wreck to the edge of the cliff. A heave and the plane tumbled like a wounded bird into the foam-filled blackness below. The bandits gave a cheer and returned their attention to the prisoners.

'Now we kill you, imperialist running dogs,' remarked Celestial Sparrow, swaggering up to Romy, gun at the ready. 'How do you like to die?' he added in a conversational tone.

'Go away, you little ghoul,' she snapped.

Otto broke into a long hysterical speech in Chinese, to which the leader of their captors listened politely, his smooth face impassive. Then he signalled to one of his men, and Romy felt the hard cold muzzle of a pistol pressed against her temple. God forgive me but Otto was right, she thought wildly. That boy was right, too. We're going to die. Here. Now. She couldn't take it in. It seemed unbelievable that her life was about to be snuffed out: an explosion, a stab of flame . . . oblivion.

'Stephen,' she whispered, reaching for his hand, afraid to move her head in case the gun went off before she could say what she wanted to. 'Stephen . . . I'm sorry. I got you into this.'

'Don't say that. Nobody's fault – just one of those things. Don't be scared, darling. You won't go alone.' His hand gripped hers hard as she waited for the end.

Then Otto shouted something in Chinese, repeating it over and over again. The Communist commander looked puzzled and angry; his face cleared by degrees and he gave another high-pitched order. The gun was lowered from Romy's head and she drew a deep, shuddering breath. Her legs were shaking so badly that she could hardly stand; she sagged to the ground.

She felt Stephen's hand pulled roughly away from hers, and in a trice she was pinioned like a trussed bird and bundled on to the back of the pony, already burdened with lumpy sacks. Whips cracked, men shouted, and the column moved forward on its interrupted march. Something Otto had said had changed the commander's mind and persuaded him to carry his prisoners along with him. Romy was too overcome with fear and exhaustion even to wonder what had earned her this temporary respite.

It was a nightmare ride. An agonizing, interminable, terrifying ride in which the only moments of peace were those when unconsciousness overwhelmed her.

The column marched all night by the light of its flares, with the officers and political workers continually urging the men to greater speed, and the men passing on the urging to their animals. At dawn they halted for a brief rest, while the soldiers ate uncooked rice and washed it down with unboiled water. Neither prisoners nor animals were offered anything, and after a bare half-hour's halt they moved off again.

Romy had long lost any feeling in her arms and legs, and was sunk in a kind of mindless coma when at last she was lifted from the packpony late that afternoon. It was some time before her senses returned, but when they did she realized that the inert figures lying a bare five yards from her were her husband and Otto, sprawled in attitudes of total exhaustion or . . . death? Heart in mouth, she crawled over to them and was relieved to find they were both alive, but deeply asleep.

She tried to rouse Stephen, without success.

'They are tired after much marching,' explained Celestial Sparrow. He looked as fresh as a daisy.

'You mean they had to *walk* all this way?'

He nodded. 'I, too.'

'I expect you're used to it,' said Romy, obscurely annoyed by his cockiness. She took the mug of hot water he was offering, however, and sipped gratefully. Her courage revived, and with it her curiosity. 'Where are we? What's going on?' she asked.

She looked around her with growing interest. They had halted in a steep wooded valley, where the Tatu river flowed with a roar like muffled thunder through echoing walls of gingery rock. On the bank occupied by the Red Army were a few battered buildings swarming with soldiers, a guard-house, and the tall twin pillars of a long suspension bridge. On the opposite bank, some three hundred yards distant, rose the crenellated wall of a fair-sized town, its houses clinging in clusters like swallows' nests to the hill's precipitous sides.

But it was the bridge itself which caught and held her interest, for it was like no other bridge she had ever seen. It hung suspended in a shallow arc from one set of bridgehead pillars to the other, and it appeared to be composed solely of chains, like a great spider's ladder flung out across the roaring torrent.

'Luting bridge,' said Celestial Sparrow, his clever, monkey-like eyes following her glance.

'How are you supposed to cross that? There's no footway,' said Romy, wondering if she was mad, or they were. What was the point of a bridge you couldn't cross? Then she realized that from the point of view of the town's defenders, a bridge that could not be crossed was extremely desirable. No doubt they had destroyed the footway themselves, to prevent the Communists making use of it:

Hew down the bridge, Sir Consul,
With all the speed ye may . . .

Whoever held the position of consul in Luting town must be laughing up his sleeve to see his enemies thwarted on the opposite bank.

'Kuomintang take away floor,' confirmed the boy, nodding, 'but now Red fighters are making bridge again. See, they cut trees.'

All round the quiet oasis where she sat was a scene of intense activity. Like Otto and Stephen, the pack animals who had marched twenty-two hours with hardly a break had collapsed where they halted, but the men who'd trudged beside them had no time for rest. Some were felling trees on the hillside, while teams of others dragged them down to the bridgehead. The regular thump of axe on wood echoed in the gorge. Whole companies of soldiers were tightly grouped round their officers, chattering excitedly; others oiled weapons or ate with ravenous concentration, scooping bowlsful of glutinous rice from the cauldrons that hung bubbling over campfires.

She was glad of the boy's company in this strange new world into which she'd been flung, and he showed no desire to move away. Perhaps he had been set to guard her.

'My name is Romy,' she said.

He tried it out. 'Lo-mee.'

'What is your name?'

'Shiow Shin-niaw: Celestial Sparrow.' He had it off pat in English, which surprised her; but before she could question him further he caught her arm, pointing to a file of men marching purposefully towards the bridgehead.

'Look, look, Lo-mee. Now attack begins.'

An atmosphere of strained anticipation, so strong that it was almost tangible, hung over the river bank; as if the entire Red force was waiting for a signal. Suddenly it came.

A bugle blew, and the stuttering crackle of machine gun fire cut through the roar of the water. It was immediately answered by spurts and flashes from the far bank. Romy flung herself flat to the ground. To her astonishment, she saw the leading file of Red fighters run forward to the bridgehead and take hold of the huge swaying chains. Clinging like monkeys to the iron links, they began to swing themselves forward, hand over hand, towards the opposite bank. Their legs dangled helplessly above the foaming torrent.

'It's impossible! It's suicide!' She could hardly bear to watch the tiny, daredevil figures as they inched across the chasm, clinging for dear life. From both banks the gunfire intensified. Bullets whizzed and thudded into the ground and chips of rock flew everywhere, but she hardly noticed. Her eyes were glued to the leading climber, who faltered as a bullet smashed into his chest; for an instant he clung motionless, then dropped into the surging waves far below.

'Ma Ta-chiu!' groaned the boy with a dry sob.

'They'll never make it. It's impossible,' she breathed. United in suspense, they watched as man after man lost his grip on the chains and vanished into the foam. There were very few of the original twenty-two climbers left now, but a cheer went up from the Reds as a second wave of soldiers ran forward and began to swing along the chains. Strapped to his back, each man carried a freshly cut plank with which to replace the footway.

'Look, Lo-mee! Look at Commander Liao!' screeched Celestial Sparrow, jumping about in ecstasy. She switched her attention back to the leaders and saw that, amazingly, one at least had made it. He stood upright, like Horatius defying the Ten Thousand, just where the arc swung lowest over the water, and Romy realized with a leap of the heart that only the planks on the near side of the bridge had been removed. The townspeople of Luting had either been too lazy or had no time to remove the flooring right across the river.

They now realized their error too late. A huge tongue of flame shot into the air at the far side of the bridge, as they frenziedly poured kerosene on to the planks that could prove their undoing, and set them ablaze; but by now Commander Liao had been joined by several more climbers. Charging across the remaining section of footway, they vanished into the smoke and flames, while the second wave of climbers reached the centre of the bridge and began to place their planks over the bare chains.

The further bridgehead could be seen through a corridor of flame, like an artist's impression of hell, into which Red soldiers plunged with grenades bursting and clothes on fire.

It was crazy heroism, but it worked. Roars of encouragement burst from the assembled Communists; Romy knew that she was yelling with the rest, though she couldn't hear her own voice. At her side, Celestial Sparrow's plangent screeches cut like a knife through the din. Bodies still rained into the water below the bridge, and at the far end the fighting was fierce, but there could be no doubt now that the defenders were in retreat.

'We've won! They're going back!' screamed the boy, beside himself with excitement. 'D'you hear the bugle? It's Lin Piao's division, attacking from the rear.'

Since he spoke in Chinese, she didn't understand his words, but the meaning was plain enough. Another Communist force had arrived to take part in the battle. Now she realized the significance of the original column of Red marchers which Stephen had spotted on the eastern bank of the Tatu the previous day. A single division of the Red Army had succeeded in crossing the river at Anshunchang before Chiang Kai-shek's bombers made the ferry impassable, and this had now arrived at Luting. The townspeople and garrison were caught in a pincer movement from which there was no escape.

Within an hour the battle was virtually over. Sporadic bursts of firing still echoed in the town's narrow streets as the three Europeans crossed the bridge under guard. Stephen and Otto stumbled along like men in a trance, speechless with exhaustion. Unlike Romy, they had walked every foot of the way from the scene of their capture, and were now too far gone even to raise their eyes when a heavy drone overhead signalled the arrival of Chiang Kai-shek's bombers – too late to save Luting. As they dropped their lethal burdens, reducing more of the town to smouldering ruins, the Red Army received orders to withdraw into the broken wooded country beyond, where planes could not follow.

The aerial destroyers, cheated of their prey, flew away to the east, and with them went the prisoners' last hope of rescue.

CHAPTER NINE

They all suffered during those first weeks of captivity, while the Red Army continued its relentless progress through the Tibetan foothills, but both mentally and physically Otto suffered most. He was forty years old, twice Romy's age and ten years Stephen's senior. Living in the East, he had grown soft, prematurely fat and flabby through indulging his appetite for beer and rich food and taking little exercise. Climbing steep hills and blundering through icy streams, sleeping rough and eating the sparse monotonous diet of millet and parched corn which was all the mountain villages could offer, rapidly reduced him to a shadow of his former self: a deflated balloon whose skin sagged loosely on now-visible bones.

He was tortured, too, by anxiety about his family. 'My poor Ilse, my poor *Kinder*,' he would groan. 'What will they do? How will they live?'

Unanswerable questions, for it was clear to all of them that their captivity was purely a practical arrangement. The moment they ceased to be of use to the Red Army would also be their last.

It was thanks to Otto that they had not been summarily executed the night they were captured. On the day following the crossing of the Luting bridge, when the general euphoria had quietened somewhat, the three Europeans were taken before a military tribunal.

In a whisper, Otto identified the stern faces of their judges across the expanse of crowded benches in what had once been a village school. 'The big one with the wart on his chin: Mao Tse-tung. On his left, Lin Piao. I know him from pictures. On the right, General Chu Teh. The other I do not know.'

You could plant seed potatoes in the dirt on Mao's face and neck, thought Romy, staring fascinated at the Red Army leader. There was no glamour about him to match her imaginings; nevertheless he appeared formidable enough. He wore a stained and crumpled tunic with a curling collar, baggy trousers and straw sandals like any peasant, but his expression was immediately arresting. His broad moon face and hooded eyes below a high, wide forehead proclaimed that rarity: a man of action who was also a man of thought. Uncouth he might appear beside the dapper Chou En-lai and neat-featured, bright-eyed Lin Piao, but there could be no doubt who was leader.

When all had taken their seats, Chu Teh rapped on the table for silence, and a slender young captain, leader of the platoon which had captured them, rose to address the tribunal. His shrill emphatic voice and sharp, angry gestures seemed to bode ill for the Europeans.

'What's he saying?' whispered Romy in an agony of suspense. She found it terrifying to be unable to understand her accusers; to be forced to rely on expression and gesture and Otto's occasional muttered asides.

The pilot was listening intently and didn't reply until she nudged him sharply. Then he turned and shook his head.

'Be quiet. I must hear . . .'

'But what's he *saying*?'

Otto ran a shaking hand across his forehead. His face was grey.

'It is bad. Very bad. They are all against us. Now I also must speak.' His voice rose and fell in a mixture of indignation and pleading. Sweat trickled freely down his temples, but the stern expressions of the men on the platform facing them did not change. Chu Teh hawked and spat. Lin Piao stared at his hands. Mao Tse-tung's hooded eyes seemed to turn inwards as if his thoughts were a thousand miles away.

Otto sat down again, and two more soldiers immediately sprang to their feet, demanding a hearing. Romy tugged at Otto's sleeve.

'What did you tell him? What are they going to do to us?'

The German shook his head. 'I don't know what they do. They say we are spies for Chiang Kai-shek. They discuss if they will shoot us.'

'*Shoot us?*' She felt as if she might faint. 'What did you say?'

'I tell them they would be foolish to kill men of such skills as us. I am an engineer, and they need engineers. Stephen also has much experience of finance.'

An argument seemed to be developing on the bench. Otto looked more and more worried. Again he rose to speak and was curtly ordered to sit down.

'What's happening now?' said Stephen.

'They do not agree,' Otto replied unhappily. 'Chu Teh says we should die. Lin Piao and Chou En-lai say Chiang Kai-shek would pay a great ransom for your return. Mao says nothing – yet, but when he leads, the others will follow.'

Romy said with a sudden flash of inspiration, 'Tell them we're friends of Mrs Bentley.'

The two men stared at her as if she'd gone crazy. 'Why on earth?'

'It doesn't matter why. Just do it,' she urged. 'Stand up and tell them.'

Otto said heavily, 'This is foolishness . . .'

Romy hesitated. She was loath to betray Abigail's secret but she saw no alternative. 'Mrs Bentley helps Communists to escape from Shanghai,' she said in a rush. 'She hides them from the Blueshirts. It's true – I swear it. Her house is a safe-house for Communists.'

She could see they didn't believe her. 'Oh, really, darling, that's going a bit too far,' protested Stephen. 'That's a ridiculous suggestion.'

'Mrs Bentley to help Communists? Absolutely impossible,' said Otto with conviction.

'It's not,' she insisted. 'I tell you it's true. I've seen them myself.'

'I think you were dreaming, then,' said Otto.

'It's true!' She was almost crying with frustration. 'Damn you: you must believe me. It may be our only chance.'

Otto shrugged. 'What harm, after all? I tell them.' Again he rose to address the bench.

Romy, straining to catch Abigail's name, saw a remarkable change come over the broad abstracted face of Mao Tse-tung. His attention sharpened visibly. For the first time he seemed fully aware of the courtroom. The hooded lids rose and his eyes looked directly at the prisoners. Then, unbelievably, he smiled.

'Ben-lee,' he said, nodding. 'Missee Ben-lee.'

'Bull's-eye, darling,' murmured Stephen. 'Bang on the gold. I think you've just saved us all.'

As Mao spoke, the whole atmosphere altered. All round the courtroom hostile expressions were replaced by looks of open curiosity. The bench conferred again and a buzz of excited chatter rose to the rafters.

Otto's hands still trembled with strain. 'I think – I hope – that you are right. Listen now . . .'

Resonant and authoritative, the voice of Mao Tse-tung rose above the chatter, which was abruptly stilled. Otto began to translate.

'He says it is proved that we are capitalist spies . . . he calls us running dogs for the Japanese invaders, lackeys of the imperialist Chiang Kai-shek . . . He says that because of our . . . association with a lady who has helped many Communists, we shall not be shot as spies . . .'

'Thank God for that!'

'Instead we must – how do you say? – repent our crimes by working for the Red Army . . .'

'You mean they're not going to set us free?' The smile froze on Romy's face. 'Tell them they must free us – for Mrs Bentley's sake,' she whispered urgently.

'Hush . . . He asks now, what work can you do?'

'Me? Glory be!' Her brain felt numb, paralysed. What could she do? She had no training, no skills.

'Think quickly,' Otto urged. 'They will not feed useless mouths. Can you nurse the wounded?'

'I could try,' she said doubtfully. 'I've looked after enough sick animals . . .'

'Ah, animals. That is good.' Otto's anxious face lightened. 'I tell them you are doctor for animals . . .'

For the moment their lives were safe.

Their health was a different matter. Otto had a huge appetite and in spite of the extra rations supplied to him he daily grew weaker. Celestial Sparrow was open in his scorn.

'Half a catty of rice, half a catty of vegetables, and still he is not satisfied but asks for bread as well. Bread! Truly all German people eat too much.'

Romy couldn't help smiling as she sponged the sore back of one of the pack horses. 'Do you know so many Germans, Sparrow?'

'Li Teh, the military expert from the Comintern is also a German,' he said with dignity, 'and he eats just as much. When we were in Kiangsi Province, a courier was sent to Hong Kong to buy wine for him, and tobacco. His feet are so big that no sandals can be made to fit him. He is indeed a giant.'

'And he gives his horse a sore back, too,' agreed Romy, recognizing the man in question. 'I didn't realize he was German. Perhaps poor Otto should share his quarters and his food – I'm sure he'd be happier. Come and hold up this leg, will you? I want a good look at that cut. If only we had some proper antiseptic, these things would be far easier to heal.'

The boy bustled to do her bidding. Her new status as regimental horse-doctor pleased him, since it increased his own importance in the eyes of his contemporaries. It was still his responsibility to guard her and see that she did not escape; although well aware that this possibility was remote, he dogged her footsteps all day long, chattering constantly, and as a result the fluent English which he had spoken as a small boy was coming back to him by leaps and bounds. Romy, in turn, was picking up a smattering of Mandarin. Their daily horse-doctoring clinics were conducted in a mixture of languages, as Romy instructed Celestial Sparrow and he passed on her commands to the other *mafoos*.

It was not too difficult a job. Very few of the animals were ridden, though occasionally a wounded man would be placed in the saddle until he was fit enough to march again. Mao Tse-tung could often be seen on the dun pony he had captured seven years before from a Kuomintang general, and Li Teh, the German, usually rode; but most of the other leaders preferred to march with their men. The drivers who handled the animals were ignorant and feckless but seldom brutal, and the sturdy little Mongolian ponies and mules were extremely hardy, able to pick up a living even on the barren foothills. The most common ailments to afflict them were girth galls and saddle sores caused by ill-fitting packs, which never had time to heal properly during the Army's brief halts.

Though the nights were still cold, the days grew stiflingly hot. Biting insects plagued them, small black flies and zinging mosquitoes from whom they had no protection. But for Romy there was one horror worse than any mosquito.

She gave a stifled shriek when she first noticed what looked like a short length of grey rubber attached to her bare leg, midway between sock and skirt-hem.

'Ugh! What's that?' She brushed at it in disgust but it continued to cling.

Otto bent to look. 'Aha, you have been caught by a leech,' he announced.

Romy went pale. 'A leech?'

'Yes. You must know that this is very beneficial to the health. In old days doctors used very much leeches to take away blood from wounds and –'

'Get it off me!' she said in a tightly controlled voice.

'Don't lecture me about doctors. Can't you see that it's eating me alive?' A trickle of blood streamed down her leg from the site of the leech's feast. Romy shook with horror. She couldn't bear to touch the obscene grey slug sprouting from her flesh, growing visibly plumper. 'Stephen, help!' she shrieked.

He came running. 'What's the matter? Oh – what's that thing on your leg?'

'It's a leech,' she shuddered. 'I can't bear it. It's sucking my blood. I can't get it off. Oh . . . it's moving! Do something!'

By now she was the centre of an interested crowd. 'D'you want me to pull it off?' asked Stephen doubtfully. 'What if it breaks and the head goes on burrowing into you? I knew a girl once who got a tick in her head, and her mother pulled half of it off, and the rest . . .'

Romy said in a rising voice that bordered on hysteria, 'Will you stop talking and *do* something before I go mad? *Get it off me*. I don't care how – just get it off.'

'What happens here?' Debonair as a young prince, Celestial Sparrow swaggered through the gaping crowd. His cap sat at a rakish angle and his pockets bulged with stolen mulberries. When he saw the leech his eyes brightened. He drew deeply on the damp hand-rolled cigarette drooping from his lower lip, and then jabbed the glowing end into the bloated grey slug. It shrivelled as if punctured, waved feebly a few times, then dropped from Romy's leg. The blood of its interrupted banquet streamed unhindered into her sock.

'Oh . . . thank you!' Heedless of his dignity, Romy flung her arms round the boy and hugged him. Celestial Sparrow looked black as thunder. He suffered her embrace, standing as stiffly as an offended kitten, and then stalked away, head held high.

Stephen began to laugh. 'Well, that's a trick worth knowing!'

Romy rounded furiously on him. 'Why couldn't you do that? All you did was talk while the beastly thing sucked my life's blood. I didn't want to know about ticks and doctors in the olden days . . . aagh!' Her voice rose frenziedly and she slapped at her socks. 'There's another . . . and another. I'm crawling with the things. Why do they pick on me?'

'You'll have to take up smoking, darling,' said Stephen, 'or else wear trousers.'

'Wait till they start eating you,' said Romy darkly. 'You won't laugh then . . .'

During the day they seldom met, for their work kept them apart. Stephen travelled with the vanguard, helping the accountant and treasurer of Party funds, which were mostly in the form of silver dollars, carried by pack horses and doled out to villagers in payment for food. Romy's supply section marched at the rear.

Remembering how the Kuomintang soldiers at the anti-Communist bases he had visited had been encouraged to live off the land and prey on helpless peasants, Stephen began to see a good reason for the extraordinary popular support which had sustained the Red Army so far.

'They pay for everything they eat. It's the last thing I expected,' he said to Romy one evening as they lay exhausted by their fire after a particularly strenuous climb. Above them, the icy peak called the Great Snow Mountain reared heavenward against the black velvet sky.

'Pay? I thought they just helped themselves,' said Romy.

'Not at all. You know the orchard we passed today – the one full of ripe apricots?'

'There weren't any by the time we got there. There never are.'

'Well, I was up in front with the bullion and I saw that the branches were absolutely loaded. I thought the marchers would fall on them like locusts. I wanted to, myself.'

'Didn't they?'

'Not a bit of it. They sat down and waited for a good ten minutes while someone ran off and fetched the owner – then they solemnly bought handfuls of fruit from her. I couldn't believe my eyes, and nor could she. Quite a change from the warlords' armies, I imagine.'

'Every branch was stripped when *we* arrived,' said Romy mournfully. 'You get all the fun up in front.'

'Here, catch!' Stephen tossed across a handful of golden fruit. 'They're a bit squashed but still edible, I hope.'

'Now I know that chivalry still lives.' She said with her mouth full, 'Did Otto get some too? I see him drifting in this direction, alerted – no doubt – by the prospect of food.'

'He won't want them, don't worry.'

'How d'you know?'

'Tummy trouble. Off his grub,' said Stephen succinctly.

Romy groaned. 'The poor man – not again! I'm getting worried about him, Stephen. He's simply fading away before our eyes. At this rate he'll soon be too weak to keep up, and then what'll happen?'

'We'll have to persuade them to give him a horse . . . Hello, Otto. How're you feeling now?'

Otto looked years older than when they'd crashed. Loose folds of skin hung round his neck and his complexion was an unhealthy grey-yellow, against which his sunken eyes peered anxiously from deeply-hollowed sockets.

'Ah, you are eating apricots, I see. You must know that these are very bad fruits for the digestion. Once when I was young I eat a kilo of apricots and *Mein Gott*! One hour later I think I shall explode. They swell and swell in my stomach. My clothes are too tight. I cannot sit, I cannot lie, I cannot stand . . .'

'Steady on, you're spoiling my supper.'

'Ah, you laugh. You have a strong stomach. You can eat such things, but I am already ill from eating bad food. I ask for medicine but there is none. I ask for men to carry me, but they say if Chu Teh and Ho Lung can walk, I must also. But these are strong peasants,' he continued indignantly. 'They are used to walking long distances. Nobody knows how much I suffer.'

It was a recurrent theme. Stephen made sympathetic noises, but when Otto moved away, Romy said, 'I am sorry for him. I really am – but I do wish he wouldn't moan and groan so much.'

Stephen said, shrugging, 'You can't really blame him.'

'That's typical. *You* never blame anyone.'

He shook his head. 'Look at it this way: if it wasn't for us, poor old Otto wouldn't be in this fix. Or so he thinks.'

'You don't know that,' she argued. 'You can't *prove* it. He might just as easily have crashed on any other flight.'

'I doubt if he'd ever have gone within feet of the enemy if we hadn't asked him to,' said Stephen dryly.

'So you're blaming me.'

'No, I'm not.'

'Oh, rot. You know as well as I do that I asked Otto to go closer.'

'He needn't have obeyed you, though.'

'That's what I mean. It's just as much his fault as yours or mine . . . Anyway,' she added impatiently, 'we're all in the same boat now, so why should he think it's so much worse for him?'

'Oddly enough,' said Stephen slowly, 'I think it really is worse for him. He's never lived rough in his life, you see.'

'No more have I – or you, for that matter.'

'Oh, my prep school was twice as tough as this,' said Stephen lightly. 'Cold baths before breakfast and near-starvation. Not to mention the most grisly marathon runs. I used to spend most of the holidays in bed recovering.'

She laughed unwillingly. 'It can't have been that bad . . . Well, all right. You may have experienced hardship before, but what about me? I didn't go to boarding-school, praise be.'

Stephen looked at her across the fire with an expression she couldn't fathom. 'Oh, you're lucky, darling. You're one of nature's survivors.'

'What d'you mean?'

'How can I explain? You're tough, darling; which is what poor old Otto will never be.'

'Tough?' She wasn't sure whether to be flattered or insulted. On the one hand it was nice to know he thought she was coping better than Otto; on the other his words seemed to imply a certain lack of sensitivity in her, an inbred peasant strength which was hardly the image she had striven to cultivate.

She said, rather huffily, 'I'm nothing like as strong as some of the Chinese women.'

'No, beside Kang Ke-ching you look quite a fragile flower,' he agreed, laughing. 'I doubt if you'd be able to carry wounded soldiers on your back as she does. All the same, if anyone had told me a month ago that my wedded wife could survive with the Red Army on the march and still look as if she'd stepped straight out of the pages of *Vogue*, I wouldn't have believed him.'

This was better: compliments from Stephen were as rare as gold-dust. 'Ah, now you're codding me! I look a fright,' she exclaimed delightedly.

'No, you might well be setting a new fashion – the Peasant Look, or the Shepherd Boy Look – you know the kind of thing they go in for.'

Cities – fashions – modern civilization – how far away it all seemed! How far away it was from his primeval night on the cold hillside, watching the velvet sky and diamond-sharp frosty stars. They lay quietly, busy with private thoughts, listening to the countless small sounds from the sleeping soldiers scattered around them. At this altitude, men from the lowlands of Southern China slept lightly, uneasily, with pain in their chests and aching temples. The slow climb up from the valleys had done much to acclimatize Stephen and Romy: all the same she shivered at the thought of the morrow's assault on the Great Snow Mountain which barred their passage northward.

The thin bedrolls with which they had originally been issued had recently been supplemented by heavy sheepskins captured from a regiment of marauding Tibetan soldiers. The skins were only half-cured and smelt rank, but their wonderful warmth more than compensated for the stench. Romy moved across and snuggled close to Stephen, lying between him and the fire.

'These mountains . . .' she whispered. 'D'you think we can cross them? No one seems sure if there's a pass at the top. What if we come to a sheer drop? We'd freeze to death before we could get down.'

It was rare to see her defences crack. He said with a confidence he didn't feel, 'If Tibetan tribesmen can come over to raid this village, as I hear they do from time to time, there must be a pass. Don't worry. We'll find it all right.'

They lay side by side in their sleeping-bags for a few moments, thinking of the morrow, then he said casually, 'By the way, if anything . . . happens to me, I want you to know that Longmarsh will be yours.'

If anything happens . . . A superstitious shudder ran up her spine and she spoke without considering the effect of her words.

'That's the last thing I'd want. Don't talk about it.'

Too late, she sensed his hurt. 'All the same,' he said stiffly, 'I'd want you to have it. And look after it.'

'Your sister Sybil would do that better than me.'

'Sybil,' said Stephen unexpectedly, 'would do nothing of the kind.'

'Oh, don't talk about it,' she begged.

'Why not? It's important. We ought to discuss it. I want to know that if I die my home will be in good hands. Your hands.'

'It's unlucky. It's tempting fate to talk about it,' she said quickly. The thought of the ancient house hung like a millstone round her neck and filled her with dread. 'Oh Stephen, I'm scared,' she said in a low voice. 'I hate heights. That mountain looks so cold and forbidding, lying in wait for us . . .'

'Stop thinking about it. Go to sleep.' He murmured as if to himself, '*Cueillez dès aujourd'hui les roses de la vie.*'

'What does that mean?'

'Gather ye rosebuds while ye may . . .'

Romy was silent for a time. Then she said in a small voice, 'Do you think we haven't – haven't got long?'

'Who can tell?'

He kissed her lightly and she responded with passion, trying to blot out the spectre of the mountain looming above them. When he wanted to draw away she clung to him. 'Don't leave me, Stephen,' she whispered. 'Hold me tight. I'm scared.'

But he knew it wasn't only fright that prompted her to press against him on the stony ground, stroking the hair at the nape of his neck with trembling fingers. Against his will his blood stirred.

'Not now, darling,' he protested. 'This is hardly the moment –'

'Don't say that,' she said fiercely. 'Why is it never the moment? What's wrong with now? You said yourself this may be the last time we have together. Why can't we make love?'

Around them the army murmured and stirred. Fires crackled, dice clicked. There was a burst of laughter near at hand, quickly stilled.

Stephen shifted uncomfortably. 'All these people.'

'I don't care about them. What do they matter? Let them mind their own business and we'll mind ours. What's the matter, darling?' Her voice was soft, caressing. 'Don't you want me any more?'

The direct question embarrassed him. Want her? Of course he did, but not on a bleak frozen hillside in the midst of a Chinese army. Had she no sense of propriety? There was a time and a place for everything.

'Don't you?' she persisted.

'It's just that I think –'

'*Stop* thinking!' she said with sudden vehemence. 'You think too much. Stop explaining and rationalizing and being so damned *gentlemanly*.' Her voice cracked on the last word and she buried her face against his chest with a smothered sob.

She meant it. This unexpected glimpse into her mind took Stephen back. After all, he reflected a moment later, there was nothing immoral about making love to your own wife in a public place – it was just not done. But why wasn't it done? Was it some foolish hangover from his upbringing which made him regard the prospect with distaste? She was right that no one was paying the least attention to them, so why was he worrying?

On a sudden impulse he pulled her closer, and as his hands moved to cup her breasts she gave a tiny whimper, but whether it was of pleasure or relief he could not tell. The body which a moment before had felt as tense and brittle as a bundle of dry twigs relaxed at his touch into the warm sinuous slenderness he knew so well. She made no other sound when he pulled her across from her sleeping-bag into his, but wriggled quickly out of her remaining clothes so that they lay naked, pressed together in a single tight cocoon of cotton.

With her warm silky skin against his chest and the

coarsely-woven material abrading his back like sandpaper, Stephen's senses at last took command of his brain, blotting out his awareness of curious eyes and ears all round them in the dark. Inside the sleeping-bag was another world, a half-forgotten world of sensuous caresses and warm soft smoothness where Romy and he were no longer people with opinions and prejudices and temperaments, but ecstatic animals revelling in giving and receiving pleasure. He no longer cared who heard their muffled gasps and half-finished phrases, nor what interpretation an onlooker would put on the bag's heaving, shifting outline against the stars. He was far away, oblivious of anything but his own desire for his wife's strong, slender body and the pain of her nails digging deep into the muscles of his back. Even if the pent-up fury of his passion hurt her, she made no sound. Time and place lose their meaning until their thundering hearts rolled over the highest peak and began the long, gentle, glide down the farther slopes.

Romy lay in a delicious torpor, dreading the inevitable moment when Stephen would draw away from her. She wished they could remain like this all night, limbs intertwined so that she hardly knew if it was his arm or hers beneath her head, his pulse or hers beating softly against her cheek. His relaxed weight pinned her against the ground but she didn't mind it. Like a puppy she could sleep in any position, adapting her contours to local pressure. She felt safe and sheltered in his arms. Her fear of the Great Snow Mountain receded; the ever-present worry of whether he loved her thawed like an icicle in the combined heat of their bodies.

But Stephen, she well knew, preferred to sleep alone. Even in a double bed he lay tidily on his own side, guarding his privacy, keeping his distance in sleep just as he did when awake. Any moment now, she anticipated, her proximity would begin to disturb him. She knew the signs, the sequence of actions. He would stir uneasily, then one by one he would collect all the outflung portions of his anatomy until reassured that they all belonged to him and obeyed his will again; then stealthily, careful not to disturb her, he would withdraw by inches to his own territory, shutting her out as decisively as if he'd slammed a door in her face.

She waited while the minutes stretched out and Stephen's chest rose and fell with rapid, high-altitude breathing, warm against her neck, but he did not stir. Of course, she thought eventually, we're in *his* sleeping-bag. He's too polite to throw me out, so he's waiting for me to make the first move. Just a few minutes more . . . She dozed and woke again, amazed to find herself still in his arms.

This time I'll have to move, she told herself. She dreaded the breaking of contact between them even more than the plunge into icy air, but it had to be done. It was worse to wait for him to ask her to go than to initiate the separation herself.

As soon as she began to wriggle upward in the sleeping-bag, he started and his arms tightened round her. 'What's up?' he whispered, 'What are you doing?'

'It's all right, darling. I'm only moving back to my own sleeping-bag,' she said through chattering teeth. The frosty air bit her bare shoulders.

'Don't go; warmer like this,' he muttered indistinctly. 'Nice having you here . . .'

She couldn't believe she'd heard him correctly. Had he really said that, or was it just what she'd willed him to say? She lay tensely for a few minutes longer, open eyes staring into the dark as she waited for the first unconscious sign of rejection – but none came. At last she relaxed and allowed herself to believe that the miracle had happened; tonight at least, in the shadow of the Great Snow Mountain, Stephen needed her as much as she needed him.

CHAPTER TEN

The bugle woke them before daylight. All around was bustle and confusion in the dank chill of a misty dawn. Packs were strapped on to carrying-poles, the sick hoisted aboard ponies and mules; units grouped themselves round their leaders and the First Front Army began to climb the steep goat-track in almost total silence, a writhing serpent of men and animals struggling upward in the thin air towards the far-off peak which glittered with rose-tinted ice in the morning sun.

Romy set off with a new spring in her step and the night's terror pushed to the back of her mind. Stephen loved her; nothing else mattered. '*One* step at a time. *One* step at a time. *Right, Right, Right* in the middle of the kitchen floor I *Left, Left, Left* my wife and five fat children . . .' Her legs moved steadily, rhythmically, in the tireless gait of a mountaineer.

Celestial Sparrow used an entirely different technique for going uphill. Like a cat, he bounced upward in short bursts, now springing forward, now sitting on a rock swinging his legs and letting the column creep past him.

Many of the marchers were already in poor shape. Romy could see the weaker ones labouring when the first halt was called after a couple of hours. Men suffering from dysentery crouched beside the track, too weary to continue. She recognized Colonel Chang Kuo-hua of the supply section, who had been ill when he crossed the Tatu river, green-faced and exhausted as he slumped across a rock. She offered him a ride on the pony she was leading, but he shook his head. 'Leave me alone,' he gestured. 'I'll get to the top in my own time.'

In fact, as the path grew steeper, riding became too dangerous, and the cloud swirling round the mountainside blotted out even the shape of the men in front. Romy drove the pony before her, clinging to its tail, trusting its instinct to find the best path. She averted her eyes from the dizzying drops below as the track snaked up the hill, vertigo made her head spin and her mouth was full of the thick, evil-tasting bile which she could neither spit out nor swallow.

For the first time she began to doubt her own strength. Her heart was pounding in a way she'd never felt before, and though she sucked in great breaths of air her lungs ached for lack of oxygen. The pony, too, was tiring. It swayed like a drunken man and she feared it might lurch off the narrow track.

Faintly the bugle sounded ahead of her: another halt. She flopped down and began to sip from her waterbottle, but she had no energy left to chew the parched wheat in her ration-pouch. She craved sweetness: honey, chocolate, glucose. Even imagining such things made her faint with longing.

'Ah, there you are. I was getting worried.' Stephen slumped down beside her with a grunt. She surveyed him wonderingly, as if for the first time. He looked gaunt and tired and *ill*, she thought with a nasty jolt.

'What are you staring at?'

'You look . . . rather tired,' she said, choosing her words with care. 'Hadn't you better ride the next stage?'

A shutter seemed to drop over his features, freezing them in the polite, noncommital blank she knew of old.

'I'm all right,' said Stephen. 'It's not far to the top now.'

'Do take this pony,' she urged. 'He's only got a light load – he'd easily carry you too.'

'I'm all right,' he repeated doggedly. 'There's lots of chaps worse off than me. You hang on to your pony. You may need him yet.'

'But you need him *now*. Please, Stephen – be sensible. How will it help if you kill yourself?'

'Don't worry, I won't kill myself,' he said shortly. 'Hello, we're off again. Go carefully, darling . . .'

He staggered away to rejoin the head of the column, where the bullion chests were being carried, and as she watched him go the sky grew dark and an icy blast of wind blew down from the summit. Her pony neighed shrilly and swung round to present its rump to the storm; there was a rattle like machine gun fire and huge hailstones the size of pingpong balls pelted down on the exhausted marchers.

Some of them cowered under rocks; others grabbed their tin bowls and clapped them over unprotected heads.

Romy tugged at her bedroll with fingers that were clumsy with cold, then flung it over her and the pony's head. Together, they waited in the gloom for the storm to abate. When at last it did, everyone was soaked to the skin and shivering, hair plastered flat to skulls and bodies shaking with uncontrollable shudders. The political workers, always the first into action, hurried up and down the column, urging men to move, but for some marchers the storm had been the last straw. They lay where they had fallen until comrades pulled their limp bodies to the edge of the path to let the survivors struggle past.

Only a few hundred yards from their halting place, still a mile or so below the summit, Romy caught sight of a familiar stocky figure collapsed in the trampled slush.

Otto.

As she drew level with him, she saw that he was still alive, his desperate eyes begging her to stop and help him. With the silent aid of a husky young peasant following her, she placed the German across the pony's back, where he slumped like a sack of flour, too far gone even to speak. She tried to get the pony to move forward with its double burden, but it lowered its head and refused to budge.

A political worker loomed out of the swirling mist. 'What's the delay?' he shouted against the wind. 'You can't stop here. Move on.' He peered closely at Otto. 'What's that?'

'The German prisoner. The pilot,' said the young peasant.

'He's done for. Shoot him.'

Before Romy, who had only half-understood the rapid exchange, could intervene, the peasant drew a pistol from his belt and put the muzzle to Otto's temple.

'Don't!' she screamed.

He glanced at her dispassionately, then pulled the trigger. Romy couldn't bear to look at the place where Otto's head had been. Casually, the young man hauled the body from the pony's back and shoved it over the edge of the path. Then he shuffled forward into the driving wind.

'Move on. *Jex jen hung joeh!* Hurry!' shouted the political worker, waving his arms to shoo the pony on. 'Don't stop at the top but keep going.'

Scalding tears stung her eyes and instantly froze on her cheeks. 'Brutes . . .' she sobbed, but she had to obey. Nothing she could do would help Otto now. Freed of the extra weight, the pony blundered on, frantic now to reach shelter, stumbling over more bodies lying on the path, and shoving past another group of pack animals, halted on a bend. She recognized the shape of bullion chests, and would have stopped, but the pony tugged her on and she could only cling to its tail and trust that it would not slip.

They must have passed the summit without her noticing, because suddenly they were over the pass and the pony was sliding downhill, hoofs rattling over loose stones. A few moments later Romy realized that she was out of reach of the wind, standing in a deep cleft between cliffs. It seemed very quiet. All around lay the survivors of the Great Snow Mountain, untidy heaps of men and baggage jumbled together while their animals stood with heads hanging and waited for the first exhaustion to pass.

Though she had been on the move since daybreak, Romy was unaware of hunger, thirst, or cold: all she felt was an overwhelming need to rest. Heedless of the snow, she crumpled to the ground with the rest and allowed herself to drift into oblivion.

When she regained full consciousness, it was growing dark and she was rigid with cold, hands and feet utterly numbed. A boy was shaking her by the shoulder. For a moment she thought it was Celestial Sparrow, then realized this was a larger, stronger child – a stocky round-faced youngster known as Shiow cho, Little Ball, the nickname earned by his habit of tripping over his own feet when running downhill. He was leading her pack pony.

On, he gestured. She must go on. She could not sleep here on the mountain. Camp was lower down.

Painfully she struggled up and followed him along a steep path to a flat upland meadow which already twinkled with cooking fires. The nomads who had fled at the Red Army's approach had left piles of drying yak dung outside their huts, and the order had been given to use these foı fuel.

Little Ball guided her to his unit's fire and brought her a bowl of buckwheat gruel.

'Where is Celestial Sparrow?' she asked, surprised by his concern for her. The boy unstrapped the load from the patient pony's back, pulling out bags of rice and wheat that would be distributed among the unit the next morning before turning the animal loose to graze. Again, this was one of Celestial Sparrow's tasks. Romy hoped he had come to no harm.

'Celestial Sparrow. Where is he? *Ta tjai na nuc?*' she said slowly, but the boy looked blankly at her and shook his head.

She tried again. 'Where is Ste-phen?'

No reply. She gave up and drank her gruel. Searching for one man in that mass of exhausted humanity would be like looking for the needle in a haystack. Huddled in her sopping sheepskins on the wet clammy bedroll, Romy slept uneasily, with Stephen's face haunting her dreams and the echo of his words – half-admiring, half-bitter – echoing through her head: 'You're lucky. You're one of nature's survivors . . .' What if he hadn't been so lucky?

With daylight came the bombers, three menacing black birds droning out of the morning sun. Romy woke to the all-too-familiar whine and thump of exploding shells as they dropped their deadly eggs on the sleeping army. Breakfastless, cold, and stiff, the marchers gathered up their untidy loads and ran for cover under the steep overhanging cliffs that bounded the nomads' grazing grounds. Several of Romy's pack animals suffered minor wounds, and she was kept busy tending them in the brief halts that alternated with scrambling rushes from one patch of shelter to the next.

By midday they were safe from the bombers, but now her worry about Stephen had reached fever-pitch. Twenty-four hours had passed since she last saw him; twenty-four hours since Otto had been so summarily executed. Had Stephen shared the same fate, back on the windswept summit of the Great Snow Mountain?

With cold dread she remembered her moment of recognition of that blurred but still distinctive outline of bullion chests halted on the way to the summit; how her own pony had shoved past the group of men surrounding the Red Army's funds. Was that where it had happened? Had Stephen fallen, too exhausted to go on, and been shot by some hard-pressed political worker or simply left to die in the snow?

Had her own pony, stumbling over fallen bodies, stumbled also over Stephen's?

Somehow she must find out. She pestered Little Ball, repeating: '*Ta tjai na nuc?* Where is he?' but he either could not or would not answer. Frantic with anxiety, she searched up and down the column of resting marchers, scanning each hollow-cheeked face in the hope of finding someone with whom she could communicate. Without Otto, without Celestial Sparrow, she was helpless – a prisoner of silence, and the tired half-starved men to whom she spoke shook their heads wearily and turned away, unable to make the effort to understand.

At last she saw a man she recognized: Ah Song, the elderly orderly to General Chu Teh. Surely he would know the whereabouts of Celestial Sparrow? The old man listened patiently to her frenzied questions, nodding like a mournful mechanical monkey. At last he patted her arm and gestured: Stay here. I will find someone who can understand you. He shuffled away.

He returned accompanied by a slim, good-looking young Chinese with an alert, indefinably cosmopolitan air. Compared to Ah Song and the other ragged, crumpled soldiers he looked like a poster advertising the Ideal Red Warrior. His Sam Browne belt shone, his trousers and tunic fitted him to perfection, the peak of his red-starred cap was razor-sharp.

Ah Song introduced him: 'Wu Tsung-jen.'

The young man bowed elegantly from the waist and smiled broadly at her. '*Parle français*,' he announced.

Jesus! thought Romy wildly. He speaks French. If only

I could too! Sister Carmela, somewhat hampered by a cleft palate and a thick Kerry brogue, had taught French at Romy's convent school, and reckoned Rosemary O'Halloran to be the least apt pupil of her year. Now as never before she tried to understand the language, straining every nerve to decipher Comrade Wu's rapid jerky speech.

He tapped his chest. '*Garçon. Restaurant français.*'

She got that, all right. He'd been a waiter in a French restaurant. So far, so good. She nodded to show she understood and dredged up a few words from her memory.

'*Mon mari. Ste-phen. Où est-il?*'

'*Mort,*' said Comrade Wu with finality.

Romy stared at him. Mor? What did he mean? It wasn't a word she remembered. It didn't sound French to her.

'*Non,*' she said, shaking her head.

'*Oui, madame. Je regrette. Votre mari est mort.*'

Oh, it was agony not being able to understand. Like in those terrible after-dinner games where one person tried to act a word for his team to guess, and they'd be so dimwitted that the actor would go nearly mad trying to get his message across in ever wilder ways. If only she had Celestial Sparrow at her elbow, cheerfully translating for her! The force of her isolation struck her like a blow.

She had to shake her head again. '*Comprends pas,*' she admitted.

'*Mort, madame. Mort, mort, mort.*'

It was no use. She couldn't understand him. The two Chinese conferred together, then Ah Song went off and fetched one of the smaller Little Red Devils, together with a pack pony.

Romy watched in complete bewilderment. Were they going to fetch Stephen? Or were they completely at cross-purposes with her?

'*Mon mari?*' she said plaintively. 'Ste-phen?'

Wu tapped his chest again. '*Voici votre mari.*' He pulled the grinning child forward. '*Voici Celestial Sparrow.*'

Suddenly she understood. He was going to act the answer to her question. They were on the same wavelength at last.

He patted the horse's back. '*Argent. Trésor.*'

He must mean a bullion chest. '*Bon,*' she said.

'Montagne.' He pointed to the sky. *'Chiachinshan.'*

The Great Snow Mountain.

He led pony and boy forward, peering to left and right as if moving between precipice and cliff; up to the left, down to the right. He mimed a man in the last stages of fatigue, body bent forward against an invisible wind, legs staggering. Suddenly, at his order, the boy appeared to trip and fell sprawling off the right-hand side of the path, into the pretended abyss.

'Oh, God!' she murmured.

Comrade Wu knelt down, releasing the pony, which wandered off. He peered to either side. Slowly he reached forward and tried to grasp the boy's ankles. Too far. He inched forward over the pretended drop, appeared to slip, then rolled himself over half a dozen times until he was out of sight behind a cluster of rocks.

'Votre mari,' he said, returning. *'Mort.* Celestial Sparrow,' he prodded the recumbent boy. *'Mort aussi. Morts tous les deux.'*

She could no longer misunderstand him. Tears were coursing down Ah Song's leathery cheeks; she remembered how fond he had been of the impudent youngster who had teased him and bribed him and insulted him in a way no Red warrior should have been teased and bribed and insulted.

Somewhere near the summit of the Great Snow Mountain, Celestial Sparrow had fallen over a precipice. Stephen had tried to rescue him – and died in the attempt.

CHAPTER ELEVEN

A pulse throbbed erratically in Abigail's throat as she stared at the letter gripped in her white-knuckled hands. It had been brought to her breakfast table in the flower-filled courtyard by Chen Cheng, her new Number One boy, with the explanation that the gatekeeper, the *k'aimenti*, had found it pushed beneath the gate when he rose to unlock it.

Abigail didn't altogether trust Chen Cheng not to have read it before bringing it to her. It was still sealed, but steam and deft Chinese fingers were more than a match for any sealed flap. Rather than open the envelope under his knowing, inquisitive eyes, she sent him to find her spectacles, and while he was gone slit the cheap ricepaper with her fruit-knife.

The message bore no greeting and was frightening in its simplicity:

Your servant Li Ping has purchased a pardon by telling the Blueshirts of your subversive activities in helping Communist bandits to evade justice. You would be well advised to leave Shanghai for a prolonged holiday until police interest in your doings has died down. As you may be aware, the climate of Sianfu is beneficial and the area rich in archaeological interest. Young Marshal Chang Hsueh-liang urges patriots to join his fight against Japanese imperialism.

A WELL-WISHER

By the time Chen Cheng returned with her spectacles, Abigail's heartbeat had returned to normal. She had feared a 'confession' from poor one-eyed Li Ping ever since his disappearance – presumably kidnapped by Chiang Kai-shek's police – a month ago; and though she could not blame him for revealing the secret of her involvement, she hoped it had not been the illusory offer of a pardon which had finally broken his resistance. A month . . . Li Ping was certainly dead by now, but she felt sick at the thought of what he had probably suffered before he died. The Kuomintang police never pardoned Communist sympathizers; nor did they release them to tell tales.

She took the proffered spectacles. 'Thank you. That will be all.' She managed to speak in a perfectly normal tone.

He left – reluctantly, she thought. She re-read the letter; it puzzled her. If Li Ping had confessed, why had she received no visit from the International Police? They were usually quick to follow up any line given them by the

Blueshirts. Her own position here was respectable, certainly; but she'd be a fool to imagine herself inviolate. She'd have expected a stern warning, at least.

Did that mean the letter was from a friend, as it claimed – or an enemy? On the whole, she suspected the latter. Friends did not send anonymous letters full of veiled threats. And why the hint that Sian was a suitable place for her to take a holiday? Why not Peking, or Hong Kong, or even faraway England?

As you may be aware . . . Obviously the writer, whoever he was, knew that she and dear Alexander often spent their leave in Sian in the old days, when he was collecting material for that uncompleted book on the great Chin emperor, the unifier of China.

And the Young Marshal's fight against Japanese imperialism? Well, it was an open secret that Marshal Chang no longer saw eye to eye with his Generalissimo over the question of how to deal with the Japanese invaders. 'Stamp out Communism first, then drive out the Japanese from a united China,' said Chiang Kai-shek. 'The Japanese are only a skin disease; but Communism is a disease of the heart.'

'Push out the Japanese before they push you out,' responded Marshal Chang. 'Three provinces are in their hands already, and five more are threatened. Stop fighting your own countrymen and unite against the Japanese imperialists.'

The attitudes were irreconcilable. Rumour had it that the Young Marshal even went so far as to welcome Communist sympathizers to his base at Sian, provided they were determined to fight the Japanese.

Healthier . . . thought Abigail. Yes, it certainly would be a healthier political climate for me. Besides, I should like to see for myself just what *is* going on in the North-West. The spirit of adventure which had led her to China in the first place stirred in her again. The more she considered her position, the stronger it grew. Why cower in Shanghai waiting for the axe to fall?

'A nod's as good as a wink to a blind man,' as wise old Alexander used to say, so what did it matter who had written the anonymous letter? Whatever his motive, he had succeeded in warning her: now it was up to her to make use of the warning.

Finishing her cup of jasmine tea, she went indoors to her writing desk and dashed off a few chits to friends, cancelling all her immediate engagements.

A little later she rang for Chen Cheng and informed him that she planned to take a working holiday in North-Western China.

'I have decided to finish writing the book which my late husband started,' she explained. 'I may find it necessary to remain in Sian for several months – perhaps until Christmas. If that proves to be the case I will rent a house there and send for you. In the meantime, I would like you to stay here and take care of my property.'

'Velly good, missee,' said Chen Cheng in the pidgin English she abominated. 'Missee send for Chen Cheng, comee chop-chop.'

'Excellent. Now go upstairs to the master's library, please, and bring down the two black tin boxes containing his notes. I must sort out which to take with me. Oh, and if anyone calls, tell them I am Not At Home.'

A genuine indifference to fate tends to put a guardian angel on his mettle. In the weeks that followed Stephen's disappearance, Romy's angel seemed determined to work overtime; but his efforts went unthanked since she had ceased to care whether she lived or died. The sense of aching loss was aggravated by a feeling of waste: why did he have to throw away his life for the sake of that wretched child? Didn't he realize how badly she needed him?

The knowledge that Longmarsh now belonged to her, if she lived to claim it, gave her no particular pleasure. Let it revert to Sybil, she thought dully. What good was it without Stephen? All the same, it was chiefly the memory of his half-joking, half-serious command that she must survive – for the sake of Longmarsh – that kept her plodding on, day after gruelling day, while around her men and women collapsed and died, worn out by cold, hunger and exhaustion.

In many cases it was the unaccustomed food which finished them off. The abrupt change from a rice diet to one of corn, often uncooked, proved too much for the Southern Chinese. Their stomachs rebelled and the food went straight through them.

More accustomed to roughage in her diet, Romy suffered less at first, but as they climbed higher into the barren hills and even corn grew scarce, she too began to experience gastric disorders and to sympathize, too late, with Otto's complaints. Nausea and dizziness alternated with violent stomach cramps which left her trembling and exhausted. There was no privacy on the open hillside. Men and women squatted wretchedly beside the track, racked by uncontrollable gripes, and she had no choice but to do the same. She was fortunate in sharing Ah Song's nightly fire, for his culinary skill could make even a leather hide palatable, and the old man extended to her the same small kindnesses he'd shown towards Celestial Sparrow. Even so, she grew daily thinner and more liable to lag behind the main body of the march.

This was extremely dangerous, for in these hills lived fierce nomadic tribesmen with centuries of Chinese ill-usage to avenge. Like birds of prey they watched from the crags, swooping down to murder and mutilate Red Army stragglers, as eagles will strike down the slowest birds in a covey.

All too often small parties sent to forage in tribal villages failed to return. Once, as a grim warning, Ah Song led Romy into a hut where a dozen Red marchers sat round the ashes of a fire. They seemed to be leaning forward in earnest discussion, shoulders hunched; it was a second or two before she realized with horror that every one of them was headless. After that she made more of an effort to keep in the thick of the column: death from exhaustion she could accept, but mutilation at the hands of savage tribesmen was a different matter.

Personal cleanliness became a serious – even debilitating – problem. Without soap or toothpaste it was hard to keep her teeth and skin clean: a painful crop of boils developed where the straps of her pack chafed her shoulders, and small cuts, scrapes, and blisters festered and refused to heal. Her hair, frequently soaked but never washed, felt greasy and stiff. She tied back the bulk of it in a single plait as the Chinese women did and borrowed Ah Song's treasured scissors to chop a rough fringe straight across her forehead. It was a small relief to her that her monthly periods, always unpredictable in timing, now ceased completely; in her general state of debility she found this hardly surprising.

It was not until midsummer, when the battered, tattered remnants of Mao Tse-tung's First Front Army straggled down from the hills into the steamy valleys of Szechuan to join forces with their sleek, well-fed comrades belonging to Chang Kuo-tao's Fourth Front Army, who had already spent the best part of a year in this fertile countryside, that Romy began to wonder if this convenient suspension of her bodily functions might not, after all, have a different explanation.

Chang Kuo-tao's men were eager to press food on their half-starved comrades. Ah Song's cookpot bubbled with savoury offerings: the smells were delectable but Romy found herself unable to eat more than a few mouthfuls. This is ridiculous, she thought, as her stomach heaved and Ah Song, the eternal stockman, turned a lizard-like gaze on her in which enquiry was rapidly replaced by speculation. She could guess what he was thinking. There could be no secrets in an army on the march – especially a Chinese army. They lived, ate, washed, slept, and died in public and no doubt every marcher within earshot had been aware how she and Stephen had spent the night before the crossing of the Great Snow Mountain. Strangely, the thought did not embarrass her. Among the Chinese, she had observed, the least sign of affection between husband and wife was rare and they appeared to treat one another with brusque disdain; nevertheless there were pregnant women on the march whose condition could not be attributed to a shower of gold.

She tried to imagine having a baby of her own, Stephen's baby, but the mental effort was beyond her. How could anything as fragile as a human embryo have survived the conditions she'd existed in since Stephen's disappearance?

She'd reached the stage of hand-to-mouth living where she could throw her mind no farther forward than the next day; it was impossible to envisage any remoter future.

With deep relief she heard the order to make camp. The Red Army was to have a much-needed rest and re-fit while its leaders conferred over future plans.

Despite the joyous welcome given by the rank and file of the Fourth Front Army to their travel-weary comrades, Chang Kuo-tao himself was by no means effusive in his greeting of Mao Tse-tung. Before a week had passed they were in total disagreement. Chang wanted to spend the coming winter in Szechuan, where food was plentiful and many of his men had their homes. Mao was determined to press on northwards.

'We haven't marched all the way from Kiangsi in order to rot here while the Kuomintang traitors hand over province after province to the Japanese dwarf devils!' squeaked Little Ball in high indignation one evening flinging himself down beside Romy as she sat watching old Ah Song plait straw soles for her sandals. The stout walking shoes which she had fortunately been wearing when the plane crashed, had served her nobly across the mountains, but here in the steamy monsoon heat they were too heavy for normal use.

'What's the matter? Aren't you glad of a few days' rest?' enquired Ah Song tartly. His fingers flashed back and forth like the shuttle of a loom.

'A few days! The Fourth Army wants to stay here all winter! They've gone soft. They haven't been politically educated. They don't care if the Japanese imperialists cut up their homeland,' spluttered the boy. He was parrotting the words of his elders, but Romy knew that most of Mao's men would agree with him. Almost without noticing it, she had picked up enough Chinese to understand what was said around her. The tired First Front Army's resentment against Chang Kuo-tao's well-fed troops reminded her of hard-riding foxhunters who had followed a straight line, necks for sale, and arrived muddy and exhausted at the kill only to find that cannier men who had trotted gently round by road were there ahead of them.

Ah Song, however, was a native of Szechuan and glad to

be home. He saw a good deal of merit in the plan to remain there. 'You'll sing a different tune when you're wallowing up to your neck in the Grasslands of Chinghai,' he grunted. 'Even the chance to fight the Japanese won't seem so delightful then.'

'Oh, I didn't realize you were a coward. I thought you wanted to fight them too,' said Little Ball in a tone nicely calculated to annoy. Although he had taken over Celestial Sparrow's duties and place by Ah Song's fire, he had by no means succeeded in usurping the old man's affections. Ah Song took any opportunity that offered itself to make the stocky youngster look foolish, and Little Ball was quick to respond.

'What are these Grasslands?' asked Romy to avert a row.

For a moment Ah Song's hands were stilled and his eyes looked far away. 'It is the country of the dead, where neither bird nor beast can live. The sea of grass with never an island, its waves higher than a man's head, its roots in black stinking mud that will suck a horse down and swallow him without a trace. Men, too. Only the nomads can live on its fringes, and they guard their secrets. Evil plants grow there, turnips full of poison and fungus that turns a man's bowels to water. Nothing good grows in the Grasslands; nothing to eat, to drink, nowhere to rest. Nobody knows where its hidden paths lead and there are deep dark traps set by evil spirits to catch unwary travellers. Truly, it is a terrible place.'

'It won't stop the Red Army,' said Little Ball stoutly, though his face belied his bold words.

Ah Song smiled mysteriously and resumed his work. 'Wait until it comes to the vote,' he said. 'Then we'll see how many Red fighters want to leave their bodies in the Grasslands of Chinghai. Comrade Mao is a great leader but what he has not seen he cannot know; and he has never seen the Grasslands.'

But when the leaders emerged at last from their conference, Ah Song's prediction was confounded for a majority had voted to press on northwards, as Mao wished, and Chang Kuo-tao's efforts to remain in his lush pastures had been rebuffed. Old Ah Song seemed unperturbed when the news was announced, and Romy regarded him with suspicion. It was as if he knew some secret denied to the rest of them. All the time the army was re-grouping, preparing to march again, he smiled serenely and became unexpectedly generous in doling out small luxuries fom his own pack. 'Take this . . . I won't be wanting it. You may need that . . . Perhaps this will come in useful in the Grasslands . . .'

A roll of thread and two needles. A handful of dried mulberries and a handsome sunhat made of oiled paper, equally useful in a sudden downpour. Romy accepted this largesse with gratitude, but couldn't help wondering if he planned to desert from the Red Army himself, and so avoid crossing the Grasslands. However, a glance at him fussing round his stocky little General, Chu Teh, preparing his food and brushing his threadbare clothes with touching devotion seemed to make the idea of desertion unthinkable. She was still puzzling over the matter when the supply unit to which she was attached reached the edge of the Grasslands.

Holy Mary, that must be the biggest bog in the wide world! she thought with awed horror, staring down from a little promontory at the ocean of waving grass which Ah Song had described. No wonder the poor man was scared to cross it. Never had she seen anything like it. Here, at a height of eight thousand feet, the last thing you expected to find was mile upon mile of marshland, grass growing on grass which was itself rooted on the decomposed grass of countless years' growth. Sere and sedgy on top, it grew out of slimy black muck which assaulted the nose from several miles' distance, and showed flashes of that treacherous vivid emerald which she knew and distrusted of old. It looked an impassable obstacle, stretching away to the east as far as her eyes could see; but the thin line of the advance guard was already descending the hill, stumbling and splashing through the shining black pools of stagnant water, men and animals disappearing like wraiths into the dark mist that hung over the whole sinister landscape.

Little Ball grinned and waved her forward, and she had no alternative but to follow them on to the black quaking surface, trying not to imagine what it would feel like to be sucked slowly down into that evil-smelling morass. For the first time since Stephen's death she felt afraid, and in a curious way welcomed the fear because it meant that she wanted to live once more. It was a strange feeling: as if a limb, long numb, had begun to feel the circulation of blood again, painful but indisputably alive. Stephen was right, she thought with surprise. I'm a survivor. I'm not going to give up. No matter how long we march or how bad it gets, I'm going to survive.

Sian

I wonder how long he'll manage to last without it? thought Harvey Lombard, watching with clinical interest the small muscle that jumped and twitched below Marshal Chang's left eye as he stared fixedly at the Chinese chessboard. The Young Marshal's handsome face was prematurely lined, his skin parchment-pale, and his plain long robe of grey silk topped with a padded surcoat made a stark contrast to Harvey's own flamboyant mandarin's jacket of brilliant green satin, embroidered back and front with writhing red-and-gold dragons, bordered with black satin and splendidly sashed in cloth-of-gold.

The nip of winter was already in the air, and charcoal braziers warmed this red-pillared pavilion of the Young Marshal's headquarters in the walled city of Sian, once the capital of Chinese emperors, and still the strategic nerve-centre of the whole North-West. He had taken up residence near by the handsome old clock tower from whose topmost storey the signal was given to open and close the city gates. It was now three hours past sunset and those gates were shut, but the same north-east wind which in bygone ages had blown the topsoil of the Gobi Desert into Shensi Province howled like a banshee around the city walls and puffed clouds of fine dust along its busy streets.

He's been losing weight recently, thought Harvey, still watching his patient with close attention, alert to every tiny movement of facial muscles that might indicate his thoughts. I wonder how long he'll fight the craving before he gives in to it? That's the worst of morphine addiction. You may think you've broken the habit, but you never quite lose the craving, and in idle moments like these, moments of doubt or uncertainty, even of humiliation, you begin to yearn for the prick of the needle which will make you all-powerful, all-serene . . . He'd have done better to stay on the opium. That, at least, is a sociable habit in his circle. Most of the generals smoke between battles; even the old Empress Dowager used to relax with a pipe at the end of the day, I'm told. I enjoy it myself . . .

But morphine's a different matter. Morphine's a killer. That fool of a French physician should have known he was throwing him out of the frying pan into the fire when he tried to break Chang's opium habit with morphine injections. He probably did know, and grew fat on the knowledge. At one time Chang was spending two hundred dollars a day on the stuff. Two hundred dollars a day for . . . medication! I'm a better doctor than the Frenchman. I've cured him, if anyone has; but I'll never be able to touch him for two hundred dollars a day, more's the pity. Still, if I win tonight . . .

He's watching me, thought the Marshal with inner amusement, no trace of which appeared on his lean face with its deep-set slanted eyes. He thinks that my debility may favour his own aspirations. He wonders how best he can profit from my . . . weakness. Poor Harvey! He sees his power over me dwindling, for I have cured my addiction while he must still suffer his. He craves money just as I once craved opium and here in Sian, away from the spreading tentacles of the Green Gang which he used to serve, he finds little opportunity for the 'squeeze' on which he's grown to rely. Or has he found another source of 'squeeze'? When I lived in opulent luxury, warlord-style, Harvey was content; but he does not at all like this new regime of hard exercise and simple living. At heart he is far more extravagant than I am.

Covertly he studied the handsome coppery head bent over the board, thick straight eyebrows drawn together in apparent concentration.

I could, thought Chang Hsueh-liang, dismiss him and let him return to Shanghai now that my health no longer depends on his skill, but I think I prefer to keep him here under my eye. He has been close to me too long: he knows too much about me. If he were tempted to report recent changes in my thinking to the wrong ears, it would undo much of my patient work. Yes, he is better here; even if what he treats me for no longer exists. Artistically, he allowed his thin hand to shake a trifle as he moved one of his red ministers in a swift diagonal flight across the board to menace Harvey's sole remaining charger.

Harvey frowned and bit his lip. God, he thought, I should have seen that coming. What's the matter with me? I've got to win this game. I've *got* to! It had been a mistake to allow his thoughts to wander even for a moment, regarding the man opposite as patient instead of opponent. A very wily opponent. Anyone who played *Xiang qi* with the Young Marshal needed his wits well about him. Now Harvey's black army was in lamentable disarray, with the Marshal's red pieces crossing the river in droves to threaten the Nine Palaces where Harvey's general helplessly awaited defeat.

It was all or nothing: he had little choice left. Recklessly Harvey threw his last officer in the path of an advancing chariot.

'*Jiang!*' exclaimed the Young Marshal with quiet satisfaction. Harvey's general took a pace to the rear. Smiling, the Marshal moved up a minister to reinforce the attack. '*Jiang si!*' The game was over. 'Checkmate. You are still a gambler, Harvey. You trust to luck. You prefer to improvise rather than calculate.' He sighed. 'My father, Chang Tso-lin, was the same. If you and he had played together there would not be one piece left on the board by the end of the game.'

'I'm a doctor, sir, not a soldier,' Harvey protested, trying to speak lightly, not to give away how badly he'd needed to win that game. 'I haven't your skill in handling armies – even chess armies.'

He watched carefully to see if that dart would reach the mark and was rewarded. The Marshal's smile vanished.

He said sombrely, 'Perhaps chess armies are all I'm fit to

command now. Certainly the Generalissimo seems to think so.'

Harvey's senses were instantly alert. Perhaps there was some truth in the rumour that Chang Hsueh-liang was going to be superseded in his command. 'But he knows all your officers are loyal –'

'Loyal! Do you know how many of my officers have surrendered to the Communists in the past month? Surrendered without a fight, because they don't want to fight their own countrymen any longer. Can you blame them? Every day I find it harder to tell them they must stamp out this Red Army before they turn to fighting the Japanese.'

'But the Generalissimo –' began Harvey.

Chang Hsueh-liang held up a hand. 'Don't tell me: I know it already. Chiang Kai-shek will not hear of forming a united front with the Communists. Ah, if only he would listen!'

Harvey drew in his breath sharply. He knew that the disaffection among Tungpei officers was spreading daily, but if the virus had affected the Marshal himself he would have to report it. He said tentatively, 'You believe that we should unite with the Communists, sir?'

Chang's smile was bland. 'I believe we should fight the Japanese. You know that, Harvey.'

'With the Red Army's help?'

'Not unless the Generalissimo commands it.'

'Your loyalty does you credit, sir.'

'Loyalty to my blood-brother is all I have left.' Chang wondered if he sounded too glib. Had he injected sufficient quantities of bitterness and resignation into his voice to convince Harvey that he spoke the simple truth? Once it *would* have been the simple truth, but this last fruitless campaign in the North-West had made Chang Hseuh-liang question ideals and loyalties he'd once thought sacrosanct.

Too many of his officers, captured by the Reds and later released, had told the same tale. Far from being the ogres depicted by Kuomintang propaganda, Mao Tse-tung and his Red Army were brave and resourceful warriors, dedicated to the task of chasing the Japanese from Chinese soil and reclaiming the Middle Kingdom's lost inheritance. His own lost inheritance. Following Chiang Kai-shek's orders, he had meekly allowed the invaders to overrun his Manchurian homeland. Now he itched to unite his own army with Mao's seasoned warriors, and sweep to victory beside them.

Harvey must not be allowed to suspect.

'Another game?' suggested the Young Marshal, turning the board. 'You will want your revenge on me.'

'I'm afraid I've nothing left to wager.'

'Oh, come. Your Ming elephant against my gold phoenix cup.'

'Both your gold cups?' Almost automatically Harvey began to haggle, but before they could decide the stake they were interrupted.

A handsome young staff officer in the grey Tungpei uniform entered and saluted smartly. 'Permission to speak to Doctor Lombard, sir!'

The Marshal raised haughty eyebrows. 'Permission granted.'

'Sir!' The staff officer saluted again and turned to Harvey. 'One of our patrols attacked an enemy-held position this morning and captured a Red Army supply section. Among the wounded is a woman who was tending the mules. She claims to be an Englishwoman. The patrol brought her to the hospital, and Colonel Yang has asked if you would see her.'

Harvey frowned, annoyed at the interruption. He had long coveted the Marshal's gold phoenix cups and this looked like his chance to acquire them. 'Surely the matter can wait till morning?' he said.

'She's wounded, sir. The surgeon says she's lost a lot of blood. He would like your advice,' said the staff officer unhappily.

'She's probably a missionary. Tell the surgeon I'll be along to see her in the morning.'

'No, you must go now,' said the Marshal making a sudden decision. 'It is the penalty of a doctor's profession, Harvey. Imagine what Madame Chiang would say if it became known that you had allowed an English missionary to bleed to death while we gambled! Neither of us would ever hear the last of it. Besides, I am curious. How did this Englishwoman come to be tending mules for a Red Army supply unit? Perhaps she is their new secret weapon. Certainly you must go and solve this mystery. I shall not sleep until I have your report.'

'Very well, sir.' Harvey bowed to the inevitable. He followed the staff officer into the courtyard where a long black car was waiting.

The military hospital lay on the outskirts of the city, and throughout the fifteen minutes or so it took for the Chinese driver to blare a passage for the staff car through the narrow crooked streets, beneath wildly flapping banners, edging with no more than an inch to spare on either side between loaded trestles and benches in the main shopping alleys, Harvey's mind wrestled with his money problems. It was ironic that he, who had despised his own spendthrift father for losing a fortune before his thirtieth birthday, leaving his widow to bring up three sons on an English teacher's salary, should find himself in the same position at the same age. Without the wife and children, of course; but sometimes he couldn't help wondering if a thrifty English wife would not be a better investment than his two luxury-loving baby-faced concubines. He shuddered to think of what Fan Mei-ling and delicate lily-footed Li Wu must have cost him since he installed them in his house, but even their demands were modest compared to his own passion for Chinese treasures. After years of careful buying, Harvey possessed a fine library of Chinese books and scrolls and an outstanding collection of jades and bronzes from the great dynasties; but the more he acquired the more he wanted, and it was to satisfy this collector's lust that he had undertaken to act as an agent between Chiang Kai-shek's police in Sian and the Young Marshal's headquarters.

Everything he learnt in his capacity as physician to Marshal Chang, every straw in the wind which indicated the direction of Tungpei sympathies, was carefully evaluated and passed on by him to the Blueshirts, whose master paid handsomely for the service. Chiang Kai-shek trusted no one: not even the deputy commander of his armed forces. Over a hundred Communist sympathizers now behind bars in Sian were there as a result of information laid against them by Harvey. His position of trust in the Marshal's household gave him excellent opportunities for surveillance of all who came in contact with his patient.

If Chang Hsueh-liang were ever to dispense with his services, however, both Harvey's sources of income would vanish simultaneously. So far he had resisted the temptation to resuscitate the Marshal's addiction by introducing morphine into his metabolism once again: now he began to wonder if it would not be politic to do so by degrees. It would make his dependence more certain; it might even counter this distasteful new tendency towards fresh air, hard work and physical exercise. On the other hand, if the Young Marshal's tolerance towards Communists were to wane again, there would be fewer Reds for Harvey to denounce and a consequent drop in his income. The problem, as he saw it, was very finely balanced.

Then there was the question of Abigail Bentley. It was not for the sake of her health that Harvey had sent her the anonymous warning of her former servant's collapse under interrogation. Far from it: Harvey regarded Abigail as a possible source of 'squeeze.' If she could be lured back to her former haunts in Sian, two things were liable to happen. She would gravitate to her friends among the Communists, and possibly lead Harvey to them. She would probably also want to resume her husband's researches into the burial grounds of the Han emperors. Here, too, her activities might prove to Harvey's advantage.

When she arrived in Sian – assuming that his warning produced the right effect – he would do all in his power to ingratiate himself with her and dispel the unfortunate coolness which had existed between them ever since she had learned of his involvement in the silver-smuggling racket two years ago. She had accused him of being an agent provocateur employed by the Japanese: in this she was mistaken, because the only person Harvey ever wanted to benefit was himself. His need for money was becoming daily more pressing, but the last resort solution of selling part of his art collection was one which he refused to contemplate until all other intrigues failed.

In a more optimistic mood, Harvey descended from the car at the military hospital and was conducted through a series of courtyards where wounded soldiers lay on the bare ground beneath makeshift shelters to the former temple where more serious cases were housed. These were granted the luxury of rough plank beds, each covered with a thin rush mat and furnished with a block of wood as a neck rest. The two charcoal braziers at either end of the building did little to dispel its dank chill. Harvey shivered, thrusting his hands up the wide sleeves of his satin jacket.

The white-overalled surgeon who accompanied him halted by a bed distinguished from others by the addition of an elderly grey blanket.

'Here is the Englishwoman,' he said quietly.

Harvey glanced casually at the emaciated form beneath the blanket. Then his eyes narrowed and he bent swiftly for a closer look. '*Good God!*'

Surgeon and staff officer politely ignored his lack of manners in allowing himself to betray astonishment. They looked away to give him time to recover. The foreign doctor might have lived long in their land and spoke the language of the sons of Han with ease, but when all was said and done he was still a barbarian, and in moments of stress would behave as one.

Harvey cared nothing for their unexpressed contempt. He could hardly believe what he saw. Instead of the wrinkled weatherbeaten countenance of some tough old missionary, he recognized the beautiful girl he'd sat next to at the Shanghai opera six months ago – Stephen Russell's wife – who'd been given up for dead when their plane crashed in the Tatu gorge. It couldn't be – and yet it was. She wasn't beautiful now, of course. Her skin was grimy and deathly pale, so that the twin arcs of her eyebrows and the black sweep of lashes on her cheeks stood out in sharp contrast; her hair had been roughly cropped in a heavy fringe which gave her face a curiously blank, shield-shaped appearance. The hands which lay neatly on the grey blanket were thin as claws, with blackened, broken nails, and her neck looked far too frail to support the heavy head.

'Is it true, then? She is an English woman?' asked the

surgeon, judging it time to intervene.

'Yes . . . yes,' said Harvey abstractedly. He made an effort to pull himself together, to plan. 'She can't stay here, of course. She must be taken at once to my house.'

The surgeon's almond eyes were expressionless but he allowed his tone to indicate disapproval.

'I cannot allow my patient to be moved, Dr Lombard. As you see, she is seriously ill.'

'Nonsense, man,' said Harvey impatiently. 'She'll be far better off with me – you know it as well as I do. I'll be responsible for getting her moved, if you'll let me have a couple of stretcher-coolies. You must see that it's quite unsuitable for an English lady to be nursed in the military hospital. I'll take charge of the case from now on and you can wash your hands of the whole affair. Well, damn it,' he added as the surgeon hesitated, 'that's what you wanted, isn't it? That must be why you sent for me?'

'Yes, but . . .' The surgeon shrugged and decided not to pursue the matter. He realized it was absurd to feel protective about this particular patient, or reluctant to allow her removal to what would no doubt be better nursing conditions, just because the order came from a quarter he instinctively distrusted. The woman was a foreign devil: let her be cared for by foreign devils, then. What did it matter to him if she lived or died? He had many more cases to attend to and would be glad of the empty bed.

'That's settled, then,' said Harvey and clapped his hands to summon the stretcher-bearers.

CHAPTER TWELVE

Loud voices tried to urge Romy back to consciousness. Lights flashed in her eyes and needles pricked her flesh but still she clung to her dreams. In dreams she could return to the sun-dappled green hills of Tipperary, or canter along russet tracks soft with leaf-mould from Longmarsh beeches, with Stephen at her side.

She didn't want reality. Reality meant hunger and cold, exhaustion and pain. If she woke she would find her back propped against some rock or tree, legs drawn up to her chest and feet deep in foul-smelling icy slime. Another day of stumbling misery would stretch out before her. But if she lay here with her eyes tightly closed she could imagine that the distant squeak and clank she heard was the courtyard well at Lissanissky registering its standard protest against any kind of work, and the yapping dog would turn into Paddy the gardener's aggressive terrier.

Like frames from a badly-spliced film, scenes from the past months flickered behind her closed eyelids: herself ill with swamp fever, which blackened the skin and swelled every joint, sweating and delirious while Little Ball and his companions scoured the countryside for food to save her. For three days they had starved: then they found that, beneath their red and green paint, temple idols were made of hardened wheat and butter. They had melted them into a gluey porridge and fed it to Romy.

Another image showed her waking in the Grasslands, frozen to the ground by the water in her clothes. Little Ball had chipped and torn her free, but the rest of their group was already beyond help, frozen to death as they slept.

'Romy?'

That must be Little Ball's voice, trying to rouse her to another day of gruelling toil. But Little Ball was dead, shattered into a hundred bloody fragments when the Kuomintang shell landed on their picket line. She'd run towards him . . . then what?

The flickering film became distorted: pain, darkness, pain, flashes of light; noise, jolting, her own voice screaming . . .

'Can you hear me, Rosemary?'

Once she had been Rosemary, not Lo-mee. Who had called her Rosemary? Her mother, and Stephen, and someone else with a deep, husky, faintly familiar voice. A woman . . .

Her mind grappled clumsily with the puzzle then gave up. The only comfort was oblivion. She shut her senses to the sounds around her.

'I think she'll soon regain consciousness,' said Abigail

Bentley to Dr Lombard as they stood looking down at the patient. 'Just for a moment, this morning, I really thought she was listening to me.'

Lombard snapped shut his instrument case. 'I hope you're right. It's always difficult to predict how things will go. As far as I can tell there's no damage to the brain itself. Her reflexes are functioning normally. It seems more a question of mental withdrawal. She's unconscious principally because she chooses to be. Talk to her as much as you can, Mrs Bentley. Sooner or later something may provoke a reaction.'

He paused, then said with a casualness that gave no indication of the hours of careful thought behind the question, 'I've been wondering whether you'd care to leave the guest-house and move in here for a while? It's awfully good of you to spend so much time with my patient, but I'm afraid you must find it very inconvenient. You'd be most welcome here.'

Abigail gave him a sharp, surprised glance, wondering what had prompted the offer. She knew Dr Lombard well enough to suspect an ulterior motive. But then, she reflected, he wasn't the only one. Her brain raced as she considered whether or not to accept the offer. To walk straight into the lion's den . . .

Since her arrival in the old Chinese capital two weeks ago, she had lodged adequately if not very comfortably at the Sian Guest House, and spent her time looking up old friends and discussing how best to end the civil war. Mr Lu, who hid his political activities behind the respectable cover of a tailor's shop, told her that many of the Young Marshal's more forward-looking officers were already disenchanted with Chiang Kai-shek's policies were already disenchanted alliance with the Red Army. It was rumoured that Marshal Chang himself was coming round to that viewpoint.

But although the political climate was healthier here in the North-West than it was in Shanghai for opponents of civil war, just as her mysterious letter had indicated, Abigail soon realized that Chiang Kai-shek's faction was still strong – and dangerous. Mr Lu's friends were still being arrested with frightening regularity. Evidently there was someone close to the Young Marshal – someone with access to Tungpei military secrets, who was using his position to betray Red sympathizers on the Marshal's staff. Abigail had come to the tentative conclusion that the traitor in Marshal Chang's entourage might very well be Dr Lombard. At least, she and Mr Lu agreed, he should be carefully watched.

Now he was offering her the opportunity to keep him under close surveillance. She ought to jump at the chance. Still Abigail hesitated, wondering . . .

Was his concern really for his patient, or did Dr Lombard, in turn, suspect her of illicit contacts with Reds? Perhaps he was as eager to keep an eye on her as she was to watch him. *Quis custodiet ipsos custodes*? she thought with inner excitement. Who takes care of the caretaker's daughter when the caretaker's busy taking care?

His concern for Romy was certainly genuine enough. Since receiving the news of the girl's astonishing reappearance more than a year after she had vanished in the interior, Abigail had spent most of her waking hours at Romy's bedside, and knew that Dr Lombard was doing all he could to save both her and the baby she carried. The Young Marshal, whose reconnaissance plane had crashed with her aboard, was also taking a keen interest in the case. If Romy ever regained consciousness she should be able to provide answers to a number of present puzzles. Where had she been all that time? Where was her husband? What was she doing with the Red Army patrol?

Dr Lombard cleared his throat. 'Of course I've no right to ask this of you,' he said with a charming, rueful smile. 'You've done such a lot to help me already that I feel guilty even suggesting you should do more. The truth is, I can't give Mrs Russell as much attention as I'd like to because of other professional commitments.'

'Of course, I understand. It must be very difficult for you,' said Abigail earnestly.

'But if you were living here, as my guest . . .' he left the sentence artistically trailing and gestured with open hands, indicating she would be mistress of all she surveyed.

'Well, I don't know . . .' said Abigail, apparently flustered; but her mind was made up. If you were fighting a man with a long-range weapon, the safest policy was to hug him. Not that she could ever imagine hugging Dr Lombard: nevertheless the principle was correct. She assumed the vague, silly-old-woman expression which so successfully camouflaged her cool alert intelligence.

'It's really much too kind. Poor Rosemary – if you're sure I wouldn't be a nuisance to you . . .'

'On the contrary, it would be a great weight off my mind to know you were here when I can't be,' he assured her smoothly. 'Mrs Russell should have constant companionship and conversation to try to stimulate her brain into activity. I don't know anyone who could do that as well as you. Of course, it's asking a lot of you.'

'Not in the least.' Abigail peered earnestly through her gold-rimmed spectacles. 'I feel somehow *responsible* for the poor child. If you really think I could help her I'll arrange to have my baggage brought here today. I'll move in at once.'

'Excellent. Believe me, I'm deeply grateful,' said Lombard with another of the warm, confidential smiles which made him such a popular physician among ladies of a certain age. Hooked her! he thought triumphantly. I've got the old trout just where I want her now. It would greatly simplify his task of unmasking Mrs Bentley's confederates if she were living under his roof. He took his leave with many expressions of pleasure.

Abigail maintained her look of captivated bewilderment until he was safely through the door, then returned to Romy's bedside with a little skip of excitement. Mr Lu, who had tried in vain to infiltrate Dr Lombard's domestic staff with a man of his own, would be delighted to hear she was tackling the job in person.

When Celestial Sparrow had slipped off the path near the summit of the Great Snow Mountain, Stephen distinctly saw his slithering descent arrested by a rock some twenty feet below. Then swirling flurries of snow blotted the boy from sight.

'He's down there!' he yelled into the howling wind, plucking at the sleeve of the man leading his pack mule.

The soldier didn't understand. As far as he was concerned, the gale had blown the boy off the edge of the mountain and that was the end of him.

None of the struggling marchers wanted to follow him into that abyss. Neither did they wish to be blamed for the death of the crazy foreign devil who was urging them to lower him over the edge of the path. With difficulty he persuaded two young peasants to hold his ankles while he inched forward on his stomach, waiting for the snow flurries to part and show him where Celestial Sparrow was crouching, but the muleteers were plainsmen who knew nothing of climbing skills.

The moment Stephen's weight was over the edge of the path, the man holding his ankles let go. Helplessly, Stephen began to slide forward down the steep incline. Sticking out his arms in an attempt to brake and digging his toes desperately into the soft snow-crust, he vanished from the sight of the watchers above.

Seconds later he was on the ledge beside Celestial Sparrow, who huddled back against the steep slope, eyes dilated with fear. Below them a sheer drop yawned into space. The ledge was no more than eighteen inches wide: rock with a treacherous coating of ice which blurred into a snow-crust at its outer edge. It was impossible to tell how far the rock extended, and how much was ice which might melt under the warmth of their bodies. The wind howled and screamed round the corner of the mountain, tugging at their clothes as if eager to pluck them from their refuge, and though Stephen knew that twenty feet above them men and animals were still on the path, fighting their way through the blizzard, they might have been a thousand miles away for all the help they could give.

'Don't move,' he said to the boy, who stared into the abyss as if mesmerized. 'Keep quite still and we'll be all right.'

He cursed himself for not waiting to explain. A rope could surely have been found: a human chain formed to rescue the boy. But his months in China had already taught Stephen something about Oriental fatalism: life was cheap and since death was inevitable sooner or later, why should they take steps to avoid it? Even if he'd managed to make himself understood, it was unlikely that he could have persuaded the muleteers to help. He'd had to act at once – and alone.

For nearly two hours they had crouched half-frozen on the tiny ledge, afraid to move even a muscle as the blizzard swirled dizzyingly round them. Stephen's whole body was numb with cold and life had retreated into a small core of diminishing warmth round heart and stomach. Pressed against him, Celestial Sparrow shook with uncontrollable shudders. It seemed an eternity before there was a break in the storm. The wind died down and the sky cleared. As it did so, the depths below them swam into focus and Stephen's head reeled as he saw the drop over which they were poised. Eagles were planing and wheeling above a silver thread of river thousands of feet below – one slip, one shift of weight, and they both would have fallen to certain death.

As if to emphasize this, a chunk of snow broke off their ledge and dropped lazily into space, seeming almost to float as it vanished from sight. Stephen felt a surge of vertigo. At any moment the whole ledge might break away from the mountain.

'Come on,' he croaked. 'Now's our chance. I'll lead the way.'

It was easier said than done, but using a chunk of rock as an ice-axe and inching upward with the greatest caution, he began to carve notches for their hands and feet. The slope was very steep, and as the exertion brought his numb hands back to life, the fingers became too weak and floppy to grip his primitive axe. The worst danger lay in sliding back on top of Celestial Sparrow and precipitating him over the edge. Every time his feet failed to grip, Stephen's heart gave a sickening lurch, thinking the end had come, and every few feet they were forced to rest, pinned against the slope like two bluebottles on a starched linen tablecloth.

Throughout the climb Celestial Sparrow never spoke, grunting with exertion but making no other sound: but when at last they reached the lip of the path and hauled themselves to safety, he rolled on the ground, hugging himself in an ecstasy of relieved tension, and giggling hysterically till Stephen picked him up and shook him into sobriety.

'Stop that and pay attention,' he said sharply. 'We're not out of trouble yet. We'll have to get down the mountain fast, before that storm hits us. Look at it.'

A heavy dark purple cloud, pink-tinged at the edges, was bearing down on the mountain's steep conical peak. Stephen briefly considered pressing ahead to the pass, but he didn't fancy their chances of surviving a night on this mountain, nor did he see much prospect of catching up with the marchers.

'We'll have to go down,' he decided. 'Tomorrow the weather may be better. We'll go back to the village and ask for shelter.'

'Find proper house to sleep,' agreed Celestial Sparrow, who liked his comforts. Nimble as a goat, he skipped ahead down the path they had climbed so wearily that morning, apparently oblivious to the many blue-clad forms, lightly dusted now with snow, which lay where they had fallen or been dragged to on either side of the path. How many lives had the crossing of the Great Snow Mountain cost? Stephen, plodding grimly behind, could not ignore the dead so easily. The sight of Otto's body, distinctive in its black flying-suit and boots, his shattered head half-buried in snow, confirmed his worst fears. They had killed Otto when the going got tough: *what had they done to Romy?*

Fearing to look, yet fearing more not to look, he examined the face of every dead marcher he passed, but she wasn't among them. Gradually his hope grew: perhaps, after all, she had survived this terrible day. The army would be sure to rest and recover on the other side of the mountain. Tomorrow he and the boy would start at dawn, and try to catch up with them.

Wu To-ching, who lived in the old earthen house cut into the side of the hill where Celestial Sparrow beat on the door and demanded shelter that night, was a gentle, lean old man, with a straggly white beard and a cranium as brown and smooth as a newlaid egg. He was a simple peasant, but he had lived all his life in the shadow of the mountain and was wise to its moods. His half-dozen scrawny sheep and goats browsed up to the highest slopes, and he knew every path among the rocks.

When the Red Army had marched into his village at noon the previous day, he and his wrinkled old wife had prudently hidden themselves and their livestock in a cave some distance from their home; but as soon as he realized that the footsore bedraggled marchers were not soldiers belonging to the dreaded warlord but weary peasants in need of food, he had come out of hiding and offered them what he could: millet bread and garlic and dried red peppers. He had even offered to kill one of his few fowl for their general's meal – an offer he was glad to have refused.

Now he extended the same courteous hospitality to Stephen and Celestial Sparrow, calling to his wife to prepare beds and soup, and serving them himself at his own table. Stephen felt ashamed that he had neither money nor goods, nothing to offer in return for their night's lodging. He was further embarrassed the next morning, when they woke to find the mountain peak hidden in cloud and lightning bouncing off the rocks to the rumbling accompaniment of thunder. Clearly, there was no chance of reaching the pass that day.

Celestial Sparrow didn't share Stephen's fear of battening on an unwilling host. With excellent appetite he tucked into everything the old couple offered him, meanwhile complaining loudly at the poverty of the fare, and ordering the old man hither and thither in sharp, peremptory tones.

For a while Stephen let him have his way, but when he noticed the old woman weeping next morning, while her husband gloomily sharpened a long knife, something in the resentful looks they cast at their uninvited guests triggered off Stephen's suspicions.

'Why is the *lao t'ai-t'ai*, the old woman, crying?' he asked Celestial Sparrow.

'Because she is sad,' replied the boy cheerfully.

'Why is she sad?'

'Because she does not wish her man to kill the sheep.'

'Then why must he kill it?'

Celestial Sparrow shrugged. 'Because we are important lords and must be fed.'

'But we don't need . . .' Stephen broke off and stared at the boy with dawning suspicion. 'Did you *tell* him to kill his sheep for us?' he demanded.

'Certainly. For if I had not found them he would have given us nothing but garlic and bread,' said the boy indignantly. 'He is a bad man. He offered the general a fowl when all the time he had six sheep hidden.'

'All the same, he mustn't kill any of his animals for us,' said Stephen. Uneasily he wondered what other orders Celestial Sparrow might have given in his name. 'Go on, tell him we don't want his sheep.'

Celestial Sparrow looked mutinous. 'You will lose face,' he warned. 'I tell him you are a powerful foreign devil and a minister of the government. If this old man no longer fears us he may kill us secretly or turn us out to starve.'

There was a grain if ignoble truth in what he said. Stephen considered for a moment, then said, 'All right, tell him I have taken a vow to eat no meat. You did not know of this when you ordered the sheep killed.'

'If I say this, I shall not eat meat either!' cried Celestial Sparrow woefully.

'Too bad. All the same, I don't think you'll starve,' said Stephen, hiding his laughter. 'Mr Wu has been very hospitable and I won't allow you to behave like a warlord towards him.'

'I am not a warlord,' said Celestial Sparrow between his teeth. 'I'm a Red marcher.'

'Then tell Mr Wu to stop sharpening that knife or I shall spank you, Red marcher or not,' said Stephen firmly.

'You would not dare!' But Celestial Sparrow had felt Nanny's slipper often enough to know from bitter experience that the persons of little boys, even of exalted rank, were not regarded as sacred by barbarous foreign devils. Unwillingly, therefore, he countermanded the order for meat, and peace fell once more on the Wu house.

All the same, both he and Stephen were heartily tired of a

diet of millet bread and garlic by the time the storm finally blew itself out and old Wu To-ching agreed to guide them over the pass as far as his First Brother's son's house in Chengsha, where he had business to transact.

The silk-merchant sat in his stately guest-hall to receive his visitors. Beneath the ancient network of red and green cantilevered beams the lacquered floor shone like black ice, and the great teak chairs and couches and the carved table topped with marble glowed with sombre splendour in the soft, evening sunlight filtering through ricepaper lattices all down the southern side of the hall. Over the chair of carved blackwood in which the merchant was enthroned hung the portrait of an emperor of the Ming dynasty, ousted by the usurping Manchus, whose painted smile and half-closed eyes echoed those of the living man below him.

Wu the silk-merchant was a very different personage from his uncle, the scrawny, work-worn farmer. In the generation which separated them, the family had prospered. The younger Wu was as sleekly rounded as a well-fed cat and there was something feline, too, about his still dark eyes and the little pointed fingers which occasionally peeped from the wide sleeves of his robe of rose brocade. His head was shaven, with the top hair gathered in a queue in the old, pre-revolutionary style, and his broad smooth moon face with its thin arched brows and heavy jowls proclaimed his fondness for food and ease. His robe and sleeveless black surcoat were of traditional cut, but beneath them – as if to demonstrate his ability to move with the times – he wore Western shoes of shiny black leather.

Like his fellow merchants, Wu had been a worried man when the Red Army came down from the encircling hills and set up camp only twenty *li* from Chengsha. He had hastily dispatched his most treasured furniture and valuables to a place of safety, and had been preparing to follow them when a message reached him from the governor himself, proclaiming that the Red Army leaders had sworn not to molest Chengsha.

Nevertheless he had left his treasures where they were,

and the imposing guest-hall now bore witness to the recent removal of some of its furnishings. Large dusty patches showed where chests and tables had once stood, and several of the satin hangings and gold-bordered scrolls were missing from the walls.

Wu greeted his uncle with courtesy and welcomed the unexpected guests, offering them tea in bowls of eggshell porcelain and tiny sweet cakes on red lacquered trays.

Stephen, watching and listening in silence although he could now understand enough to follow the gist of the conversation, was struck by the ease with which Celestial Sparrow comported himself in the presence of this obviously rich and high-ranking merchant. He appeared perfectly conversant, even familiar, with the conventions of *k'o-ch'i-hwa*, the traditional 'politeness-talk' which required the speaker to praise his host's possessions and person while roundly abusing his own; indeed, the boy seemed far more assured in these grand surroundings than did the old hill-farmer, who stammered nervously and showed signs of wanting to escape even before their host drained his teacup, signifying that the interview was at an end.

Slowly, as befitted a Chinese conversation, information was exchanged. Stephen heard himself described as a high-ranking foreign devil, adviser to General Chu Teh. Wu the silk-merchant stroked his smooth chin as he digested this news, eyeing Stephen covertly. Then he announced that he would count it a privilege if his venerable uncle and honoured guests would condescend to pass a night or two in his unworthy house and partake of his poor hospitality.

Celestial Sparrow demurred. If, of his benevolence, the honourable Wu would provide them with a guide, they would rid his magnificent house of their abject personages, which were in any case far too lowly to deserve his bounteous hospitality. But his protests were overruled. Wu was determined they should remain there. When he dismissed them, servants carrying flaring torches escorted them across many flagged courtyards roofed with straw and heavy with the scent of lilies and syringa. The stiff, waxy blooms of tree-paeonies glimmered in the gloom and paper lanterns like huge glowing fruits shed soft light on a miniature lake where a heron stood immobile by a little humped bridge, head tucked beneath his wing. In the warm dark, frogs croaked companionably; a fleeting streak of black-and-white against a wall betrayed the presence of a hunting cat.

At last they reached an inner court surrounded by red-pillared pavilions with flying eaves, where the servants indicated that they should rest and refresh themselves. Stephen prowled to and fro, exploring. Behind a paper screen stood a tub of green-glazed earthenware, some three feet tall and wide enough to sit in, full of warm scented water. This was a welcome sight, and so were the clean cotton jackets and wide trousers laid on the beds.

Celestial Sparrow regarded the clothes with open contempt. 'He gives us cotton to wear. Does he offer lodging to coolies?' he snorted, and fired a volley of words at the servant, who bowed and disappeared. A few minutes later he reappeared carrying an embroidered satin jacket fastening high on one shoulder and black silk trousers.

'*Hao!* It is well,' said the boy, graciously accepting them.

'Aren't those a bit fancy for a Red marcher?' asked Stephen, to tease him, but Celestial Sparrow shook his head. Splendidly dressed he would acquire face in this rich man's house; if he wore coolie's clothes he could expect to be treated like a coolie. Clean and bathed for the first time for weeks, he and Stephen were escorted back across the courtyards to Wu Yuan's table.

Along with his rice, Celestial Sparrow picked up much information that night, which he later passed on to Stephen.

Wu Yuan's air of serene prosperity was misleading: his family was divided against itself and he was in urgent need of money to offset the extravagance of his elder son. This young man, adored and indulged by his mother since babyhood, had grown up wilful and demanding. He constantly urged his father to make the House of Wu into a place befitting the family's rank; in the past years new courts had been constructed with the finest materials, the marble basins filled with rare fish, the terraces with plants that bloomed all year from earliest spring to deepest winter.

First Son had bowed to his parents' wishes in marrying the plain, countrybred wife they had chosen for him, but she had not contented him for long. Only a few months after she had given birth to a second weakling daughter, First Son installed a pretty concubine from his favourite tea-house in an inner court of his father's home. This Second Lady – as she was known – had lost no time in presenting her new lord with a bouncing son, much to First Wife's chagrin. However, before the child was weaned, First Son's roving eye lit on yet another fancy, a dancing-girl from Soochow, and he was now absent from home negotiating her purchase from her close-fisted family.

The Second Lady was outraged by his fickleness, but there was nothing she could do to prevent the new concubine taking the place which had been so briefly hers. Naturally enough, First Wife was delighted by her rival's discomfiture; she and her obese, sharp-tongued mother-in-law were united and untiring in their efforts to make the Second Lady's life a misery.

Beneath such an onslaught of misfortune, most Chinese concubines would have bowed their pretty heads and succumbed to their fate, but the Second Lady was a girl of spirit. Though outnumbered and outgunned by her enemies in the household, she still planned her revenge, and her instrument lay close at hand.

Besides his extravagant elder son, Wu Yuan had two other children. Liu, the Second Son, now lived with his aunt in a coastal town full of foreigners and steadfastly refused to return home to marry the bride his parents had chosen for him. Nor was Liu's unfilial behaviour the last of Wu Yuan's problems. His daughter Pao-ching – Bright Treasure – was a pretty child who had always been her father's darling. She had begged and pleaded until he allowed her to attend a little school in Chengsha, where she started to learn her characters.

Not content with this, she'd later wheedled her father into sending her farther afield – much to her mother's disapproval – to an academy for girls in Canton, where Wu Yuan's Fourth Brother was a high official. Wu had imagined his precious Treasure safe in the care of Fourth Brother's wife, but that modern, town-bred woman had allowed Treasure to unbind the tiny feet which her mother had so carefully wound with long strips of cloth when she was five years old.

Now, instead of possessing the admired 'golden lilies' only three inches long, Treasure's feet had grown as huge and ugly as palm fans. When the husband to whom she'd been affianced as a baby heard of this outrage, he had wanted to break the betrothal. Only by substantially increasing his daughter's dowry had Wu Yuan been able to hold the bridegroom's family to the contract.

Bright Treasure had been brought home in deep disgrace. Her mother had tried to rebind the offending feet, but the damage done by three years of freedom was irreparable. Worse soon became apparent: the dutiful, obedient daughter whom Wu had despatched to Canton had turned into a rebellious, unfilial young woman who was even now imprisoned in her own quarters on a diet of rice and water until she withdrew her stubborn opposition to marrying the man she was betrothed to.

'If he doesn't want to marry her and she doesn't want to marry him, why don't they call the whole thing off?' asked Stephen.

Celestial Sparrow's hooped brows rose in unutterable scorn at such simplicity. 'Of course it is impossible. She will have to obey her parents. The dowry has already been sent to the bridegroom's home.'

'What's to stop them sending it back?'

'They would lose face,' said the boy with finality.

'What a wretched business this "face" is! From what you've told me, I gather that both sets of parents are worried, the bridegroom is resentful, and the poor girl is being starved simply because of a matter of face.'

Celestial Sparrow cleared his throat importantly and spat.

'Three times has Treasure tried to kill herself,' he announced. 'First she threw herself in the water, but First Son came by and pulled her out. Then she swallowed raw opium, but it was not enough and only made her sick. The last time she tried to hang herself from a silken girdle, but her mother came into the room and found her. Now she is guarded night and day, for if she kills herself both families will lose face.'

Stephen groaned with disgust. 'What a stupid business! Who told you all this?'

'The Second Lady. She likes to make trouble for the First Lady and for the Venerable Ancient One who is her mother-in-law,' said Celestial Sparrow with a grin. 'She wants you to help Bright Treasure to escape from her father's house.'

'Me? Oh, I say . . .' Stephen felt this was carrying his interest altogether too far.

'What do you say?' enquired Celestial Sparrow.

'I mean, that would hardly do. I can't accept Wu's hospitality and then spirit away his daughter. Especially since he's been so good and promised to find us a guide.'

'If he speaks truth about the guide.'

'Why shouldn't he be speaking the truth?'

Couldn't a foreign devil see what was right under his great ugly nose? thought Celestial Sparrow in wonderment. Wu Yuan was a rich man, and he hadn't acquired his riches by making deals that showed no profit. It was crystal clear to the boy that Wu's amiable reception of the wayfarers was because he saw a way to profit through them. Given the unsettled state of the country and the ransom possibilities inherent in any foreign devil, one way of making money out of Stephen was easy to guess. Too late, Celestial Sparrow wished he had not mentioned that his companion was a high-ranking official. Leaving Stephen's question unanswered, he pattered off into the courtyard and came back with dragging feet.

'They have locked the gate,' he announced.

'I expect they always do at night,' said Stephen, unperturbed. He blew out the lamp and was quickly asleep; but the boy lay for a long time listening to the croaking frogs and other night noises, and wishing he had not accepted hospitality in this house of many pavilions which might so easily become a prison.

After a week as the unwilling guest of the fat silk-merchant, Stephen had been obliged to face the fact that Celestial

Sparrow was right. Wu Yuan was keeping them under his roof for some purpose of his own, and the guide he had promised was a myth.

His uncle had returned to his mountain home two days after they arrived; whether he was to blame for their incarceration or whether he had acted in good faith when he confided them to the care of his brother's son was impossible to guess. Stephen remembered the old man's closed, resentful face while Celestial Sparrow hectored him in his own house, and drew certain conclusions.

Since old Wu's departure the treatment they received had deteriorated. No longer were they allowed to leave their courtyard, and requests to speak to their host were ignored. Meals were brought to them in the pavilion on the east side of the courtyard, and Celestial Sparrow worked hard to establish a friendly relationship with the man who served them.

Since he had little faith in human nature to lose, he was less shocked than Stephen by their predicament. Besides, he had one ally in the house already. All he needed now was a bribe – a big, fat bribe that would unlock doors and turn watchful *k'ai-men-ti* into blind deaf mutes.

Critically he examined Stephen's belongings. A signet ring, gold. A fine wristwatch, also of gold. Would they be enough? Would Stephen be prepared to sacrifice them to regain his freedom? He decided to tackle the first question first, and embarked on a long haggle with the servant who brought their meals. For three anxious days he met with little response.

Chang, the servant, was a cautious man. Risk his master's wrath for the sake of a foreign wristwatch? What an idea! He would suffer the *bastinado*, or the torments of the *kong* if he were discovered. His wife and children would starve in the streets. He would need much more than a paltry gold watch to compensate him for taking such a risk.

Celestial Sparrow persevered. If, he insinuated, the master had sent messages to the Kuomintang, offering them his prisoners for ten thousand silver dollars, what would his servants get from the deal? Nothing at all. And when the Red Army triumphed, as it undoubtedly would very soon, and Wu Yuan and his like were subjected to the slicing process while their goods were distributed to the peasants they had robbed, would it not be worth something to have a Red Army general for a friend?

Chang wavered. When Celestial Sparrow judiciously added the gold signet ring to the bribe, at long last the bargain was struck.

That night, while Stephen slept, Celestial Sparrow was silently admitted to the inner court beyond the moon-gate, where the pretty, intrigue-loving Second Lady had her apartments, and by the light of bean oil lamps the two of them conferred earnestly, far into the night.

CHAPTER THIRTEEN

The prisoners left the silk-merchant's house by stealth, on a warm, wet, moonless night when the summer rains deluging down from the mountains swirled in yellow torrents along the unpaved streets of Chengsha. That same morning Wu Yuan had ridden out to meet his *Chung-jen*, the intermediary who was negotiating with the Kuomintang general over the ransom for the distinguished foreign devil held in captivity. When this news reached Celestial Sparrow he was in a fever to be gone before the silk-merchant's return.

'Tonight when it is dark, we go,' he said positively.

'But how?'

The boy raised his hand in a sharp, imperative gesture. 'You do nothing, say nothing, Ti-fen. I fix.'

Stephen was obliged to obey. He hated his dependency, the fog of uncertainty surrounding present and future, but there was nothing he could do to penetrate it. He had to trust Celestial Sparrow to lead him back to the Red Army.

With Stephen at his heels, the boy scrambled nimbly up a bamboo ladder which mysteriously appeared at dusk against the wall of their courtyard; they crossed the angle formed by two pavilions, and dropped into the adjoining flagged court. Thereafter it was easy. They tiptoed across further courtyards, slipped through flat-topped *p'ailous*, and crept past latticed ricepaper windows glowing with yellow lamplight. They skirted the pond where the heron slept by his humped bridge, ducked under the rain-drenched branches of a clump of willows, and found more ladders set either side of the gatehouse's outer wall, where the sleeping *k'ai-men-ti* faithfully kept his part of the bargain. Gusts of wind plucked at the springy bamboo ladder, but someone had his foot on the bottom rung and Stephen, descending into the stream which was the street, found Chang, three donkeys, and two other muffled figures waiting at the foot of the ladder, sheltering from the downpour beneath large oiled-paper umbrellas. It was a wet night for conspirators.

Stephen had a sense of total unreality. Where was he going? Into what folly was he allowing this domineering small boy to lead him? Should he have refused to leave Wu's house, and waited there for whatever fate the fat merchant planned for him? Celestial Sparrow had hinted at ransom, and Stephen had heard enough horror-stories of foreigners held hostage by Chinese bandits to be anxious to avoid the experience. Ransom was a slow, tortuous business which frequently turned out unsatisfactorily for all parties concerned. It was conducted through intermediaries who wanted their own cut of the ransom money and were unscrupulous in their methods of obtaining it. If the negotiations dragged on too long, the hostage's ears and fingers were at risk; if the ransom offered proved too small, he would be murdered.

All in all, Stephen preferred to trust the Red Army: at least its leaders had shown no desire to make money out of him. Besides, he must know what had happened to Romy. Hope that she had survived the crossing of the Great Snow Mountain alternated with hideous doubt whether any white woman could endure such conditions for long. When he thought of her alone and unprotected his brain shied away from imagining what her fate might have been.

As if in a trance, he allowed the boy to divest him of his watch and signet ring and hand them to the grinning Chang.

'Get on the donkey.'

Stephen obeyed, wondering if the little grey beast would sink into the mud beneath his weight. One of the muffled figures also mounted, the other made a gesture of farewell. Beneath the umbrella, Stephen caught a glimpse of the pouting lips and mischievous almond eyes of the Second Lady.

'*Tsai-chien!*' called Celestial Sparrow softly.

They splashed away down the street in the rapid amble peculiar to Chinese donkeys, with the rain to hide their hoofprints and the warm wet night to protect them from curious eyes. When Wu returned, he'd find his birds flown.

The guide was a taciturn youth, Stephen decided, after several attempts to converse with him had been ignored. Though he hadn't Romy's quick ear and his knowledge of Chinese was still rudimentary, Stephen knew that his questions were clearly put and must have been understood; but for reasons of his own the guide preferred to ride in silence. Stephen was irritated. There was so much he wanted to know: how far was Moukung, where the Red Army was encamped? Were there other soldiers in the region? How long would it take to reach safety?

The torrential rain soon died away, and all night they rode through a drenched and dripping landscape on a track that more nearly resembled a river-bed than a main thoroughfare. As dawn broke in pink and primrose streaks over the conical peaks of the eastern mountains, they reached the ferry which would take them across the swirling yellow waters of the Wa-tung river. Stephen stood apart and was careful to keep his face hidden as Celestial Sparrow haggled with the bronzed, half-naked ferrymen, though he had no doubt that news of their crossing would reach Wu's ears soon enough. Small parties of soldiers in baggy grey uniforms, wearing the pink armband of the local warlord and with paper umbrellas strapped to their backs, stood idly about the river bank, smoking and spitting, but they made no move to interfere with the passengers as they led the donkeys on to the ferry. In the dawn light Stephen got his first good look at their guide. It was not reassuring. He was a slight, delicate-looking youth, slim as a willow sapling, dressed in a peasant's baggy dark-blue trousers and tunic from whose over-large collar his thin, childish neck and freshly-shaved head stuck up like a turnip on a broom-handle. His scalp gleamed like ivory through the soft dark stubble covering his head. Despite his rough clothes, he didn't look like a peasant. There was a certain casual grace to his movements and his oval face was pale and smooth. It was easy to see that his small soft hands with their finely-tapered fingers had never held a hoe or guided a plough.

Aware of Stephen's scrutiny, the boy shifted uncomfortably. His eyes were demurely downcast, and something in the curve of his lips, the almost translucent pallor of his long eyelids increased Stephen's uneasiness.

'Just who *is* that boy?' he muttered, edging nearer to Celestial Sparrow. 'Yes, I know he's our guide, but who is he? Where did he spring from?'

Celestial Sparrow withdrew his attention from the absorbing spectacle of the ferrymen poling the low-sided, flat-bottomed boat in which they stood towards the slab-like yellow rocks on the far side of the river. He turned an innocent face towards Stephen, who nonetheless suspected him of inner laughter.

'He is a poor peasant boy of Chengsha,' he said dismissingly. 'He will guide us to where the Red Army is encamped.'

'How does he know the way?' Stephen persisted. 'Why won't he answer when I speak to him?'

'Do not trouble yourself, Ti-fen,' said Celestial Sparrow politely. 'The boy is shy and finds your speech strange.'

'Other people understand it all right.' Stephen stared at the boy again. It was no good Celestial Sparrow telling him not to trouble himself in that airy way. He wanted to trouble himself. He wanted to know what was going on. He had an uneasy feeling that somehow he was being duped, deliberately kept in the dark.

'What will Wu do when he finds we've escaped?' he asked.

'He will be angry,' said Celestial Sparrow serenely.

'I imagine so. But what form will his anger take? Will he send people after us?'

A flicker of apprehension crossed Celestial Sparrow's insouciant features. His eyes slid away from Stephen's and rested on the slight figure of their guide, now seated on the boat's square-cut prow. Stephen followed his gaze. The light breeze ruffling the water's surface pressed the baggy cotton tunic against the boy's slender body, and suddenly, with the certainty of one solving a crossword clue correctly, Stephen had the answer.

'My God,' he breathed. 'That's Wu's *daughter*, isn't it? The one who wanted to escape. Oh, Celestial Sparrow! What have you been and gone and done now?'

'The silk merchant will be angry,' repeated the boy mechanically. His eyes searched Stephen's face.

Resisting the impulse to pick him up and shake him, Stephen said severely, 'Why didn't you think of that before? It's no good worrying about that now. The damage is done. The question is, what are we going to do about it?'

Irresistibly his eyes were drawn back to the graceful, fragile figure seated on the prow, head drooping low as she watched the swift-flowing river, her pose at once dignified and defenceless. Something tugged at Stephen's heart. What sort of hell could her life at home have been, he wondered, to force her into the desperate step of cutting herself off from her family, running away into the unknown with a foreign devil for company? Was even freedom worth so much? Would he, in her place, have taken such a risk?

He wondered how old she was. Sixteen or seventeen, he guessed. It was difficult to estimate Chinese ages. Just a slip of a girl defying the weight of Confucian tradition, striking a blow for a new China.

She would have to be returned to her mother, of course. *Of course*. What her mother would do to bring her to heel was no concern of his. But again he felt that strange little lurch of the heart and recognized his old enemy, the traitor within the gates.

Damn and blast, thought Stephen as the flat-bottomed boat grounded and the passengers began to stream ashore. I'm a rational human being. A normal, civilized specimen of homo sapiens, not a caveman. When I meet a problem I use my brain to solve it. I don't allow my animal instincts to overwhelm me. That girl must be returned to her father's house, the sooner the better. I shall not look at her, speak to her or – above all – touch her. I shall have nothing whatever to do with her.

But even as he made this resolution he knew he would not keep it. Feeling his gaze upon her, the daughter of Wu turned her pale, flowerlike face towards him and smiled, not with prim, downcast lids like most Chinese girls, but a look of sparkling mischief. The red lips curved and lifted at the outer corners, one delicate hand stole up to hide her laughing mouth.

In that instant he knew he could no more send her home to her angry mother than he could abandon an unwanted puppy on a road. For better or worse she was his responsibility now. All the same, she couldn't travel with them. That was out of the question, and he must tell her so himself. This was a piece of translation he dared not entrust to so unreliable an intermediary as Celestial Sparrow.

Almost without realizing he had moved, he found himself beside her, staring down at the small cropped head. 'Pao-ching,' he said slowly, struggling to find the Chinese words, 'you must go home. I am going to take you home.'

He knew she understood, for she shook her head so violently that the dark stubble rippled like the feathers on a fledgling blackbird. With a sudden imperious gesture she beckoned to Celestial Sparrow and rapped out words in a clear high voice that made Stephen think of chiming temple bells.

'What does she say?'

'She has no home but yours now, Ti-fen. When a Chinese bride goes to her husband she ceases to belong to her father's house.' The boy shrugged, disclaiming responsibility, but his complacent tone made it clear that he approved of Pao-ching's attitude. Stephen was horrified.

'She's not my bride! How on earth did she get that idea? Tell her I'm married – I have a wife already.'

'She knows this. She consents to become your Second Lady,' explained Celestial Sparrow. A trace of embarrassment in his manner gave Stephen a shrewd idea as to how the misconception had arisen.

'So this is your doing, you little wretch!'

Celestial Sparrow skipped nimbly out of reach. 'Ti-fen! People look at us!'

Stephen glanced at the interested onlookers and controlled his temper. He thought the matter over. Somehow Pao-ching must be told there was a mistake. He had no intention of burdening himself with a Second Lady, no matter how lovely or desirable; no matter how sorry he might feel for her.

Celestial Sparrow said rapidly, 'If she returns to her father's house she will die. We will all die. Her mother will beat her to death because she is dishonoured and her father will throw you in a pit because you have dishonoured his house.'

'I suppose *you'll* get off scot free?' The sarcasm was lost on Celestial Sparrow who gave a histrionic shudder.

'And I, although I have done no wrong, may even be beaten with bamboo rods,' he said faintly. 'When Wu the silk-merchant frowns, even the innocent must tremble.'

'Innocent!' Stephen knew it was useless to argue with Celestial Sparrow. His fertile brain had hatched up this scheme to escape from Wu's bondage, and Stephen would have to accept the consequences of his meddling. He turned away, frowning, and stared at the muddy yellow water, lost in thought. Perhaps he would be able to leave the girl with missionaries . . . After her sheltered upbringing she couldn't be abandoned to take her chance in the world. He groaned softly and was careful not to catch her eye.

A gentle hand touched his arm. She stood beside him, silently pleading, but even now he sensed that laughter was not far away. The slightest sign that he had relented would be enough to bring the sparkle back to her long almond eyes, the dancing dimple to her cheek. Her skin was as fine and soft as magnolia petals and the dark lashes lay against her wide cheekbones like the wings of a moth. He fought down a mad impulse to take that fragile body in his arms, and said with deliberate coldness: 'If you refuse to return to your home, I shall take you to the nearest mission station. You can't come with me, and that's final.'

It was an empty threat and she knew it as well as he did.

'My home is my husband's home,' she said meekly, but the naughty sidelong glance she flashed at Celestial Sparrow told Stephen they had planned the whole thing together.

He turned and strode away without waiting for either of them, squelching up the red mud track with an energy better suited to marathon walking than a journey in the torrid heat of a Chinese summer. For the rest of that day he held himself aloof, refusing to acknowledge his companions who followed with the donkeys at a respectful distance.

Stephen ate alone that evening in the courtyard of a deserted temple, accepting the food the girl prepared and the water Celestial Sparrow offered as if they were the ministrations of servants.

I will not be forced into this position, he thought angrily. I will not be made responsible for an obstinate, self-willed, disobedient Chinese female. He rolled himself in his quilt and lay for a long time tensely listening for an approaching footstep. Frogs croaked; a light breeze sighed in the pine tree's branches; the high-pitched whine of mosquitoes came intermittently to his ears. Over by the cookfire he heard low chatter punctuated with laughter.

He slept restlessly with fantasies crowding his dreams, wrestling with memories and desires. Fever gripped him in a redhot embrace; he heard his own voice pleading: 'Romy . . . forgive me . . .' His arms encompassed her soft warmth as they had on the Great Snow Mountain's slopes but when he gazed on the face of his dream she had long tilted eyes and brows like young willow-leaves against a magnolia skin.

Towards dawn he slipped into a deeper slumber and did not waken until the sun was well risen and smoke from Celestial Sparrow's cookfire rose in a thin blue column to the aquamarine sky. He felt refreshed and strengthened, ready to move mountains. Birds sang joyously in the temple's flaking eaves and the rosy-tinted fluffy clouds promised a glorious day.

Slowly his gaze shifted from the heavens and focused on something nearer at hand – right beside him, to be exact. A hump in the cotton quilt, hair as soft and dark as a fledgling's down, a cheek like magnolia petals . . .

'Oh, my God!' said Stephen, flinging back the quilt.

Naked and beautiful, Pao smiled dreamily up at him and he drew the cotton over her again with haste. Her full lips curved and parted to reveal teeth as white and even as matched pearls.

'Ti-fen,' she murmured.

Near their feet there was a snort of ill-suppressed merriment and a moment later the impish face of Celestial Sparrow rose cautiously to peer down at the two of them.

'Velly nice Number Two Lady!' he chortled.

Stephen ground his teeth. He waited until the boy came in range and caught him a neat clip on the ear. 'You doped my food, you unspeakable brat!' The sandpaper dryness of his mouth confirmed this guess, but the delicious languor that lay heavy on his limbs made it difficult to sustain anger.

'Bring me hot water and then make yourself scarce unless you're looking for the hiding you deserve,' he growled; 'and you get out and make yourself decent,' he added, speeding Pao-ching on her way with a smack on the rump.

They withdrew, exchanging laughing looks.

The hollow where she had lain was warm with her scent; his eyes followed her hungrily as she pattered across the courtyard and when she vanished behind a pillar it seemed to him that a cloud obscured the sun. In that instant he knew that not only had he lost the skirmish; he had lost himself as well. He was bewitched by a pair of laughing almond-shaped eyes, and now he had known the pleasures of that smooth supple body he would never feel desire for any other. That night, or one soon after, River Pearl was conceived.

CHAPTER FOURTEEN

Spring in North-Western China has a magical quality. While the sere yellow-brown earth still lies in wintry camouflage, untouched by even a hint of green, the bare branches of plum and pear, cherry and almond burst forth in cloudy billows of pink and white and ivory blossom that looks too heavy for the slender black boughs to support. Pine trees sprout frivolous golden tips to their venerable green needles; the tamarisk blooms rose-and-green. Mimosa opens yellow balls as pale and fluffy as newly-hatched chicks, and the curved bronze wands of willows turn the softest, tenderest green.

As the iron grip of winter slackens on the soil, the fields themselves seem to sprout diligent blue-cotton-clad figures bending, hoe in hand; and even the warlord's careless soldiers are moved by some inborn impulse to make detours round the pale-green spears of wheat and millet springing so bravely from the narrow terraces. At last the tearing searing wind from the North-East which can flay skin from an unprotected face is transformed into a zephyr and then only a memory; rolypoly Chinese children begin to shed their padded winter clothes day by day, layer by layer, until their chubby golden arms and legs are revealed to the admiring eye of the sun. They tumble and play about the courts like happy puppies, and the warm air is full of their shrill shrieks and the admonishing cries of their mothers.

It was during this season, when the healing sun began to beckon green plants from their winter's sleep, that Romy's mind stopped drifting in the mists of fantasy and she woke to reality once more.

On a blue-and-gold morning in early March, she sat beneath a pink drift of flowering almond in a sunny corner of the inner court, idly watching the unsteady steps of the Number One boy's two-year-old son as he staggered to and fro in pursuit of a gaily-hued butterfly. She was well wrapped in rugs, for the wind still held a nip, and on her lap lay a tiny pair of red satin slippers. Abigail Bentley had suggested she embroider them with tiger faces, like the slippers the cook's baby sported on festival days, but Romy was no needlewoman. The design had gone wrong somewhere and resembled a fox more than a tiger; and now her small burst of energy had spent itself.

The slippers lay neglected on her lap, and she tried to turn her thoughts to the child she was carrying. It still didn't seem real. As far as Dr Lombard could ascertain, it would be born in a month's time, but Romy was vague about dates. She had lost track of time during the last weary stages of the long march, when days and nights blurred into an unending sequence of privation and exhaustion. How many weeks had elapsed between their capture beside the Tatu river and Stephen's death on the Great Snow Mountain? How long again before they had reached Shensi and her supply unit had been blown to pieces by Kuomintang guns? She could not tell.

She knew that Dr Lombard and Abigail were worried about the baby, afraid that it would prove too great a drain on her slender reserves of strength. She had heard them talking while she pretended to sleep.

'She won't hear of a termination,' he'd said. 'I did my best to persuade her but she became upset and irrational. She's still emotionally unstable. I thought it better not to persist.'

'I never liked the idea,' Abigail said shortly. 'Poor girl, she's been through a lot. It's hardly surprising she's clinging to the only thing she's got left.'

The slippers had been Abigail's idea. She was always trying to encourage Romy to think ahead and plan for the future when she would be well enough to leave Sian and travel home, but Romy didn't want to think ahead. Her exhaustion was mental as well as physical. It was enough to be here, sheltered and fed and at peace. She couldn't imagine catching trains and boats, organizing her own life. The thought of Longmarsh filled her with dread. It lay there, waiting to swallow her up, like an ancient dragon demanding its toll of human lives, and because of Stephen's child she must return to claim it – to allow it to claim her. Not yet, she thought with a shudder. I'm not strong enough to stand up to it yet.

Letters arrived from Stephen's sister Sybil, who was looking after the estate in their absence. She urged Romy to return, but reading between the lines her sister-in-law deduced that Sybil was enjoying having Longmarsh to herself, and luckily Dr Lombard would not hear of her travelling for some time.

Dear Harvey, she thought, smiling. He was her rock, her

shield against the world's troubles. Abigail thought she leaned on him too much and was inclined to urge her to make her own decisions; but how could one ignore the advice of a man who had pulled you back from the very brink of death? To him she owed her recovery, if not her life.

He came towards her now, striding across the courtyard, radiating energy and confidence. His sleek copper hair gleamed in the sun, and a smile broke over his freckled face as he saw her. He had been riding and wore an open-necked white shirt with a blue-spotted cravat tied like a stock, his long legs encased in whip-cord breeches. I wonder why he's never married? she thought irrelevantly.

'Good, I hoped I'd find you enjoying the sun – just what the doctor ordered. Are you sure you're warm enough?'

Romy hesitated. He was so strong and positive, so quick to sum up a situation, he made her feel more helpless than ever. 'Well, perhaps my feet . . .'

'*Lai!*' he shouted.

Li, the watchful Number One boy, immaculate in white jacket and dark trousers, appeared at once. 'Footstove for Missee, chop-chop,' ordered Lombard. He picked up one of the tiny slippers and examined it critically. 'Sewing? What's that odd-looking beast?'

She stared at it, trying to remember.

He smiled. 'Let me guess. Is it a tiger?'

'Oh . . . oh yes.'

'Well, if you want it to look like one, you'll have to change the ears. May I?'

She nodded listlessly. With deft movements he unpicked a few stitches and rethreaded the tiny needle. She watched it flashing back and forth, incongruous in his big square hands.

'How about that?' He displayed the long-whiskered, handsome tiger he had stitched. 'You can copy it on the other slipper. What's so funny?'

'You holding that needle,' said Romy, smiling. 'It looks lost in your hand. Oh, do go on, finish the other one. I'm too tired.'

'You must be careful not to strain yourself,' warned Lombard. 'You're still very weak, you know.' He began work on the second tiger-face. He enjoyed embroidery; it helped keep his hand in for some kinds of surgery, though he seldom employed a needle in his work at the Blueshirt interrogation centre. The stoicism of Communist suspects never ceased to amaze him.

As Li crossed the courtyard carrying the smouldering charcoal-filled footstove and placed it carefully beneath Romy's feet, he said casually, 'I came to find you because I wanted to warn you I've got to go to Nanking with the Marshal. It's a flying visit. He's been summoned to discuss a new offensive against the Communists.'

Romy made a face. 'The same old thing.'

'I'm afraid so.'

She didn't want him to leave her. Without Dr Lombard she felt lost and defenceless. 'Why have you got to go? You're not a soldier?'

'My dear girl, I have to follow the Marshal. He hasn't touched opium for months and wants me to help him resist temptation in the big bad city.' He dropped his flippant tone and said seriously, 'You mustn't worry. I hate leaving you, but Mrs Bentley will take good care of you and I'll be back almost before you know I've gone.'

'You're going in the Marshal's plane?' She couldn't keep the anxiety out of her voice.

He squeezed her hand reassuringly. 'Don't worry,' he said again. 'Stay here in the sun, get plenty of rest and build up your strength. I want to see some colour in your cheeks when I get back.'

He strode away across the courtyard, leaving her tired and chilly. She called the Number One boy and asked him to carry her indoors.

Gene Lyon arrived in Sian with a secret purpose; he was determined to visit the Communist base in Yenan and interview the Red leaders. Cautious enquiry among Chinese intellectuals and students in Shanghai had provided the address of Mr Lu the tailor; from Lu he learnt with great surprise that the person most likely to be able to arrange the interviews he sought was his old acquaintance Mrs Bentley.

'Are you sure?' he asked, wondering if Lu could have his facts straight. It seemed inconceivable to Gene that a respectable English widow of Mrs Bentley's standing could be mixed up in such a business.

Yes, Lu was sure. She, if anyone, could persuade Mao Tse-tung and Chou En-lai to grant interviews to an American journalist. Why didn't Mr Lyon take a rickshaw to the Street of Tranquil Wisdom where she was staying, and ask for her help?

Puzzled but obedient, Gene followed the tailor's directions. He found an interested crowd outside the gates of Dr Lombard's residence, gathered round a small black Ford car with a flat front tyre. At the centre of operations Mrs Bentley, splendid in solar topee, purple chiffon dress and white gloves, was instructing two half-naked coolies in the correct use of jack and wheel-brace.

He pushed through the crowd. 'Good morning, Mrs Bentley. Can I be of assistance?' he asked.

She turned. 'My dear Mr Lyon! What an unexpected pleasure. Have you come to call on Rosemary? It will do her good to see an old friend.' She waved away his offer of help. 'No, no. These fellows will do very well now. I get so many punctured wheels on these dreadful roads that they're really perfectly capable of changing a tyre without my supervision. Do come in.'

He was conscious of a quickened heartbeat; a sudden tightening in the stomach. 'Mrs Russell's still here? I didn't know. I thought she'd have sailed for home by now.'

Mrs Bentley frowned. 'So she would have if I'd had my way, but Dr Lombard won't hear of it. He says she's not fit to travel yet. She's been very ill, you know. Her husband . . .'

'I heard. I'm so sorry. That's why I thought she'd have gone back to England as soon as she could. China must have unhappy memories for her.'

'I know.' Abigail hesitated, and he wondered if she was regretting her invitation. She said, 'I must warn you she is a good deal . . .changed. She still tires very easily. Don't be surprised if she doesn't recognize you immediately.'

'Don't worry, I won't stay long,' said Gene easily. He added in a lower voice, 'As a matter of fact, Mrs Bentley, it was you I wanted to talk to. I'm told you're the person who can help me.'

'Me, Mr Lyon?' Behind the gold-rimmed spectacles her eyes were blank, utterly ingenuous. 'I'm flattered, of course, but I hardly think –'

'I went to see Mr Lu the tailor today. He took a bit of persuading, but in the end he told me if I wanted to get in touch with the Red bases, you were the person I should approach.'

'Ah, I see.' She stood silent for a while, apparently lost in admiration of a shaggy-headed peony of truly improbable size. When she spoke it was so softly tht he had to strain to hear. 'It won't be easy, Mr Lyon, and it may well be dangerous. Are you sure you really want to undertake such a journey?'

'Yes.'

'Very well. You'll have to be patient but I may be able to arrange it. If you will drive out with me tomorrow to Mount Li, where we can talk more freely, I'll see what can be done.'

'Thank you very much.'

She waved aside his gratitude. 'Don't thank me yet . . . Come now, let's see if we can find Rosemary.'

Even Mrs Bentley's warning had not fully prepared Gene for the shock of seeing her so altered; her vivid face was drained of colour, almost as white as the pillows she leaned against, and her dark eyebrows and springy black curls seemed too harsh a contrast to this pallor, like the make-up of a clown. More shocking still was the stick-like frailty of her bare arms, narrower at the bicep than the elbow, so that the great mound of her stomach under the light covering rug seemed grotesque in comparison. No one had told him she was pregnant. He was aware of Abigail's eyes, watching his expression, and forced a smile.

'Why, hello, Romy!' he said with deliberate breeziness, though his heart ached with regret at this cruel metamorphosis. 'I was passing and thought I'd look you up. How are things with you?'

Her eyes fluttered open and focused on him. For a moment he thought she didn't know him; then an incredulous smile transformed the sharp features, softening outlines to reveal a shadow of the Romy he remembered. 'Gene!' she said on a choking, breaking note. To his dismay tears sparkled suddenly on her lashes and spilled down her cheeks. 'I never thought I'd see you again.'

'Don't cry, honey.' He forgot propriety and Abigail's watchful presence. He knelt swiftly and wiped away the tears with a silk handkerchief. 'I didn't mean to upset you. I just wanted to say hello.'

She made an obvious effort to control herself. 'I'm not crying, not really. It's too stupid, the least thing makes me blub nowadays,' she said shakily, and the schoolboy slang wrenched at his heart. She returned the handkerchief with a final sniff. 'There, that's better. It's wonderful to see you, Gene. What brings you to Sian?'

He avoided the question. 'I'd have come before now if I'd known you were sick. I imagined you'd gone back to England.'

'Harvey doesn't think I'm strong enough to travel,' she said with a faint sigh, and he experienced a small unpleasant shock at her use of Lombard's Christian name.

'What do you feel yourself? Aren't you longing to get home?'

She looked surprised. 'Oh no. I mean, I've got to do what Harvey says. He takes such care of me. And Abby too, of course,' she added hastily.

'I say fresh air and exercise are what she needs now,' said Abigail robustly. 'All this lying about is *keeping* her weak.'

'Oh, Abby . . .'

Gene glanced from one to the other, sensing conflict. He said diplomatically, 'While I'm in Sian I want to visit all the ancient monuments hereabouts. If you could see your way to showing me round, Mrs Bentley, I'd be more than grateful. You mentioned Mount Li . . .'

'Oh, there's *nothing* I'd enjoy more.' Her spectacles flashed with enthusiasm. 'Are you free tomorrow? We'll drive over and take a picnic. There's so much to see, you wouldn't believe.'

'Splendid. I'll be ready whenever you say.'

Romy felt left out and somehow betrayed. Since Harvey's departure she'd found the time hanging heavy on her hands.

One couldn't spend all day resting and eating and resting again. Abigail came and went about her own business, and her brisk, cheerful manner lacked the soothing solicitousness to which Romy had grown accustomed. Now, just when Gene had appeared to alleviate her boredom, Abigail was proposing to whisk him off on a round of sightseeing without a thought of the long solitary hours Romy must endure. For the first time since she regained consciousness she had a sense of being cooped up, stifled. The sunny tranquil courts with their red-pillared pavilions seemed all of a sudden more of a prison than a refuge.

On impulse she said, 'Can't I come too?'

'You?' They both looked startled.

She went on persuasively, 'You're always saying I ought to make an effort to get out and about. Don't say I can't now that I really want to.'

'It's rather a long way,' began Abigail. Romy's mouth drooped ominously, and she added, 'Of course, dear, if you think it wouldn't tire you too much. After all, you can rest in the motor while we're scrambling about the hill.'

'I *would* like to come,' said Romy, like a fretful child, and Abigail shot Gene a glance compounded of triumph and complicity. It was clear to her that the arrival of the attractive young American had acted better on her patient than any tonic. As she'd suspected for some time it was chiefly Dr Lombard's pampering and over-indulging that had undermined Romy's physical confidence and reduced her to this state of helpless inertia. Without him in constant attendance, she would soon be leading a normal life once more. Abigail hoped the doctor's business would keep him in Nanking as long as possible.

'We'll start at eight o'clock, before it gets hot,' she said. 'If you'll wait outside the guest-house, Mr Lyon, I'll collect you there.'

That first visit to Mount Li, the man-made hill some forty miles from Sian where the great Emperor Chin Shih Huang Ti was entombed and Mrs Bentley's radio transmitter carefully hidden, was a success from everyone's point of view.

For Romy, the world outside seemed more beautiful than

she remembered after her long illness. Sitting beside Gene in the back seat, bumping shoulders whenever the little black Ford lurched over a pothole, touching his arm to point out sights that caught her interest, she felt alive for the first time in months. Gene was content to watch her animated features and temporarily forget Linda's bitter voice and white, accusing face as she announced that their marriage was at an end. She was going home to her father. *He* loved and understood her even if Gene didn't, and he needn't think he could soft-talk her out of it this time! She'd had as much as she could take of this horrible dirty disease-ridden country with its hellish climate and unsympathetic people, and a husband who was never there when she wanted him but spent his time chasing after non-existent news and anything in a skirt. And so on. And so forth.

'You'll never make the big time,' she'd said scornfully. 'I could have helped you a lot, with my connections. The trouble with you is you're so damned dumb you can't even tell which side your bread is buttered. Dad offered you the French posting, but you wouldn't take it even though you knew I've always loved Paris. Well, I'm through with you. I've got better things to do with my life than swelter in a filthy Chinese town waiting for you to come home. Research! I know what that means. People aren't blind and deaf, you know, and plenty of friends have been kind enough to tell me where you spend your evenings. I'm going home, Gene, and I'll make sure everyone knows exactly why. You won't have a friend left in China by the time I've done with you.'

She had, indeed, gone within the week, sailing back to America on the very ship they'd arrived in, leaving him with a heap of unpaid bills, embarrassed looks from his colleagues, and a lot of useless lacquered furniture which she'd bought before things went sour between them. Had it been his fault? He couldn't say, but he knew she'd keep her word and do everything in her power to make things uncomfortable for him. No doubt once she was safely back with 'Daddy' she'd start divorce proceedings and then look around for another man – someone who didn't mind being pushed around. He'd made the mistake of letting her see he valued independence: she couldn't stand that. Her efforts to cut him down to size might even extend to getting him sacked from his job – after all, she was still the boss's daughter. Maybe when he returned from the Red base he'd find another man in the Shanghai office and a curt note telling him he was fired.

Oddly enough, at this moment the prospect didn't worry him. He felt Romy's hand on his arm and tried to hear what she was saying, and his spirits rose until he felt like singing.

Abigail glanced in the rear-view mirror and a small crease appeared between her eyebrows. I ought to warn her, she thought worriedly. I don't want Rosemary hurt again. She's had a rough time; now she needs a chance to get back on an even keel, emotionally speaking. The last thing she should do is fall in love with a handsome face and an easy manner. That young man has more than his fair share of charm – I'm conscious of it myself – but if half of what I hear is true, he has no conscience where women are concerned.

The Shanghai grapevine, nourished by dinner-party gossip, had lost no time in reporting the rift between young Lyon and his beautiful wife. Rumour spoke of constant arguments terminated only when Mr Lyon marched out, slamming the front door. It also hinted that Mrs Lyon's complaints were well-founded. Her husband was a womanizer, and not a discreet one, either. He had been observed in a dance-hall with a pretty Eurasian girl two days after his wife had suffered a miscarriage, and there was evidence to suggest that his newspaper work took him all too often into the lowest type of tea-house.

Certainly Romy should be warned – but how? She was a grown woman, not a giddy girl. She might very well tell Abigail to mind her own business.

I'll have to risk it, thought Abigail gloomily, bumping over the potholes. She took another look in the rear-view mirror. Li was perched on the jump-seat beside an enormous picnic hamper; his monkey features proud and solemn. Mr Lyon now appeared to have his arm round Rosemary's shoulders, no doubt to protect her from the bumps.

'Will your wife be joining you in Sian, Mr Lyon?' Abigail asked pointedly, meeting his eyes in the mirror.

His jaw tightened perceptibly. 'No, she's had to go home for family reasons,' he said with wooden politeness. 'I'm on my own now.' He stared back at her challengingly and did not remove his arm.

Impasse, she thought, and stamped savagely on the accelerator. The sooner I send him off to the Red base the better for Rosemary's sake. The little black Ford bounced like a pingpong ball along the rough track.

They crossed the Wei river, the water now so low that it meandered in a dozen narrow channels, and took the left-hand fork in the road while the convoys of army trucks which had been belching dust over them for the past ten miles swung to the right on their way to supply the Front. Romy dozed, her head against Gene's shoulder, waking only when they reached the little town of Lintong, which straggled up the craggy side of a mountain. At its foot lay the temples and shining pools of the pleasure-garden where long ago the lovely concubine Yang Wei-fei used to disport herself in natural hot springs for the delectation of her imperial lover. Steam hovered over the water's glassy surface.

Abigail noticed that foreigners were evidently in residence: several long black motors were drawn up in the temple's forecourt and uniformed Chinese chauffeurs gambled in the shade.

She turned left into the plain, hoping that none of the temple's visitors had any interest in archaeology. She didn't want some amateur antiquarian poking around her own little excavation on Mount Li. The local peasants considered it a haunt of evil spirits; an idea she took care to foster. However her fears were groundless. When she switched off the engine at the foot of the man-made hill silence and dust settled around the car. Her secret was still safe.

'Here we are,' she announced. Reluctantly, it seemed, Gene and Romy disentangled their limbs and got out, yawning and stretching. Li busied himself with the picnic hamper and a folding table.

'Before we eat I'd like to show you my little excavation site, Mr Lyon, I'm sure you'll find it interesting.' She gave him a look so loaded with meaning that he couldn't help smiling, and was obliged to turn away with a pretended coughing fit. What a character the old dame was! Sixty-five if she was a day, and still driving over the rough country tracks like Boadicea in her chariot, up to her eyes in intrigue. He hoped he'd be the same at her age.

'I'd like to see it too,' said Romy unexpectedly. 'I've always wondered what you find so fascinating about Mount Li.'

'Good gracious, no, child! It's far too steep for you in your condition. There's nothing much to see – just a few broken pots . . .'

'Then why should Gene want to look at them?' Romy's lower lip had a mutinous droop.

Gene said, 'Mrs Bentley's right. It's too hot for you to climb uphill on your first outing. Wait here in the shade and enjoy the view, and if there's anything interesting I'll photograph it for you. How about that?'

'All right.' She flopped on to the canvas chair Li had produced from the boot of the Ford. Her legs did feel wobbly, and she was glad enough to sit and watch as Gene and Abigail scrambled up the side of the hill and vanished into the trees.

The heavy brooding silence settled round her, and despite the heat she shivered a little, imagining the bloated body of the great Han emperor being laid to rest in this immense tomb two thousand years ago, surrounded by his wives and concubines, his horses and hounds, grooms and servants and rank upon rank of bowmen, chariots, infantry and cavalry – an army in effigy facing East, from whence the new empire's enemies would come. Abigail had told her how, when the Emperor Chin Shih Huang Ti died at last, his courtiers were afraid to announce his death for fear of popular uprising. Propped in the palanquin, the imperial corpse had been escorted back to his palace by the whole of his usual retinue, with a cartload of stale fish preceding the palanquin to disguise the smell of decomposing human flesh.

She wondered what drew Abigail to this eerie sombre spot, which local peasants shunned. Built by conscripted labour, watered with innocent blood, even now Mount Li seemed to be a haunted, evil place, where the air cried a tale of ancient cruelty. Yet day after day Abigail drove here from Sian and climbed the hill alone . . .

Perhaps, thought Romy with an inward laugh, she has a still hidden on those tree-lined slopes, and there she takes selected visitors for private orgies. She might have included me in the party today! Perhaps she prefers the company of good-looking men . . . Whatever they're up to I wish they'd come back. I've had enough of this spooky place. I'd hate to be here alone at night.

'*Lai!*' she called, more to break the brooding silence than because she wanted anything.

'Yes, missee?' It was reassuring to hear Li's high-pitched voice.

'Bring me – oh, something to drink. Whatever you've got, it doesn't matter.'

'Lemonade, missee?'

'That'll be fine.'

'Open rice, missee?' he suggested.

Romy hesitated. She was hungry and it was too bad of the others to disappear up the hillside without a hint of when they'd return. It would serve them right if they got back to find she'd finished the picnic. After a moment her better nature prevailed. 'No, we'll wait,' she said reluctantly. 'I'll have just the lemonade now.'

It was an hour before she heard their voices as they descended the steep slope. Both gave off an air of suppressed excitement which made her wonder if her guess about the secret still hadn't been far from the mark.

'I'm sorry we took so long. Are you starving? We'll eat at once,' said Abigail. 'Mr Lyon asked so many questions I could have stayed up there all afternoon. It's such a treat for me to show my finds to an expert.'

Gene looked a little embarrassed. 'Well, I can't claim any special knowledge –'

'You underrate yourself, Mr Lyon!' Abigail's tone could only be described as arch. Romy felt that if she'd been holding a fan she would have given Gene a playful tap. 'You're far too modest. I hope you'll give me the benefit of your *scholarship* more often. Sometimes it's so hard to interpret what I discover.'

It seemed to Romy that they were no longer discussing the tomb of Chin Shih Huang Ti. They had strayed to some other topic of absorbing interest to both of them, from which she was excluded. She felt hurt and resentful. Why didn't they trust her? She said, 'Do tell me what she showed you, Gene. I'm bursting with curiosity. Why did it take so long? What does she keep in her secret hideyhole on the top of that hill? I'm beginning to think she must make moonshine up there.'

Abigail laughed heartily. 'Oh Romy, how could you suspect me of such a thing? I'd no idea you had such a vivid imagination.'

Something in her voice, some hint of patronage combined with the gloating confidence of one who possesses a secret, provoked Romy to another guess. A switch seemed to click in her brain as half-remembered hints and minor puzzles slid smoothly into place: Abigail's mysterious absences, Gene's unlikely interest in archaeology, the choice of this grim, haunted hill which superstitious Chinese peasants shunned . . .

'If it's not a still, it must be a radio transmitter,' she said clearly.

There was a crash close behind her as Li dropped a pile of plates, and Abigail's laughter froze on her lips. She looked astonished – and scared.

'W . . . What makes you say that?' she faltered.

Only Gene seemed undismayed. He crossed the little clearing in a couple of long strides and put his arm round Romy's shoulders. He was smiling. 'I told you it wouldn't be long before she tumbled to it,' he said. 'Now you'll have to let her into the secret.'

On his return from Nanking, Dr Lombard noticed a definite and displeasing change in his patient. Without hesitation he blamed the influence of Mrs Bentley and cursed the necessity which had taken him from Romy's bedside long enough for his ascendancy over her to wane. No longer was she content to lie becomingly draped on a chaise-longue, languidly acquiescing to his proposals for speeding her recovery. Instead she rose and dressed for breakfast, and only his direct warnings prevented her from accompanying Mrs Bentley on her daily trips to Mount Li.

'I went there while you were away, and it didn't do me any harm,' she protested. 'In fact, since I've been getting out a bit I feel much better.'

'Then you've been extremely lucky,' he said gravely. 'Nothing could be worse for a woman in your condition than bouncing over those rough roads. Frankly, I'm horrified to hear that Mrs Bentley encouraged such folly.'

Romy shrugged – another departure from precedent. Lombard wondered what else he could say to undermine Mrs Bentley's influence without actually causing the older woman to leave his house in a huff. His plans were at a delicate stage and he had no wish to upset the careful balance of his household. If either Romy or Mrs Bentley left, she would take the other with her; with Mrs Bentley would go his chance of identifying her Communist contacts. So far the big fish had eluded him, but he was convinced that someone in Sian was in regular communication with the enemy and his instinct insisted that if he were patient Mrs Bentley would lead him to the traitor. She had managed to keep him in the dark so far, but sooner or later she would, he was sure, relax her guard.

He said emphatically, 'As your doctor, I must utterly forbid any more careering about the countryside. It's quite unnecessary and highly dangerous for your baby. Do you understand?'

Bully! thought Romy. I don't believe a word of it. This time last week I would have, though. I'd have said, 'Yes, Harvey; no, Harvey,' and obeyed without question. I wonder how long I'd have stayed in that state?

Aloud she said, 'I understand,' although she had no intention of taking his advice.

Gene and Romy stood together in the wooded shadow of Mount Li a few days later, waiting for Abigail to signal the arrival of the Red guide who was to smuggle Gene through the front line. Here in enemy territory a Red Army man was bound to be wary and suspicious of strangers, so Abigail had gone alone to meet him. The voice of 'Missee Benlee,' at least, was known and trusted.

Now that he was about to leave her, Romy felt nervous and depressed. What if the Reds mistook him for a White, or the Whites a Red? What if he never returned but disappeared just as Stephen had done? But she knew that if she voiced her vague fears and begged him to stay he would think her another Linda – a clinging, demanding woman as incapable as ivy of standing alone.

Linda had had some reason to cling: after all, she was his wife. Romy had no such claim on him. Nor do I want one, she thought quickly. I can stand on my own feet. A woman who can't live without a man's support is a poor creature! Look at Abigail: she makes the most of her independence. If her husband was still alive I doubt if he'd encourage her to operate a secret transmitter. The most reckless activity of her life would probably be the weekly game of *mah-jong*. I'm free now, too. I don't want to be tied to a man again. Nevertheless, the treacherous words, 'Don't go!' revolved ceaselessly in her brain and she had to bite her lips to prevent herself saying them aloud.

'Look after yourself while I'm away,' said Gene.

'Of course.'

'Don't let Lombard push you around.'

Her eyebrows rose. 'What have you got against Harvey? Why don't you like him?'

'I'll tell you some day.'

'Tell me now.'

Gene said seriously, 'I'd like to, but I can't. But please believe I've got my reasons.'

Romy shrugged. 'Oh, all right, keep your silly secrets. I don't care.' She bent so that her hair fell forward to hide her face as she pretended to examine a large iridescent beetle which was clambering laboriously over a boulder.

Gene wasn't fooled. 'Tell me honestly,' he said, turning

her round so that she had to look at him. 'Would you rather I didn't go away until after the baby's born? You've only to say the word, you know.'

Her throat felt tight and she put up a hand to ease it, forcing a laugh. 'Don't be ridiculous! There's no point in you hanging around for the next three weeks – what good would that do? If you don't interview the Red leaders now someone will get there before you and all Abby's trouble will have gone for nothing.'

'You really think it won't be for three weeks?'

'That's Harvey's guess. Personally, I'm sick of waiting and it can't be too soon as far as I'm concerned,' she said with a nonchalance she was far from feeling. 'You buzz off to Pao An and forget all about me. I'll be all right.'

'I can't forget about you, Romy, not for a single minute. I thought you knew that,' he said softly. He was close to her, much too close. She fought against the current that seemed to draw her towards him into his arms, but his mouth was suddenly against hers, and her treacherous heart was ignoring all her instructions and crying out, 'Don't go! Stay with me. I need you!'

He cupped her face in his hands and kissed her eyelids; then gently traced a finger along the line of her brows, over the high cheekbones and down to her chin. 'You're so beautiful,' he said with a kind of wonder; then smiled. 'You must be tired of men telling you that.'

Her eyes crinkled suddenly and dimples appeared either side of her mouth. 'It's not something that's easy to tire of!' Pulling away from him she bent and addressed the beetle, which had surmounted its stone and now seemed to be contemplating an ascent of her shoe. 'What's he after, Beetle? What shameless flattery will we hear next? Listen carefully, Beetle, because I may have to call you as a witness later on, when he denies he ever said such a thing.'

The insect's jewel-like eye regarded her, unwinking. 'You see,' she added to Gene. 'You'll have to be careful how you strew compliments around now. You're under observation.'

'Then let's give him something to observe,' suggested Gene, pulling her into his arms again; but when he tried to kiss her she turned her face away. She lowered herself to sit beside the beetle and began to use her paper fan with short, jerky movements. He could see a small pulse beating fast in her neck.

'We ought to go back,' she said. 'Abby must have found him by now.'

'She said she'd call . . .' Gene tried to recapture the mood of a moment ago. It was like trying to catch hold of a rainbow. One minute he thought he had her in his grasp; the next she had slipped away where he couldn't reach her. 'Has anyone ever painted you?' he asked at random.

The fan stilled for an instant, then moved even faster. He went on quickly, 'I'd love to have a portrait of you posed just like that. Will you get one done for me before I come back? Mrs Bentley will know where to go. These Chinese artists don't take long – just one or two sittings. They're very good.'

'Stephen used to draw me. He was quite good, too,' she said in a faraway voice as if she was looking down a corridor of memory. In the early days of their marriage she had posed for Stephen dozens of times; even now she seemed to hear the scrunch of crumpled paper and his impatient, disappointed voice: 'It's no use. I can get your features all right but I can't get *you*. As soon as I've pinned you down on paper you're not Romy any longer.' Eventually he'd given up trying.

She sighed. 'I don't think he found me a very good model.' She rose rather laboriously, ignoring his outstretched hand, and brushed down her skirt. 'I'm sure we should be getting back.'

'No – wait a minute. There's something I've got to ask you,' he said with sudden urgency. For the first time since she'd known him he sounded hesitant, unsure of himself. The shadow of a premonition touched her. She felt curiously hollow, as if her heart had sunk several inches leaving a gaping hole in her ribcage.

'Surely it'll keep? We mustn't delay your guide,' she said quickly.

His hand on her arm was tense, almost painful. 'No. I must say it before we go. I've been wondering all week how to put this to you. I didn't want to rush things, but it's driving me crazy. I've got to risk it and ask you straight out. Will you . . .'

'Oh, no! Don't, Gene . . . not you. Don't say anything!'

'I've got to. Will you marry me?'

Romy's shoulders sagged as if a heavy weight had been spread across them, and she let out her breath in a sigh of pure exasperation.

'Oh, why do you have to ruin it all?' she exclaimed in tones of deep disgust.

Gene stared at her, taken aback. It wasn't at all the reaction he'd anticipated. 'Don't you like the idea?'

'Like it? Of course I don't! How would *you* like it if someone tried to slap a brand on you two minutes before he waved goodbye and galloped off into the sunset?' she demanded furiously. Sparks danced in her snapping eyes and her pale cheeks were suddenly pink.

'You know that's not what I meant,' he protested.

'I know nothing of the kind. What *did* you mean, then?'

'Well . , . I hoped we could have some kind of – of understanding. I wanted to know that when I come back you won't have forgotten me.'

'Exactly. Just like a dog who buries his bone because he can't eat it now and may feel more like it later. I understand all too well! Sorry, Gene, but the answer's no. I've had enough of marriage to be going on with, and I thought you had too. That's why . . .' she stopped abruptly and swallowed.

'Why what?'

'Why I liked being with you,' she gulped and suddenly burst into tears. Her voice ran out of control, 'I thought you were different, but now you've shown me you're just the same as all the rest of them! Kisses and pretty speeches until you've trapped a girl into loving you, and then you wave goodbye. Work's more important than a wife to men like you. I've made that mistake once and I'm not going to do it again. Go off and get your b – beastly interviews but don't expect me to be waiting with open arms when you return.'

'Romy, it's not like that. Nothing matters to me except your happiness. Of course I'll stay if you want me to.'

'I don't want you to,' she said fiercely, scrubbing at her eyes.

'All right, then. I'll go, but I certainly won't give you time to forget me. I'm going to think of you every minute I'm away, and I warn you that I don't take no for an answer.'

'Words!' she said contemptuously. 'Words don't mean a thing.'

From the grove below Abigail's voice floated up faintly. 'Romy! We're ready!'

He tried to detain her, but she spun on her heel and hurried away down the path. Gene followed more slowly. They arrived separately in the small clearing where Abigail stood beside a thin young Chinese boy in a baggy uniform. His quick eyes darted here and there like an animal sensing danger.

They've quarrelled, thought Abigail after a single glance at Romy's tear-stained face. She felt absurdly relieved. Her warning to the girl wouldn't be necessary after all. Briskly she introduced Gene to his guide and sent them on their way.

When the dustcloud of their truck was well out in the yellow-brown plain, Abigail turned to Romy with a crease of anxiety between her eyebrows. 'You're very pale, dear. Would you like to rest before we start home?'

'I've got a tummy-ache,' Romy admitted. 'Too silly. I must have overdone those pork rolls at lunch – I can never resist them.'

'A *tummy-ache*?'

Abigail sounded so horrified that Romy hastened to add, 'Only sort of on and off. It's not too bad.'

'You foolish child! When did this begin? Why didn't you tell me before?'

'I thought it would soon stop,' said Romy apologetically. Her face twisted suddenly as the pain gripped her. 'I knew it was a mistake to eat so many, but . . .'

'What are you talking about? This is nothing to do with food, you little nitwit!' exploded Abigail, torn between exasperation and alarm. 'Don't you realize? This is the *baby*. If we don't get you home in double quick time your baby will be born here. Come on, into the car with you.

We've no time to lose. Of all the inconvenient moments to choose!'

Romy thought she was overreacting. She couldn't believe that the long wait was finally over and her baby about to arrive. The very idea seemed absurd. 'But Harvey said it would be *weeks*!' she protested.

'I would remind you that Dr Lombard is not gifted with second sight,' said Abigail tartly. 'Come on, don't argue. Even if you can contemplate the prospect of giving birth to a child on the slopes of Mount Li with equanimity, I cannot.'

Ignoring Romy's protests, she hustled her down the hill and settled her in the back seat of the car. The pain had vanished as abruptly as it struck. Romy said chirpily from her comfortable nest among the cushions, 'I'm sure you're panicking unnecessarily, Abby. Truly. I feel perfectly all right again. It's only a false alarm.'

But Mrs Bentley had seen the red light; she was taking no chances. 'False alarm!' she snorted, letting in the clutch with a bang and roaring forward in a cloud of dust. 'Pork rolls! I never heard such nonsense. Can't you see what's staring you in the face? Have you no sense at all? Now hold on tight and don't talk because I won't be able to hear a word you say. I'm going straight to the Catholic Mission just as fast as I can drive. Pray Heaven we're not too late.'

'Oh, the darling, the little pet,' crooned Abigail a few days later, bending over the rose-pink cradle and beaming down at its tiny occupant. 'She's the prettiest baby I ever set eyes on.'

'Only a slave,' murmured Romy, to tease her. In China the birth of a female child – a slave – was a matter for commiseration, and had Stephen been alive Romy suspected he might have been disappointed that this was no male heir to Longmarsh. But despite her deprecating tone it was impossible for her to hide her pride and joy in this perfect small girl who was so completely her own. She longed to show her to Gene.

'How can you say such a dreadful thing? Have you no maternal feelings at all?' responded Abigail indignantly, rising to the bait. 'She's a princess – a little English rose!' She wasn't going to admit to Romy that her pleasure in the baby's looks sprang from another cause. For the past months she'd been haunted by the fear that Rosemary's child might have slanted eyes and a head of straight black hair. Though neither she nor Dr Lombard had voiced this dread, each knew the other was aware of it. Abigail had even made enquiries about adoption from the nuns at the Catholic Mission. She was deeply relieved to find that no arrangement of that kind would be necessary. Rosemary was well; the baby undoubtedly Caucasian. She could forget her fears.

'Have you decided on a name yet?' she asked.

Romy nodded. Propped up on a bank of pillows, her shield-shaped face framed in tendrils of dark curls had a luminous, almost translucent quality. Her skin glowed and her wide-set amber eyes had regained all their old sparkle. 'I'm going to call her Clare, after Stephen's mother.' She hesitated, then added shyly, 'Clare Abigail. Will you be her godmother?'

'Nothing would give me greater pleasure, my dear. I shall enjoy telling her how she nearly entered the world via the sarcophagus of the great Han emperor. Talking of which . . .'

'Have you heard anything?' said Romy eagerly.

'I was going to say I had news of Mr Lyon this morning. Indirectly, of course. He seems to have made a good impression, as far as I can tell.'

'Will he be back soon?'

With a gesture Abigail warned her to keep her voice down as two gardeners pattered barefoot past the veranda. 'Not for a bit. Apparently his hosts have planned a full programme for him. It'll take longer than he expected.'

'How long?'

'About three months, according to the message.'

'*Three months!*' Romy felt stunned. Three months was an eternity, a blow to the heart. 'But he said he'd only be away a week!'

Abigail said gently, 'You must remember that in his profession it is difficult to be sure how long anything will take. Newspapermen are notoriously unpredictable in their comings and goings. I think that was what Mrs Lyon objected to.'

'But he won't be back before I sail for England.'

A good thing too, thought Abigail. She had already decided to say nothing about the special message Mr Lyon had added, saying he'd think of Romy every minute while he was away and count the days until he saw her again. That sort of declaration was out of place on a secret radio link; she was surprised that he had prevailed upon the straitlaced Red radio-operator to transmit it at all. There was no point in encouraging groundless dreams. The sooner Romy went back to England and forgot all about Mr Lyon the better.

Romy was aware that Abigail didn't wholly approve of Gene, and managed to conceal the dismay she felt at this news, at least until Mrs Bentley was summoned from the room. Then she held the baby against her breast and allowed slow tears to trickle down her cheeks and on to the pillow. Stephen had abandoned her and left her to fend for herself, and now Gene was doing the same. She should never have allowed herself to count on him. She should have paid more heed to Abby's warning that Mr Lyon's affections were reputed to be easy come and easy go. Work would always come before women for him; the demands of his career take precedence over family life. Poor Linda had discovered that, and now it was Romy's turn to digest the bitter truth that she meant nothing special to Gene Lyon. No leopard changed his spots. She had been a fool to hope that with her it would be different; to think that if she made no attempt to fetter him he would return to her willingly. A fool learns from his own mistakes, a wise man learns from the mistakes of others, she thought. I saw how he treated Linda – why couldn't I be wise?

Romy cried for a time, then freed a hand from the baby's wrappings and sought a handkerchief on the bedside table. That was enough. Another time she would be more careful about pinning hopes on a few casual endearments, a few caresses. Now she would put Gene Lyon firmly out of her mind and plan for the future. She had a sudden overwhelming longing to see England again.

CHAPTER FIFTEEN

'*I told every little star, just how sweet I think you are. Why didn't I tell you?*' chanted Stephen, using a fine brush to apply oil to the old radio generator's cracks and crevices.

Only extreme familiarity with the song would have enabled a music lover to identify the tune, though to Stephen's own ears the low-pitched groaning issuing from his lips was indistinguishable from the mellow tenor which had made it famous. Fortunately there were no music lovers within earshot, and the baby, at least, seemed to enjoy his father's crooning.

He was a placid, companionable baby, easily moved to smiles and gurgles, his golden face as smooth and buttery-fat as a labrador puppy's. Stephen liked looking after him. If the male stickleback and the male partridge saw no shame in guarding their respective nests, he reasoned, why should the human male? Every so often he stopped work to shift the baby's box so that the sun couldn't strike on it directly. It was rare enough to see the afternoon sun in this dripping, steamy climate. He'd brought the baby out from the hut to make the most of it.

More, even, than Stephen's crooning, the baby enjoyed the steady hum of the generator, which made him coo and wave his fat arms and legs; but today, thought Stephen, wiping his forehead with an oily rag, it looked as if young River Pearl would have to forego this treat. The ancient machine had become as temperamental as a prima donna, and every attempt to start her had ended in frustration.

General Chu Teh would not be pleased. The radio generator was his, captured long ago from the Kuomintang, and it was now the sole link between the Fourth Front Army stagnating here in the wastes of Sikang and Mao Tse-tung's triumphant First Front Army up north in Shensi Province. Since the death of Chen-lu, its original operator, Stephen was the only person who understood the old engine's vagaries. His youthful enthusiasm for ham radio had landed him the job when poor Chen was killed in a bombing raid. Among his possessions Stephen had discovered the maker's instruction and maintenance manual which Chen, who couldn't read anything, let alone English, must have kept more as a talisman than for any practical purpose. For Stephen it was a godsend.

He frowned now as he thumbed through the grimy pages in search of the section headed *Engine fails to start: Causes.* The trouble was that he knew the booklet practically by heart and he'd already tried every trick it suggested. If he couldn't diagnose the ailment by dark, he would have to trudge off to the monastery at Paochen and seek expert help, and that meant a long hot walk tomorrow.

'*Odi et amo*,' he told the gurgling baby. When he'd first taken charge of radio communications it had seemed an improvement on digging irrigation ditches: now he was not so sure. What had begun as a pleasant distraction had turned into a full-time job as General Chu became daily more restless and demanded news of Mao's campaign up north.

It was clear to Stephen that General Chu now bitterly regretted leaving Mao to march north alone the previous autumn. No one knew the ins and outs of the quarrel, but in a fit of pique the comrade general had joined forces with smooth-faced Chang Kuo-tao of the Fourth Army and marched westward, hoping to winter in fertile Szechuan. Things had gone wrong. Chiang Kai-shek's bombers had driven them into the bleak hills of Sikang, where food was scarce and popular support uncertain. As news of Mao's successes in North-Western China began to trickle through, General Chu fretted and fumed, chafing to be back in the thick of the fight. Daily he pestered his radio-operator for news. Until the generator was restored to working order Stephen would know no peace.

On the question of a move northward to join Mao's army, Stephen's own feelings were mixed. He was guiltily aware that he ought to be eager to return to civilization. He should be longing for news of his home, not to mention his wife. He should crave cultural news, business news, news of world affairs. What was happening in London, Paris, New York? Had England lost the Ashes? What was the name of the

Derby winner? Strangely he cared nothing for any of these things. The world could carry on as it pleased. So long as it left him here in Western China, living like a peasant with his woman and his baby son, he was content.

He was under no form of restraint, nowadays. The farcical 'sentence' imposed on him when he was captured had long expired: there was nothing to prevent him leaving General Chu's camp except the physical difficulty of reaching a road or a railway.

'You can go tomorrow, Ti-fen,' Pao would say. 'Why don't you go and live in your great house again and eat off fine plates and count money all day long?' Then her long eyes would crinkle and she would put a hand to her mouth to hide her laughter, for she knew very well why he stayed. He was happy here with her, and his greatest fear was that one day he must wake from this idyllic dream and lose his Chinese love.

Not that most Europeans would find this life idyllic, he thought now. The earth-floored hut they lived in was more primitive than the poorest farmhand's cottage at Longmarsh. The climate was harsh, the diet sparse and monotonous. To keep his small household fed, Stephen spent most of his waking hours in search of food or preparing it, collecting sticks for the fire, carrying water, washing clothes, tending vegetables. Subsistence living, physical drudgery. The age-old life of the Chinese peasant, though without the age-old taxes. Yet he, owner of three thousand English acres and a house full of historic treasures, who had never cooked or cleaned or washed clothes before, had never in his life been so happy.

The reason, of course, was Pao. A year after their meeting, a year lived in close physical proximity with total lack of privacy, he was still bewitched by her. He loved her voice, her quick gestures, her tinkling laugh. The fluid grace of her movements enchanted him and so did the bubbling playfulness which made a joke of every hardship. Yet beneath this laughter-loving surface lay a surprising depth of purpose. Pao had not left her comfortable home to join the Red Army on a sudden whim, as he'd at first imagined.

Far from being the pretty, helpless victim of parental

tyranny she was a dedicated Communist of long-standing, a seasoned campaigner, who had already been arrested for her part in student demonstrations in Shanghai and only saved from execution by her father's frantic bribes to the authorities . . . It was principally fear for her daughter's safety which had led her mother to incarcerate her at home. When Pao's repeated attempts to escape were frustrated by family vigilance, she tried to force her mother's hand by committing suicide. At last, realizing that her mother wouldn't give in to such moral blackmail, Pao resolved to throw in her lot with Stephen.

'I watched you through the screen and saw you were not the same as the other foreign devils,' she told him one evening by the fire. 'The Second Lady told me the Red Army was near. It was then that I made my plan.'

'Not the same? How did you know I wasn't the same?'

Her pointed fingers scratched softly at the nape of his neck. 'You have no hair on your lip and your eyes are kind,' she said, smiling. 'I knew I could make you love me.'

'Oh, you did, did you? You may be surprised to hear I nearly sent you packing the moment I realized who you must be. You had a lucky escape, young lady,' he said with mock severity.

'Lucky? Yes, I am lucky. Even when my mother beat me and bound my feet it was a lucky day, for that was when I decided I would not be as other Chinese women.'

He took one of her small feet in his hands, turning it this way and that. Unlike the tiny deformed hoofs of so many Chinese girls, Pao's feet were naturally shaped.

'But your feet are not bound,' he said, puzzled.

By degrees he extracted the story of her first act of defiance. After much persuasion she had coaxed her father into sending her, at the age of eight, to live with his Third Sister in Shanghai and attend a school for girls run by the redoubtable Miss Chen. A servant had been despatched with her, whose duty it was to tighten the binding-cloths on Pao's feet daily.

'Miss Chen found me crying because I could not run and play with the other girls,' Pao explained. 'She took me back to the house of my Third Aunt and asked was she not ashamed that a child of her house was crippled because of an old and evil custom?

'Then my Third Aunt said, "What will the revered wife of my husband's brother say if I allow her daughter to unbind her feet?" And I – I cried yet more loudly, and said, "How will I get a husband if my feet grow too big to wear the red embroidered slippers of a bride?" Miss Chen laughed, and she said, "Do you really want to be a man's bride and live within four dull walls all your life? Look at me! I am no man's wife. I am a modern woman."

'I said, "Yes, I want to be a modern woman too. I will unbind my feet, whether my mother beats me for it or not." But still my Third Aunt lamented and said, "What shall I do? I cannot defy the wishes of First Brother's wife."

'Then Miss Chen said scornfully, "Well, and what is the good of unbinding a child's mind if you fetter her body? Unless you will unbind Bright Treasure's feet, I will not teach her in my school." And she went away.

'When she was gone Third Aunt and I looked at one another and at last she said, "Well, and perhaps she is right. She is a modern woman. These are new ways." She fetched hot water and cloths. She unwound the long strips of cloth that kept my feet so small and soaked them, and put them back on more loosely.'

'Were they all right after that?' asked Stephen.

Pao shivered at the memory. 'That night I learnt what pain was. As the blood stirred in my feet which had felt nothing for so long, they swelled and ached until I had to bite my mouth not to cry aloud. I could neither stand nor lie. Whatever I did the pain tore at my heart. It was worse by far than the binding, though for that I had wept a salt lake of tears. All that night and the next I sat with my feet under me, rocking and moaning, struggling not to give in and beg my aunt to tighten the cloths again and give me peace. That was the beginning.'

As she grew older, it seemed, her personal rebellion had shifted its focus, become openly political. Twice she had narrowly escaped death. Once her father's bribes saved her from a firing squad, and once she had to flee from a friend's house clutching leaflets printed on a forbidden press. At the thought of the risks she'd taken – was still taking as she strove to free Chinese women from domestic slavery – Stephen felt his blood run cold. He worried about her all the time she was away from the hut, but knew he could no more keep her at home than he could cage a wild bird.

Putting down the brush at last and wiping his hands, he took a small earthenware bowl from beneath its cotton cover and began to spoon millet mush into River Pearl's mouth, which opened and shut with the eager regularity of a fledgling's beak. Pao had weaned the baby early – scandalously early, according to the sharp-tongued wife of Lin Li-tao, their nearest neighbour, who considered herself an expert on baby-rearing and was always ready to criticize Pao's methods of housekeeping and childcare. Pao didn't mind in the least. 'If she can look after him better than me, let her do so,' she said serenely. 'Everyone must do the job he is best fitted for and I am not fitted for domestic work. That is why I left my father's house. My work is teaching the people, not feeding little babies.'

Even Lin Li-tao's critical wife had to admit that Pao was an excellent teacher. Peasant women flocked to her lessons in the old schoolhouse at Kansing, a few miles outside the Red base, and later brought their shy sheepish menfolk to learn their first characters. Sometimes, too, she would speak at political meetings, pitching her soft voice to an ear-piercing nasal whine that carried the message to the farthest members of her audience. Freedom from taxes, from warlords, from the foreign imperialists who were bleeding China white. Freedom above all from the Japanese invaders.

While she was thus engaged, Stephen would take charge of little River Pearl, and by degrees assumed complete responsibility for their domestic economy; a move which delighted Pao, who had neither time nor talent for such matters. She would cheerfully sleep on a bare board or march all day with only a handful of parched wheat for sustenance; but the time-consuming traditional arts of the Chinese housewife were not for her.

To his own surprise, Stephen found he enjoyed cooking and was good at it. Nor did Celestial Sparrow, Ah Song, and the other Red warriors consider this occupation in the least degrading. In China the preparation of food was too noble and intricate an art to entrust to mere women. The men of his unit were willing, even eager, to teach him their age-old culinary skills.

How shocked Mrs Marriott would be if she could see me now! thought Stephen, as he replaced River Pearl in his cradle and began to chop vegetables for the evening meal, using the square-bladed cleaver with neat, deft movements as Ah Song had taught him. He grinned, imagining the outraged heaving of the Longmarsh housekeeper's black satin bosom and the popping of her round brown eyes as she declared it wasn't fit to see a gentleman engaged in such a task, and demanded rhetorically whatever things were coming to?

Then Baynes the ferret-faced chauffeur, a barrack-room lawyer if ever there was one, would proclaim darkly to the servants' hall that Mr Stephen was taking the bread out of working men's mouths and there should be a law agin' it. Working men! And what did Baynes, who sat on his backside all day long, think he, Stephen, did with his time? Play? Oh yes, it was easy enough to imagine Baynes' reaction to the sight of the master slicing cabbages.

But Romy: what would she say? At the thought of Romy his amusement died. Poor Romy! She lay heavy on his conscience, spoiling the idyll whenever she entered his mind. He'd given her a raw deal, trying to force her into a mould she couldn't fit and blaming her when she failed to fulfil her role as mistress of Longmarsh. Neither of them had really wanted to be burdened with the problems of Longmarsh, but only Romy had been honest enough to admit it.

As the youngest of three sons, Stephen had never expected to inherit the estate. Growing up in the shadow of his older brothers, black-browed impatient Hugh and fair, fat William, Stephen and his sister Sybil – the afterthoughts – led a life as independent from the rest of the household as that of the mice in the wainscoting. They were seldom seen by their parents' political guests or the laughing, dashing girls and young men who came to dance and hunt and play tennis with Hugh and William. The children had their own ways in and out of the house, avoiding the front door, hall, and drawing-rooms. They ran and slid on lino-covered corridors behind the sprung green-baize doors, kept rabbits in the under-gardener's potting-shed and only visited the dining-room – with water-slicked hair and clean clothes, scrubbed nails – for Sunday lunch. When Stephen outgrew Sybil's governess and started at boarding-school, his brothers were already about to leave university; when Stephen went up to Oxford, Hugh came home to learn to manage the estate, and William joined the navy.

A few years later, when Stephen had found his niche in Sir Charles Curtis' financial empire and had already made a name for himself as one of the brightest young economists of his generation, tragedy struck savagely at the Russell family. Within months, Hugh was killed in a car crash, driving home from a Hunt Ball, and poor gentle William was drowned when his yacht capsized in a freak August gale. Stephen was left, reluctant and unprepared, sole heir to Longmarsh.

Not that he'd allowed his father to sense his reluctance. To Sir James, aged and saddened by the sudden deaths of his sons, it had appeared that Stephen was willing and able to step into their shoes. Able, yes; willing, no. He recognized now that it was only a sense of family duty which prevented him from presenting the whole place to the nation as soon as his father died.

But in the golden August of 1932, when he saw Romy O'Halloran ride her own mare to victory in the Dublin Horse Show, and fell head over ears in love with her, Sir James was still hale and hearty and the shadow of his inheritance seemed a small cloud on Stephen's personal horizon.

'You poor man! What a dreadful thing to have hanging over your head!' Romy had exclaimed when their courtship had progressed far enough for him to touch delicately on future prospects. She'd looked solemn for a moment, then added, 'We'll have to hope your father lives to be a hundred, for I'd rather live in a turf-cutter's cabin than a great old house like Longmarsh Park.'

He'd been surprised by her reaction. Most girls thought

that his inheritance made him more rather than less of a catch.

'What's so dreadful about an old house? Yours isn't exactly new,' he'd pointed out, and she laughed.

'Oh, Lissanissky's . . . different! Nobody minds if sheep mow the avenue or rain comes through the roof. If that happened at Longmarsh, I'm sure the butler would have a fit.'

He hadn't taken her seriously. 'Do you think you can still put up with me in spite of my great expectations?' he said jokingly. 'You've just promised to marry me, Miss O'Halloran, and I don't expect you to go back on your word.'

She'd given him that disconcerting upward glance from her amber eyes and taken a long time to consider the question. 'I think so, if I try very hard, but I'll still pray every night for your father's good health,' she said at last.

After their marriage, Stephen bought a pretty, fashionable little house in Pelham Place, and hoped that weekend visits to Longmarsh would gradually cure his wife's strange aversion to the place. Another five years might have done it, he thought now, putting the chopped vegetables into the round-bellied *wok*. If only Father had lived just a little longer . . .

But death had not finished with the Russell family. Sir James succumbed to a pulmonary infection in the spring of 1933; his widow promptly announced her decision to move into the Dower House, and Romy found herself the unwilling mistress of Longmarsh Park within two years of her marriage. From then on, everything seemed to go wrong between her and Stephen.

Was it my fault or hers? Stephen shrugged. It was too late to worry about that now. In the courtyard the shadows were lengthening. Soon his Bright Treasure would come home to light the smoky hut with her presence. Stephen cast an automatic glance at the baby, peacefully asleep in his box, then wrapped the starting cord round the generator's spindle. One last try!

But his pull produced no more than a sulky splutter from the machine and Stephen gave up. He packed away his tools and picked up a twist of dried grass from the fuel store.

Ducking back through the leather-curtained doorway, he thrust it into the grey embers in the stove and blew steadily until the fire caught hold. Then he fetched a pan of water from the big jar he carried up from the stream every morning, and set it to heat on the stove. Pao would need hot water to refresh her after the long walk. If he passed the town on his way to the monastery next morning he might find someone who would sell him a few tealeaves. First, however, he must face the climb up to General Chu's eyrie and report the generator's breakdown.

Stocky and low-browed as the monkeys whose home was the steep terraced valley below him, General Chu sat at the door of his hut and gently scratched his itching head with the stem of his long-handled pipe. Lice and bedbugs flourish in the steamy heat of a Chinese summer, when laden clouds cut off the hills' triangular peaks and sudden spates sweep away frail cantilevered bridges; but it was not only Chu Teh's shaven head that itched. He wanted to go north.

No longer could he pretend, even to himself, that he'd made a wise decision when he parted from Mao Tse-tung. It had been a mistake to listen to that smooth-spoken sea-slug Chang Kuo-tao who, when all was said and done, wanted power and glory and personal profit far more than he wanted revolution. Chang had always been jealous of Mao.

In his mood of self-criticism General Chu had to admit that he, too, had sometimes found it very hard to bear Mao's lofty disregard for any opinion but his own. That was why he, Chu, had been ready to listen when Chang suggested in his persuasive way that it was time Mao lost a little face. If he wanted to go north and fight the Japanese on his own, let him try it. Soon he'd come creeping back with his tail between his legs, begging wiser heads to share the burden of leadership with him.

Unfortunately it hadn't worked out that way at all. Mao didn't appear to find leadership a burden; indeed, Chu suspected he regarded it as a right. Thanks to his radio link with the First Front Army, Chu had been able to follow every stage in Mao's fortunes, and there could be no doubt that his star was still ascending.

While his erstwhile partners kicked their heels in bleak Sikang, Mao had established a powerful base in Shensi Province, which was a much better place to feed an army; and far from fighting for survival, he had managed to convert so many captured enemies to the cause that it was rumoured the Young Marshal himself was prepared to join Mao in a United Front against the Japanese. The Marshal had secretly invited Red instructors to teach in his new officers' training school. Chu yearned to be in the thick of the action once more, but it was difficult to see how he could do so without serious loss of face. The plain truth was that he had put himself in Chang's power, and that wily individual was not going to let him go.

Although the local warlords in this corner of the country were temporarily friendly, if once they sensed they were stronger than Chang Kuo-tao, the balance would quickly tip the other way. The Sikang base would be overrun and a whole year's work wasted. Already there had been instances of Red warriors and political instructors being molested by roving bands of *t'aiping*, as the unemployed and unpaid mercenary soldiers of warlords were called. It was all most unsatisfactory.

Still, the latest news was that Ho Lung's Second Army was on its way to join them and that, thought Chu Teh, brightening, might give him the opportunity to escape from Chang's irksome company. Ho Lung was a man he liked and understood: a big burly rumbustious peasant who spoke his mind freely. If he and Chu Teh both insisted on marching north, Chang would be unable to prevent them.

On the track below a man was trudging towards him. Sun glinted briefly on his pale hair and Chu recognized the loose-limbed walk of the English prisoner. He called Celestial Sparrow from his kite flying to take up interpreter-duty.

'What news from Pao An?' he asked eagerly as soon as Stephen was seated with a cup of hot water to refresh him.

Stephen shook his head. 'Tell the comrade general there is no news today.'

'*No* news?' Chu Teh's eyes bulged dangerously, reminding Stephen of a Peke whose tail had been trodden on. 'There must be news. The Fifteenth Army Corps is moving towards the Yellow River. The Seventy-Third Division is fighting near Kansu. *T'a ma-ti!* How can there be no news?'

'Tell him the radio isn't working. There's something broken or missing – I'm not sure what.'

'Well and it must be made to work again,' snapped Chu Teh when the boy had translated this.

'I know,' said Stephen wearily. 'Tell the comrade general I'll walk over to Laochen tomorrow. Apparently there's an Italian monk in the monastery there who's a bit of a mechanic. He may be able to help.'

Chu Teh nodded. 'Good. It is essential that we keep informed of events in Shensi.' He hawked and spat impressively, then drank off his cup of hot water, dismissing them.

'Certainly, Comrade General,' piped Celestial Sparrow. He gave a snappy salute that was only slightly marred by the cheeky grin which accompanied it. Chu Teh laughed and cuffed him affectionately as he scampered back to where he'd left his kite.

When Stephen got back to his own hut he found Pao-ching already there, tending the baby. She looked pale and tired.

'Where have you been? Why did you leave the child?' she said edgily.

'I had to report to the comrade general,' he explained, surprised by her tone. 'I knew you'd be back soon, and it didn't seem worth carrying him all the way up the hill. He's all right, isn't he? You didn't find him crying?'

'No, he was asleep,' she admitted, but she still looked strained.

'Then what's the matter?'

'Oh, Ti-fen . . .'

'Come on, darling. Tell me what's up.' He pulled her into his arms and felt her whole body shaking. 'What's happened?'

'I nearly didn't get back at all,' she said, making an effort to control herself.

He frowned. 'Why? Where were you today?'

'We went to that village to the south of Lungchien. Tehsien, it's called. We were holding a political meeting in the school there. Only a few villagers came. I wondered why. And the ones who did come were very quiet – frightened. They didn't ask any questions; just sat silently when Lin Tsu-han told them what the Red Army would do for them and asked for their support. I was watching them all the time, wondering what was wrong. They kept turning their heads . . . listening.

'Then it was my turn to speak. I had just climbed to the platform of planks we had constructed and had not yet said anything when there was a great cry from the door of the school. "The warlord is coming! Run! Fly! Ma Ku-fan is coming to kill us!" Suddenly all was turmoil. I jumped or was pushed down from the platform on to the floor, and for a moment I could see nothing but legs and feet. I thought I would be trampled to death. Then someone pulled me by the arm and dragged me to a door at the back of the school. I heard screams from the peasants, and the thunder of hoofs as the warlord's soldiers rode over them. I jumped over the terraces and fled down the hill. Shots came cracking past me until I was safely hidden in the trees.' She paused and drew a long shuddering breath. 'I stayed hidden a long time, until the soldiers went away at last. I dared not go back to see what they had done, but the screams were terrible . . . horrible.'

'What about the others?' asked Stephen. 'Who was with you besides Lin Tsu-han?'

'There was only Lin. He escaped too. But if River Pearl had been with me, I would not have been able to run. They would have killed me.' She clutched the baby to her in remembered terror.

'Don't think about it,' Stephen said quickly. 'You mustn't go anywhere near that village again – it's too dangerous. Ma Ku-fan's a devil, they say, but I didn't think he'd dare to molest the Red Army. Have you put in a report?'

'Lin is making one.' She relaxed against him, exhausted by fear. Stars were pricking through the blue-black dusk, and the smell of dung cooking fires came pungently to their nostrils. 'Do you know what I thought, while I lay hidden?'

'Of this fine fellow?' He tickled the naked baby.

'No,' said Pao seriously. 'I was thinking of you. I have been in danger before – oh, many times! – but I have never been afraid. Today . . .' her voice was little more than a whisper '. . . today I was afraid of death.'

He held her close. 'It's not surprising. People run out of courage, you know . . . I'd have been scared stiff. You've been living on the edge of danger too long, my love; I wish you'd give up this teaching and have a bit of a rest. Stop rushing about and stay here in camp with the baby. Very soon we're going to be on the march again, and you'll need all the strength you've got.'

She smiled and shook her silky black head. 'No, there is too much to do before we leave . . . Besides, you are wrong, Ti-fen. I have not run out of courage. I only feared death because I love you.'

'How does that follow?'

She said hesitantly, 'Tell me, Ti-fen. If I die, will you forget me as you forgot your First Lady? That was my fear.'

'Of course I won't. How could you think that?' he demanded, almost roughly. He couldn't bear the look of strain on her delicate features, the shadowed eyes. He paused, then added more gently, 'I could never forget you, Treasure. You mean the world to me. I can't forget people . . . who've been close to me.'

Pao's head came up and her eyes flashed. 'Why do you never speak of your First Lady? Why do you keep her in your heart and say nothing to me? Oh, Ti-fen! You fill all my heart. How can you keep room in yours for another woman? I told my mother I could never love a man. I believed it was true and the Cause was enough to be husband and father and brother to me. But now I think of you day and night and I am afraid – afraid of so much love. Tell me you'll never leave me. Tell me you'll keep me safe in your heart and then my fear will go away.'

'I won't leave you, Treasure,' said Stephen quietly. 'I'll keep you safe in my heart.' He bent and kissed the long eyelids beneath the willow-leaf brows.

'Always?'

'Always.'

'Then I shall not be afraid any more.' She smiled radiantly.

'All the same, darling, while we're making promises, please promise me you'll stay out of Ma Ku-fan's territory from now on. There's no need to go there again. In a week or so we'll be marching north to join Mao and any teaching you do here will be undone the moment we leave.'

'We join Mao?' Her eyes shone. 'Oh, such news! When the liberation starts I will have so much to do.'

'You'll stay away from Kansing?' he insisted.

'Yes, Ti-fen.'

'Can you stay here tomorrow and take care of the baby? I must go to the monastery to mend the radio.'

'Then he must come with me. There is a big political meeting of the Cadre Corps, and some former landlords will be struggled against. I must be there.'

'Where's this meeting?'

Her eyes flickered briefly. 'At Ping-liang.'

Stephen swore under his breath. 'That's quite close to Ma Ku-fan's stronghold. I've seen it on that map we captured.'

'Oh no, you are mistaken. Many villages have this name,' she said blithely. 'Also we will be a strong band; strong enough to scare away a hundred Ma Ku-fans.'

He had no power to stop her. 'Be careful then,' he said. 'Remember I love you.'

She flashed him a smile and stood on tiptoe to put her slim arms round his neck. 'I am always careful, and if I am also in your heart I will be safe,' she whispered. 'Wherever you go I will stay with you.'

CHAPTER SIXTEEN

The Franciscan monastery of Laochen occupied a commanding position at the head of a broad and fertile valley, and Stephen's first thought as he approached from below was that the monks had chosen their site with an eye to defence. Standing as it did between the curve of a fast-flowing river and the steep crags of Mount Hokien, whose needle-like pinnacles rose to ten thousand feet behind the monastery, it would be a difficult place to attack. In addition to its natural defences, the monks had encircled their domain with an eight-foot double wall with loopholes on the outer side and watchtowers at each corner.

Fruit orchards and nut plantations, the trees symmetrically pruned and as precisely spaced as soldiers on parade, lay inside the wall, over which Stephen caught glimpses of monks, their coarse robes hitched up to give freedom of movement, busily mulching these trees from handcarts full of manure. Obedient to their vows, they neither looked up nor spoke as he passed, but all the same he was aware of intense curiosity following him as he mounted the long stairway of shallow steps leading to the archway, where great wooden doors studded with nails marked the entrance to the monastery.

Further up the hillside, outside the wall, more monks worked on terraced fields blooming with sulphur-yellow oilseed rape; the tall pale spears of maize were interspersed with bushy soy and potatoes, tobacco, and elaborate trellis-work of bamboo canes supporting runner beans, while the luxuriant growth of marrow and squash trailed along the neat crisscross of irrigation channels.

It was a scene of triumphant husbandry: nature at her most fecund brought to heel as only Chinese gardeners know how. Like an immense vegetable garden, it made a brilliant patchwork against the stark backdrop of mountain.

The Chinese brother who appeared at one of the watch-towers in response to Stephen's vigorous hammering on the great door regarded the visitor with deep suspicion. Motioning him to stay where he was, he hurried to fetch a florid, red-haired monk whose stomach bulged over the cord of his habit. It was clear that he had been roused from a midday siesta and was in no mood to deal kindly with mendicants.

'Who are you and what do you want?' he shouted roughly in Chinese as primitive as Stephen's own.

'I'm English and I need your help. Can I come in?' called Stephen.

'You are from the Red Army,' accused the other.

'Well, yes, in a way, but –'

'We will have nothing to do with the Red Army,' thundered the red-haired monk. 'Thieves, parasites, Anti-Christ . . . Be off before I set the dogs on you!'

'I want to speak to Brother Anthony,' said Stephen steadily. He stood his ground although an unpleasant snarling and rattling of chains gave warning that the watchdogs were indeed being unleashed.

The red-haired monk sneered. 'There is no Brother Anthony here. Go away and tell your Communist friends there is nothing for them at Laochen.'

'Is this your usual welcome to weary travellers?' shouted Stephen. After sweating for six hours over muddy tracks with the awkward weight of the generator strapped to his back he was in no mood to be chased away from his objective by this officious bad-tempered monk. 'No wonder all your converts are leaving you if this is how you treat strangers. Let me in. I demand to see the abbot.'

'We have a visitor, Brother Athanasius?' enquired a new voice. The red-haired monk, who had just opened his mouth to deliver a final blast, shut it and turned round hastily.

'Yes, Father,' he admitted grudgingly.

'Then why do you keep him outside in the heat? Open the gate and let him enter.'

'But, Father –'

'Do as I say,' insisted the newcomer and Stephen sighed with relief. A few moments later the wooden door creaked open and Stephen found himself in a broad paved courtyard surrounded by the monastery buildings, whose glistening blue-tiled roofs dipped and soared like the hem of a ballerina's skirt.

A glowering Brother Athanasius led him across the mosaic pavement to a long, whitewashed refectory, where he was welcomed by the abbot, a tall, stately Belgian with startling bushy brows set over large contemplative eyes of a clear pale blue.

'You must forgive this rude reception,' he apologized in correct but halting English. 'Brother Athanasius cannot forget we were attacked from within last winter, and he is understandably wary of strangers.'

'You were attacked?'

'*Mais oui*. A party of beggars whom we admitted to our evening meal rose in the night and opened the gates to the warlord, rather in the manner of the Greeks within the wooden horse at Troy. In these troubled times it is difficult to know whom to trust. But what may we do for you, my son? You seek the assistance of Brother Anthony? Alas, he has gone to the ferry to supervise the despatch of our wine to Peking. We were fortunate that Ma Ku-fan and his men did not discover our wine cellars and we have high hopes of this year's vintage. Brother Anthony will be back tomorrow; if you care to spend the night we will be glad to offer you a bed.'

Stephen thanked him and explained the generator's symptoms, but the abbot was no mechanic and repeated that Brother Anthony was the man to help him. Meanwhile, perhaps he might care for a tour of the monastery?

'We are a self-supporting community,' he explained, 'so apart from the occasions when we sell our surplus produce, we have little contact with the outside world. All the same, we are fortunate in the skills of our brothers, and I think you will agree that we make good use of their talents.'

As he followed his host from the mill to the carpentry shop and thence to the wine-cellars and store-rooms, Stephen thought the abbot was altogether too modest. The whole monastery was a model of order, industry, and productivity. European inventiveness allied to traditional Chinese crafts and husbandry had achieved amazing results, but he noted with interest that all the Chinese brothers worked in a menial capacity, while those in charge of the monastery's major projects: the building of a dam to generate electricity, the breeding of improved strains of chicken and goat and the restoration of the chapel murals, which the warlord's men had defaced, were Europeans to a man.

The tour ended as dark fell with a thimbleful of the monastery's home-brewed liqueur, tasting of herbs and honey. As Stephen stretched out at last on his straw-filled pallet in the narrow whitewashed cell allotted to him, he reflected that this was the first time for over a year that he had felt part of the ruling race in China. It was a strange sensation. He thought of the notice he'd seen last year in a Shanghai park: *No dogs or Chinese allowed*. Then it had seemed normal to him: now it appeared grotesque. For the first time he understood Pao's anxiety to rid China of the foreign parasites who had lived off her – preyed on her – for so long. Whether it was monks or military advisers, bankers or businessmen, the results were the same. Wealth flowed into foreign pockets; the Chinese became progressively poorer. Even the bank loan which was his particular concern would have been used by Chiang Kai-shek to suppress his Communist opponents and protect the business interests of his foreign backers. There was no denying that in their own country the Chinese were regarded as an inferior breed. The trouble is, reflected Stephen, we could run China with one hand tied behind our backs, but we have no right to do it. It was a disturbing thought.

Brother Anthony stood knee-high to a grasshopper: a charming voluble Sicilian with a wrinkled nut-brown simian face, bright brown eyes and neat paws no bigger than a monkey's. He examined the radio generator with the care of a court physician, transferred valves, listened to pulses. He talked excitedly about oscillatory circuits and half-wave rectifiers, but Stephen's Italian was too rudimentary and Brother Anthony's accent too thick for him to learn much from the dissertation.

There was no doubt, though, that he had struck gold. Brother Anthony was an enthusiast. His brilliant Mediterranean eyes snapped with pleasure as he peered and fiddled, rummaging amongst his own collection of wireless spares and replacing pieces he considered outworn. Stephen was sure that if anyone could coax the old generator to life again it was Brother Anthony, and watched his busy fingers with the patient confidence of a child waiting to see the conjurer produce the rabbit.

At last, with a frenzied twiddling of knobs, Brother Anthony achieved a high-pitched whine from the speaker. He flashed a gold smile at Stephen.

More whines and squeals followed, then a woman's voice wailing a song, then the chatter of an announcer. Brother Anthony gestured: Over to you. Carefully Stephen moved the needle along the band to the frequency used by the Shensi Communists for their broadcasts and suddenly, loud and clear, he heard the unmistakable husky tones of Li Hsueh-feng, the Party secretary, urging all patriotic students to join the Red Army University.

Brother Anthony clasped his hands above his head in a boxer's gesture of triumph. The conjurer had produced the rabbit.

When Stephen did not return that night, Pao-ching was faced with a dilemma. Either she could ask another woman to care for River Pearl while she spoke at the day's political meeting at the village of Ping-liang, or she could take the baby with her. Memories of her flight from the warlord's men prompted her to adopt the first course, but an irrational desire not to be parted from her child, even for a few hours, drew her to the second.

Bending over his wooden box, admiring the bracelets of fat on his sturdy wrists and the softness of his golden skin, she wavered, unable to make up her mind. Wei ling, the only woman exempted from work on the irrigation ditches because she suffered from tuberculosis and coughed continually, was a bad-tempered slut and not a fit person to care for her precious son. Yet the country was unsettled and the baby a considerable burden; she would get there twice as quickly without him. If only Stephen had come back! The meeting was an important one. The team of political instructors was meeting the headmen of three different villages to go into the question of redistributing the fields and storehouses which the fleeing landlords had abandoned. She could not miss it.

She thought the matter over carefully and decided it would be safe to take River Pearl with her. The meeting would be well attended by peasants hoping for a share in their former oppressors' wealth. No warlord would dare to menace it.

As dawn broke over the silent mist-filled valley next morning, she tied her books in a cloth bundle to one end of a carrying-pole and slung the basket containing River Pearl on the other. Moving with the traditional bent-kneed shuffle necessary to keep the pole from rubbing her shoulders raw, she joined the coughing, spitting squad of political instructors as they set off along the track that led to Ping-liang.

Stephen was in high spirits as he trudged away from the monastery. It was wonderful, he thought, what a couple of days of rest and a decent diet could do for morale. Instead of sorghum and beans, the monks had plied him with meat and fish, eggs and poultry, milk from their own cows and vegetables fresh from the walled gardens. Goat's cheese, crisp apples, cider and wine . . . if they could grow and produce all these from a few dozen hectares of land, why couldn't the Chinese peasants?

The kindly abbot had loaded him with small presents. A jar of golden honey, fine quality tealeaves, soap, chocolate and insect repellent. Treasure would be delighted. It was satisfying, too, that his mission was successfully accomplished. The generator itself seemed less of a burden than it had on the outward journey, and he had already tuned in several times to Radio Shensi and picked up enough information to satisfy Chu Teh's hunger for news.

Swinging along at a good pace in the fresh early morning, he noted that the sorghum was nearly ripe. The tall thick stalks from which many of the peasants built their house-frames had begun to droop with heavy purple tassels of grain. Peasants clearing the choked irrigation channels in the few paddy-fields shouted a cheerful: '*Shang na'erh?* Whither bound?' and when he replied with the name of his destination he could hear the message being shouted from terrace to terrace as the titbit of information was passed to the farthest workers.

The hill-track climbed and dipped and climbed again, winding round the contours, in and out of patches of forest. As it grew steadily hotter the straps of his pack began to bite into his shoulders, and Stephen lowered his head against the dragging weight, reciting poems as he walked to take his mind off the discomfort. Absorbed in his thoughts, it was some time before he noticed a curious and disturbing phenomenon: in the middle of a working day the fields on either side of the path were deserted.

Suddenly alert, he looked in every direction, trying to remember how long it was since he last passed a bending blue-clad figure at work on the land. Now there was no one in sight and the empty terraces with their waving crops took on a sinister, oppressive air.

Hurrying in spite of his burden, he passed through a village, but that, too, appeared to be empty. He could imagine slanting eyes peeping through holes in the boarded-up lattices. Dogs, ducks, chickens and pigs would all be herded indoors with their scared owners. But what was it they feared? Involuntarily he glanced from side to side, wondering if the tall stands of sorghum concealed lurking *t'aoping*. The sensation of being watched grew stronger with every step he took, and when a jay screeched on one side of the path, to be answered by another across the stream, he felt the sweat of near-panic break out all over him. Every instinct he possessed told him he was walking into an ambush.

Ahead of him lay the fortified town of Ping-liang. He could see the crumbling encircling wall set with watch-towers, but the road leading to the main gate which should, at this hour of the day, be thronged with fodder-carts and peasants swinging buckets on their carrying-poles, was as empty as the fields around him. Stephen's scalp prickled. Something was wrong – very wrong.

It would be madness to walk straight up that deserted road, as conspicuous as a beetle on a tablecloth. A reconnaissance was needed. Gently he slid the straps from his shoulders and cached the radio generator behind a rock. Freed of his burden he stood for a moment taking stock of the various patches of cover between himself and the gate;

then he waded into the nearest irrigation ditch and struck off across the fields.

Alternately crouching and wading, occasionally wriggling on his stomach over a bare patch of ground, Stephen made a wide circle to approach the town via the eastern gate, where a tall stand of maize afforded cover right up to the wall. As he drew nearer he realized that the humming noise from within the town was being made by human voices – many voices, curiously subdued. Instead of being at work or about their business, the inhabitants of Ping-liang were gathered in the town's central square, silently – except that a Chinese crowd can never be silent – watching some drama that was unfolding before their eyes.

Suddenly, with a dizzying sense of relief, Stephen realized what that drama must be. It was the political meeting, of course! Former landlords were going to be 'struggled against' – accused of their crimes and asked to explain them. Though the Red Army incited the peasant population to rise against their oppressors, the punishment of the landlords was left to the peasants themselves.

Sometimes they merely confiscated the rich men's possessions and drove them and their families out of their homes. At other times mob rule prevailed and the helpless landlord or mandarin would be beaten or stoned to death by the angry crowd. His land and goods would then be distributed among his tenants. No doubt Pao was there now, inside the wall, haranguing the illiterate crowd on its rights. The soft voice he loved would be forced into a strident high-pitched sing-song, her gentle almond eyes beneath the willow-leaf brows would be ablaze with revolutionary fervour. Revolutionary madness. He didn't want to see her like that, drunk on words and frenzied as the Pythoness at Delphi. Nevertheless, curiosity drove him to sidle through the open gateway and thread his way through the maze of narrow *hutungs* stinking with garbage and ordure. He headed for the central square.

As soon as he reached the outskirts of the crowd he realized it would be impossible to see what was going on unless he could find a vantage point. The solid wall of human backs was packed tight, shoulder to shoulder, with children and beggars peering through the forest of legs. In the centre of the square someone was shouting. It sounded like a proclamation but he could not catch the words. A long collective sigh that was almost a groan was drawn from the onlookers.

Turning back towards the eastern gate, he climbed the steep ramp to the wall's broad top. Tiny in the distance, now, he could see a double row of kneeling figures in the centre of the hollow square formed by the tight-packed crowd. What was this? he wondered uneasily. It certainly didn't look like the kind of trial Pao had described. It looked more like a penance . . . or an execution. Surely the Cadre Corps wouldn't stand by while the landlords were murdered in cold blood?

He sensed a movement behind him. Someone else had come to share his lookout, but transfixed as he was by the scene in the square he didn't turn round.

By God, it *was* an execution! A huge man, naked to the waist, his torso glistening with oil and his shaven head gleaming like a billiard ball, had started moving along the double row of bound, motionless kneelers. The curved sword swinging in an easy rhythm from his hand was striking heads from shoulders as effortlessly as a scythe reaps corn. Stephen felt physically sick. Sweat streamed into his eyes, blinding him. He leaned shaking against the wall.

Now soldiers were kicking aside the fallen bodies, hustling more victims towards the monstrous executioner. A gleam of sun caught a bright splash of scarlet as a scarf was torn from round a prisoner's neck. A red scarf. With a jolt that hit him like a heavy blow over the heart, Stephen saw that his instinct had been right. It was an ambush – and an execution, not of the landlords but of Red Army captives. Somehow the tables had been turned on the Cadre Corps and the political meeting become a trap.

Pao-ching had been going to speak at the meeting. The agonizing realization that she could be among those kneeling to await the executioner's blade drove him to reckless action. He forgot that he, too, wore the damning insignia of a red star and if he were caught would share her fate. With a muffled groan he leapt down from the wall and began to run back to the square. He must get to her, warn her, save her. Footsteps thudded behind him.

'Stop!' called an urgent voice, but he paid no heed. He must get to her, warn her, save her . . .

A rifle butt was thrust across his path in a gloomy narrow *hutung*, and he sprawled in the filthy gutter. Hands seized his shoulders, holding him down, and he fought like a madman, using every ounce of his sinewy strength to throw off his assailant.

'Let me go, mother-defiler!' he grunted in Chinese, bringing back his bent elbow to catch his attacker a jolt in the abdomen. The man gasped, doubling up, but before Stephen could slip free the rifle butt slammed against the side of his head and a black mist spangled with stars enveloped him. Dimly he was aware of being raised and half-dragged, half-carried into a dark hole that reeked of garlic. As the mist began to clear he realized there were others in the small hut.

From behind him came Celestial Sparrow's anxious whisper. 'Make no noise, Ti-fen. Enemies are all round us.'

'Pao,' he groaned. 'Where is Pao-ching?'

The boy turned away, shoulders shaking, and Stephen knew the answer. Hot murderous rage boiled up in his heart. He would have burst from the hut and run into the square, only his hands and feet had been rapidly tied together.

'Let me go,' he hissed angrily. 'Why have you bound me like this?'

'Because we want to be revenged on Ma Ku-fan and the Nationalists who have killed our comrades,' growled a voice from the back of the hut, 'and we don't want any *hu-tu fah-tzu* – any idiot-plan – of yours to spoil it. They would have caught us all if we hadn't stopped you charging off like a mad buffalo. You can stay there tied up until your wits come back to you.'

'Pao,' he whispered in agony. 'They've killed Pao-ching and you wouldn't let me try to save her.'

Imprinted on his mind's eye was the picture of those helpless kneeling figures, the red scarf, the swinging blade.

As his imagination carried him on to what he'd been too far away to see: blood spraying from the severed necks, heads rolling in the dust, eyes and mouths still moving soundlessly, he retched emptily, unable to expunge the dreadful sight.

A bugle shrilled faintly, and soon hoofs splashed down the muddy street. Inside the hut the Reds froze into utter stillness as they passed. Through a gap in the door curtain Stephen glimpsed rank upon rank of thin shaggy ponies and the puttee-clad legs of their riders, but he was spared the sight of the grinning, sated faces of Ma Ku-fan's rabble as they rode out of the east gate, their bloody work complete.

Celestial Sparrow pressed close against Stephen. 'They will not return to their courts tonight,' he whispered in his ear. 'Beyond the river the rest of the Cadre Corps waits to revenge its comrades.'

Revenge. The choking band round Stephen's throat slackened a little, and his temples throbbed less violently. He wanted revenge, too, not only against the warlord who had been the Nationalists' instrument, but against Chiang Kai-shek himself. Ma Ku-fan and his soldiery would perish tonight at the narrow ford, but his Bright Treasure's shade would not be satisfied until her revolution was achieved. Lying there bound on the dirty, saliva-streaked floor, watching her murderers ride out of town, Stephen vowed to avenge her.

Once, as a boy, riding through the Longmarsh woods in early summer, he had spotted the gamekeeper lying on his stomach amongst the dying bluebells, his arm reaching deep into a hole in the sandy bank. Near him was his dog, sniffing curiously at a dead vixen, her ginger coat matted with mud and blood on her muzzle.

'What are you doing, Marshall?' he'd asked.

For answer the gamekeeper withdrew his arm, pulling out a tiny blind foxcub, its paws waving feebly and its stomach pink in the sunlight. Marshall knocked its head sharply against a stone and threw it to join the vixen.

'Oh, I say . . .' began the boy.

'Un'll starve else,' said the keeper stolidly. He pulled out four more cubs and dealt with them in the same way. 'That's the lot, then,' he said, getting stiffly to his feet and brushing mud from his cord breeches.

Stephen had stared at the corpses. 'What'll the dog fox think when – when he gets home?'

In his imagination he saw the purposeful sinuous shape slinking down the hedgerow, trotting towards his earth, sniffing the wind. Then the halt, paw raised, as he caught the alien scent of the destroyer, the smell of death . . .

The gamekeeper's dour face had cracked in a smile. He shook his head. 'Doan rightly know what un'll think, Master Steve. Reckon un'll be dumbfounded, that's what. Dumbfounded. 'Twill teach the varmint to come arter my pheasants, howsomever.'

Teach him? What would it teach him except how to hate? 'If I was that fox,' the young Stephen had said suddenly and fiercely, 'I'd take all your pheasants now – and your chickens too. Every last one of them.'

Now he was in the same case as the dog fox and his instinct hadn't changed. His angry helpless grief demanded revenge. He would not rest until he had it.

Fingers plucked at his sleeve. 'Ti-fen! Come. We must go quickly!'

He shook his head.

'You must come. Here is danger. The people have betrayed us.'

He said with difficulty, 'I can't go. Not until I find her.'

'She is dead, Ti-fen. You cannot help her now. If you stay here you will die too,' whispered Celestial Sparrow frenziedly. 'Come with me to safety. This town is full of Ma Ku-fan's spies.'

Stephen's throat ached. It was an effort to speak at all. He wished the boy would go and leave him alone. The rest of the Reds had already filed silently from the hut. 'I tell you I can't come yet,' he whispered back. 'Go on by yourself and I'll meet you later by the ford. I – I must find her.'

The boy gave a dry sob and vanished into the dark street. Stephen lay for a while until his body stopped shaking, then got stiffly to his feet. A numb ache was replacing the first sharp agony, but no matter how hard he tried to suppress it, a tiny flicker of hope at the back of his mind would not be extinguished. Perhaps his Bright Treasure still lived. He had not actually seen her among those bound and kneeling figures in the square. It was a fair way off, of course, but loving her as he did, surely he would have recognized her way of walking, the carriage of her head and the set of her shoulders? Surely some instinct would have told him if she was there? Perhaps, by some miracle, she had escaped the massacre. She always said she was lucky and bore a charmed life. Once he'd explained the English saying that a cat had nine lives, and she'd clapped her hands. 'I must be a cat, then,' she exclaimed, 'and I have seven more lives to live.' For a moment her laughing face seemed to float before him and the flicker of hope burned strong. She could not be dead.

He waited until the moon was well risen and the town quiet before making his way to the square, shuffling along bent-kneed in his straw sandals like any Chinese coolie, his cap turned inside out to hide the star. There were few people abroad in Ping-liang this night and from behind the paper lattices of tea-houses came none of the usual sounds of laughter and the sharp click of counters. Occasionally he heard a soft murmur of frightened voices and a keening wail. Merchants' shops were boarded up and the whole town had a blank, shuttered, wary look as its people waited for further evidence of Ma Ku-fan's wrath.

In the square the headless bodies lay in rows, just as they had fallen to the executioner's blade, but the heads had gone, no doubt to adorn the city walls. Slowly Stephen walked along the silent rows, forcing himself to look carefully at each still figure. He turned the end of one row and began the next, hope increasing all the time. Only a few more bodies . . .

At the very end of the last row he found her and stood gazing down through blurred eyes while his heartbeat slowed almost to stalling-point. Even without her head, there was no possibility of mistake. Her joined hands were cupped in a pleading gesture and her slender body lay gracefully, fallen sideways from a kneeling position so she was curled as if in sleep. With a groan he sank down beside her, as the hope that had buoyed him up through the grisly ordeal of searching changed abruptly to black despair. His Bright Treasure was dead and nothing he could do would bring her back.

'This young person was your wife?' A man was standing over him: an old man with a straggling white beard and kind, calm eyes. He looked like a benevolent lizard. Stephen stared blankly at him and did not answer.

'Was she your wife?'

When Stephen still made no reply the white-bearded man tugged at his beard and said testily, 'Even in grief respect is due to age, young man. Be good enough to answer my question. Was this woman your sister, or the woman of your house?'

'The woman of my house,' said Stephen dully. He felt too stunned and weary to search his mind for suitable honorifics with which to address this old busybody.

His questioner gave an exaggerated start and peered closely at him. 'Ha! You are not of the Sons of Han?' His speech was precise, somewhat old-fashioned, in keeping with his flowing scholar's robe and courtly bearing. He was evidently a gentleman of some standing and even in his numbed state Stephen found it strange that such a personage should be roaming the midnight streets. Then he realized that the old gentleman was, in fact, accompanied by several servants, who stood grouped about a sedan chair at a respectful distance.

'I'm English,' he admitted brusquely.

'You are of the Red Army?'

'No. Yes. Why do you ask?' countered Stephen, irritated by this interrogation. 'What does it matter to you where I come from? Go away and cease to plague me with your chatter, old uncle.'

'The wise man forgives the manners of barbarians,' commented the old man, in the tone of one reciting a well-known precept. Stephen was too preoccupied to be ashamed of his rudeness. He stared at Pao's body, wondering whether he had the strength of purpose to carry it away for burial. He couldn't leave her here to be gnawed by dogs and rats, pecked at by crows. The thought sickened him.

The old man cleared his throat noisily. 'It is a matter,' he said, 'concerning the child of this unfortunate young person.'

River Pearl! Stephen had thought the baby must be safe back at the base, left in the care of one of Pao's women friends. Surely she could not have been so reckless as to bring him with her to Ping-liang?

'Her – her child?' he stammered. 'What do you know of her child?'

'The infant is well,' the old man assured him gravely. Seeing that he now had Stephen's full attention, he bowed over folded hands and continued, 'Allow me to introduce myself. I am Wang Lo-sing, deputy magistrate of this city. My house lies yonder, in the Street of Melodious Songbirds. If you will condescend to enter my unworthy abode, you shall see the child for yourself.'

Without waiting for an answer he signalled to his servants, who immediately ran forward with the sedan chair. The old man stepped inside and Stephen had no choice but to follow as the servants carried the chair at a brisk trot through the silent streets. Lean and fit though he was, Stephen streamed with sweat and gasped for breath by the time the chair-bearers halted before a handsome iron-studded door set in a high wall. As he pursued them into a torchlit courtyard fragrant with the scent of night-blooming flowers, he felt as if he'd blundered into a dream.

White marble terraces were flanked with banks of pale blossom and life-size lions striking heraldic postures stood sentinel at the foot of a flight of shallow steps, which were softly illuminated by paper lanterns in the shape of huge pumpkins. At the top of the steps the coolies gently set down their burden, and with a stately tread the old man alighted. Stephen followed him dazedly. They entered a fine raftered hall, whose inlaid furniture, beautiful wall-hangings and handsome lacquered chests all proclaimed the home of a man of taste and refinement, not to mention wealth.

Stephen stared about him. Everything his eye took in was perfect of its kind, from the tall hand-painted screens to the tiny ivory carvings on the table beside him. The grim square with its headless corpses and the refuse-strewn alleys of Ping-liang seemed a world away from this incense-scented paradise. It was hard to believe that only a door in a wall separated one from the other.

As soon as Wang had seated himself in an imposing blackwood chair, a servant glided silently in to offer tea and small cakes. Stephen accepted them blindly, his attention fixed on the two women who entered the room by another door. The first was evidently a person of consequence, perhaps the mistress of the house. Pale, slender, and elegant, though past the first bloom of youth, she was still attractive in her simple high-collared dress of green silk, her smooth black hair drawn back in a knot at the nape of her neck. She made a graceful bow over joined hands towards old Wang, who favoured her with an indulgent smile; studiously avoided looking at the stranger, and seated herself on a small straight-backed chair to the left of the high table. Wife, daughter, daughter-in-law to Wang? Stephen couldn't tell, but a glance at the second woman stifled further speculation. She had none of her mistress' air of distinction. She was stout, broad-faced and flat-nosed, and tottered on tiny bound feet. She wore an apron over her plain blue jacket and trousers, and her hair was covered with a scarf. Those were the only details of her appearance that Stephen took in, for as she passed him he saw that she carried in her arms the sleeping River Pearl.

With a stern gesture the old man checked Stephen's instinctive move towards the baby. He addressed the fat *amah*.

'Show him the child.'

Reluctantly, she approached Stephen and held the sleeping baby so that he could see him. River Pearl whimpered and nestled closer to her broad bosom. When Stephen automatically reached out to take him in his arms, the *amah* hissed like an angry snake, and the unmistakable hatred in her narrow eyes made him draw back.

'Is this child known to you?' demanded Wang formally.

'Yes, he is my son. I am so glad . . . I was afraid . . . I am very grateful to you, honoured sir, and to these ladies. I will take him . . .'

A piercing wail from the fat *amah* cut short his stumbling

sentences. He thought that if she had not been encumbered with the sleeping child she would have flung her apron over her head. As it was, River Pearl woke up and started to cry, and she clutched him against her breast, daring Stephen with furious glances to try to take him away from her.

Bewildered, he looked from one face to the other. Why had Wang Lo-sing brought him here? What did they all want?

He said again, more firmly, 'I will take my son home,' and at last the woman in green silk raised her head and looked at him. Words began to pour from her in a shrill stream, so fast that he had difficulty in understanding her.

'He lies, my husband, he lies!' she cried. 'He is a barbarian thief, a robber who would snatch away my son. Do not listen to his deceitful tongue, for is not this a child of our own race? How can he be the son of an ignorant red-faced barbarian? He came to the square only to rob the dead, and now he is trying to steal my child away.'

'Hush, woman,' reproved Wang. 'Do not speak so. You know nothing of this man, nor have you any child of your body.'

'This is my child,' she replied fiercely, and Stephen was reminded of a wildcat at bay. 'The woman put him in my arms when Ma Ku-fan's soldiers galloped into the square, taking them unaware. She said, "Take him, older sister, for he is yours. It is the last thing I can do for him." So I held him to my breast and drew the curtains of my chair, and told the coolies to carry me home with speed. And I came safely to the house, since none dared hinder the servants of the magistrate.'

She drew a deep breath and said passionately, 'I tell you, husband, he is *mine*. You had no need to send your servant to watch the square in case one approached the body of that poor woman. Send this man away, for you are always too ready to believe the word of anyone except your wife.'

Wang said testily, 'I do not doubt your word, woman, but it was not a formal arrangement, and such weighty matters cannot be resolved by two foolish females in a city square. I ask only, is there anyone who will come later to claim this child from you when you have decked him in fine silk and made him the son of your heart? Answer me that!'

Solomon's judgment, thought Stephen. The woman bowed her head, defeated, and said no more. Tears began to trickle silently down her cheeks.

'*It is the last thing I can do for him*,' Pao had said. Her last wish was that her child should grow up safely in the care of a woman who loved him. What instinct, he wondered, had made her choose the childless wife of Wang Lo-sing, who yearned for a baby of her own? What, in any case, had the wife of the deputy magistrate been doing out in the crowded square, listening to youthful hotheads who wanted to build a new China? Was she a secret Red sympathiser herself?

In his mind's eye he saw the whole scene. The jostling excited crowd round the rostrum, urging Pao on to higher flights of rhetoric. She, with the child on her back, looking far out beyond the sea of heads and catching sight of the galloping dustcloud, the warlord's soldiers.

Perhaps she had already taken note of the curtained sedan chair parked discreetly on the edge of the crowd, and wondered about its occupant. In that desperate minute as the crowd rushed screaming from beneath the chargers' hoofs, Pao must have gambled on there being a woman behind those curtains – a woman who would save her child. Pao had always been lucky . . .

Stephen took a last long look at the baby cradled at the *amah*'s breast. The smooth golden face, Bright Treasure's face, was seraphic in sleep, one dimpled fist crammed into his mouth, the willow-leaf eyebrows slightly raised as if enjoying a secret joke.

He said loudly, 'The woman is right and I was mistaken. My son is dead. I will return now to the Red Army and fight to avenge him.'

Across the room, Wang's wife stared at him in wonder, but Stephen could not meet her eyes. He drained his cup with a single gulp and rose unsteadily. Without another glance at the sleeping baby he blundered from the room and down the steps to the courtyard, where the liquid notes of singing birds poured heedlessly, heartlessly, into the scented night, oblivious of his pain.

CHAPTER SEVENTEEN

Summer had come to Sian, and Romy was packing her trunks. Her baby was four months old and it was time – high time – that they returned to England.

She had booked passages for herself, the baby, and Clare's *amah*, a sturdy placid peasant-girl who showed a surprising readiness to travel.

This time next week I'll be boarding the boat at Shanghai, she thought. Then Tokyo, San Francisco . . . Slowly she put down the dress she was folding and leaned on the veranda rail, dreaming. Gene came from San Francisco, but she didn't want to think about Gene. The secret hope that he'd blow in one day from wherever he'd been working, full of jokes and endearments and with a perfectly acceptable explanation for his long silence, had already delayed her departure for too long. She should have put him out of her mind the day he left for the Red areas; it would have saved her a lot of heartache. So she pushed her thoughts forward from San Francisco, on to New York, London, Cheltenham . . . Longmarsh. She shivered. However long she lingered over the journey, Longmarsh would get her in the end. The old house had waited so many hundreds of years and outlived so many owners. No doubt it would outlive her, too; and Clare, and every luckless man or woman on whom the burden of ownership descended. She didn't want it. Perhaps she could persuade Stephen's sister and her husband to take over the house itself, while she removed to the graceful little Dower House in the park. After all, that was what her mother-in-law had done when she was widowed. Yes, certainly Sybil should have the big house . . .

There was a soft knock and Li entered with her breakfast tray which he placed on a bamboo table beneath the shady *p'eng*.

'Small Missee makee much cly-cly,' he announced gloomily. The melancholy, hollow-cheeked Number One boy, Li Li-san, was devoted to 'Small Missee', lavishing on her the love he would have given to his own infant daughters, born in famine years and left to die of exposure outside the city wall. He had four strong sons, but nevertheless yearned for the three poor 'slaves' he had been unable to support. He would spend hours hanging over Clare's cradle, and his angry shout of 'Small Missee makee cly!' was a summons which the lazy *amah*, gossiping with the cook's wife beneath the almond trees, ignored at her peril.

'Perhaps she's cutting a tooth,' said Romy. She lifted the metal lid from a plate of scrambled eggs and attacked them with vigour. After an early gallop on the racecourse her own appetite was keen. It was a pity she would have to sell her racing pony; he was showing promise after a few months' training. However it would be impracticable to take him back to England.

'Makee *much* cly-cly,' insisted Li.

'What? Oh, ask the *amah* to bring her in when I've had my bath,' said Romy absently, her thoughts occupied with the sale of her pony. Perhaps Harvey could suggest a buyer . . . 'Good morning, Abby; you're up early,' she added, rather surprised. 'Will you share my tray? Li, bring another cup, please.'

Mrs Bentley ran a hand through her thick greying locks, tucking wisps of hair into her ramshackle bun. She looked worried.

'I don't want to alarm you unnecessarily, my dear,' she said hurriedly, 'but little Clare doesn't look well to me. The *amah* called me just now; apparently they've had a bad night. I think she's feverish.'

Romy was instantly alert. Abigail wasn't one to fuss without good reason. '*Lai!*' she called after the retreating servant; and when he turned: 'send the *amah* to me at once. Chop-chop.'

When Clare was carried in, wriggling and moaning, a glance was enough to tell Romy that something was seriously wrong with her. During the night the baby seemed to have shrunk. Her skin was hot and dry and she wailed fretfully, arching her crumpled scarlet face away from the nipple which the anxious *amah* tried to cram into her mouth.

'Don't do that. She doesn't want it.' Anxiety made Romy's voice sharp. 'How long has she been like this?'

Stammering and mumbling, her thick brows puckered with worry, the *amah* told of a restless night. Small Missee had woken soon after dark. She seemed hungry, but soon vomited all the milk she took. After that she would not sleep, but moved and cried, 'As you see,' finished the *amah* hopelessly.

'Give her to me.'

The nurse handed over the wailing bundle with obvious reluctance. The small body was giving off heat, yet she was still tightly swaddled. Romy suddenly felt scared – scared and furious with this stupid peasant who had allowed her precious charge to suffer all night without summoning help.

'Why didn't you wake me when you saw she was ill?' she demanded.

'I was frightened the *t'ai-t'ai* would be angry.'

Romy called her a rude name often applied by Celestial Sparrow to troublesome mules.

'Steady on,' murmured Abigail. 'It's no use getting angry with her. Better send for Dr Lombard – do you know where he is?'

Harvey – of course! Harvey would know what to do for the baby. With an effort Romy controlled her urge to vent her anger on the *amah*, poor stupid frightened woman, who stood trembling and shifting nervously on her absurdly tiny feet, like little pointed hoofs in their black satin slippers, her broad face creased with worry.

Luckily she knew Harvey's whereabouts. 'He's at Marshal Chang's headquarters. He went straight on there after riding. Here, take the baby.' She thrust the moaning bundle back into the *amah's* arms, which closed round her like the fronds of an anemone.

'Put her to bed,' she ordered, 'and sponge her with cool water. Gently, mind. Don't try to make her suck – understand?'

She summoned Li and sent the rickshaw flying up to Marshal Chang's headquarters; then went to stand over Clare's cradle and watch that her instructions were carried out. It was frightening to see the change that a few hours had wrought in her healthy, thriving baby; terrifying to be able to do so little for her comfort. The baby was bawling now, a toneless monotonous 'Wah-wah-wah' that tore at her nerves. Death comes quickly in China, and cold fingers of fear clamped about Romy's heart. Clare was so small, so precious. A fever like this could burn her up as rapidly as a snuffed candle. If only Harvey would hurry!

It seemed an eternity before he strode into the shaded pavilion, but with him came that indefinable aura of confidence and comfort that doctors assume like a second skin. He looked large, competent, and dependable; more than a match for any Chinese disease.

He examined the baby, frowning as he bent over the cradle, lifting eyelids, shining a pencil torch down the small gullet.

'How bad is she?' asked Romy fearfully.

Harvey closed his bag with a snap. 'Hard to say at this stage. It's lucky I was up at headquarters, because there's nowhere else you can get medicines in this benighted place.' She nodded. She knew that because officers sold the medical supplies intended for their troops more soldiers died of disease than from fighting.

'But it happened so quickly,' she exclaimed. 'Last night she was right as rain. What's the matter with her? How could she catch this illness when she's never been outside the house gates?'

'From that filthy slut, of course,' said Harvey, eyeing the *amah* with cold contempt. The woman cringed under his gaze. 'Ten to one she's got her own diseased offspring hidden in some corner and is feeding it at the same time as yours. You'll have to get rid of her, naturally.'

'Her own baby died – she told me so,' said Romy, who had employed the woman partly because she felt sorry for her.

'Of course she did; they'll tell you anything. If your baby dies because of her neglect I'll make that woman wish she'd never been born.'

It was the start of three days of terror for the whole household, as fever mounted in Clare's small body despite all their efforts to contain it. Time and again Romy thought that the worst must have come but still the thermometer crept upward. They took it in turns to watch the baby, Li and Abigail, Harvey and Romy, while the poor *amah* nursed her congested breasts and wept silently in a corner until Romy, losing patience, sent her out of the room.

During those three days Harvey never left the house, sending the rickshaw to fetch the medicines he needed from headquarters. He would order Romy to rest when her spell of nursing was over, but she doubted if he ever undressed or slept properly as he strove to save the child. Under their eyes the baby shrivelled to skin and bone – parchment-yellow skin and knobbly birdlike bone. She was soon too weak to cry, and only whimpered a little when they touched her, moving her hot body feebly against the burning fever. It was the hardest thing Romy had ever done, to sit and watch her baby fade away, unable to help her. She prayed. She made deals with God: 'If You'll save Clare, I'll never swear again – I'll go to church every Sunday – I'll build a special chapel at Longmarsh . . .' But the futility of these promises overwhelmed her. Why should God care whether she built chapels or worshipped on Sundays? She had nothing to offer, nothing God would want.

'Please, God, save my baby. Please.'

Hour after hour she listened to the weak rasp of breath, wondering when it would stop altogether. At times a sort of madness came over her. She imagined herself picking up a cushion and holding it over the baby's face until the last feeble spark of life was extinguished and her suffering was over. Then she would make some excuse and hurry from the room, hoping against hope that when she returned there would be some change, some tiny sign that the sickness was retreating; but when, later, she tiptoed back into the shaded pavilion and asked the inevitable question: 'How is she?' all she got was a shake of the head from whoever was watching and the unvarying: 'No change, I'm afraid. She's just the same . . .'

On the third evening Harvey and Abigail exchanged a look and then he took Romy by the arm and led her outside into the scented dusk of the garden court, where double white philadelphus blossoms glimmered like stars around the limpid black oval of the goldfish pond. A young moon like a silver sickle hung low over the almond trees, and the soft air was full of the querulous croaking of frogs.

Instinctively she knew that he was searching for words to tell her that her baby was about to die.

'My dear, you've got to be brave,' he said abruptly at last. 'I've done all I can. She's not responding to treatment.'

'You mean . . . There's no hope for her?' How calm, how ordinary, her own voice sounded! It was as if she'd used up her whole store of emotion during these anguished days and now all feeling had deserted her. She could discuss the possibility – the probability – of her own child's death without any pain.

'I'm afraid so. It's extraordinary she's survived so long. Babies are tough, but all the same . . .' He sighed. 'I'm sorry, Romy. At moments like this one feels helpless against all the misery this wretched country wallows in. Dirt and disease and poverty and superstition. Helpless – and angry.'

He broke off as a strange babble of sound rose from the adjoining courtyard, where the servants had their quarters. Torchlight flickered on the garden wall and along the covered walk that led from one court to the next. A confused medley of voices, then Li's distinctive high-pitched wail: 'Small Missee, come back! Where are you hiding? Missee, Missee, you must come home!'

Others took up the clamour. A procession of torches wound into sight, threading between the sweeping boughs of willow, past the pond where lotus flowers floated on the glassy water, making towards the peace gate which led into the street. In front tottered Clare's *amah*, arms stretched out before her, holding a tiny scrap of red silk, the baby's embroidered coat, its sleeves extended in the shape of a cross.

'Missee!' she keened. 'Come back, Missee!' Those behind her – all the servants and others Romy had never set eyes on – echoed her in a cacophony of sound. They banged rattles and beat gongs.

'Missee! Missee!' echoed the shrill voices, bouncing from wall to wall.

Harvey cursed. 'The fools. The damned superstitious fools! *Chan-choh!*' he shouted. 'Stop that noise!' but his words, if heard at all, went disregarded.

'What are they doing?' whispered Romy. A shiver crawled down her spine.

'They're looking for the baby's spirit,' said Harvey disgustedly. 'They think it's lost its way and by making that racket they can show it the way home. Damned heathens –'

'But the coat – Clare's coat . . .'

'That's for the spirit to recognize, if you please. These stupid pointless rites make me wild. Why can't they learn basic hygiene instead of caterwauling in the streets like a pack of hyenas? They'll keep it up all night, hammering away at the Goddess of Mercy and greasing the palms of the priests. I'll have to send coolies to drag them back tomorrow if the household isn't to grind to a standstill.'

'Missee, Missee!' echoed the eerie voices, fading into the distance, making for the temple.

Kwan-yin, the little brown Goddess of Mercy, was Romy's favourite in the Chinese pantheon. Unlike the male gods with their bulging eyes and fierce grimaces, she was sweet-faced and calm, much loved even by the Red marchers, who sought her help when their children were ill. Legend said that she had been about to enter Heaven when she heard a child cry, and so returned to Earth. The thought of the Chinese servants begging Kwan-yin for Clare's life made her throat constrict.

She said shakily, 'I must go in, Harvey. I can't stay here while Clare – while Clare –'

He wouldn't release her. 'Stay here. You can't help her. Don't make it worse for yourself.'

'Look! Someone's coming,' said Romy tensely. Through the archway she could see a single lantern bobbing towards them down the covered path. Feet pattered quickly across the paving-stones.

It was Abigail's young maid, O-lan, a peasant girl she had bought as a toddler from destitute parents. In the lantern light her pale, round face gleamed eerily.

'*T'ai-t'ai* say come,' she gasped, her voice vibrant with drama.

'Oh Harvey, she's dying!' Romy wrenched herself from his restraining hand and fled across the paved court. She ran without feeling her feet on the ground, zigzagging across the lily garden, the middle court, through the moongate and along the wisteria-draped path that led to Clare's quarters.

'Oh God, don't let me be too late,' she prayed.

Why had she allowed Harvey to decoy her away, even for a moment? Panting, she pushed aside the heavy door-hanging and went forward into the lamplit room, dreading what she would see on the other side of the screen.

Abigail was stooping over the cradle. She straightened up as Romy entered and shook her head. She seemed dazed.

'What's happened? How is she?' Romy hardly dared ask, but Abigail's drawn face cracked into a smile.

'Wonderful news,' she said huskily. 'The fever's broken. I think . . . I think she may be all right.'

The Number Two boy stood at the door of Romy's sitting room three weeks later, waiting to catch her attention. When she looked up from her letter, he coughed gently.

'Mr Lyon askee see Missee,' he said importantly.

Romy's heart gave a heavy thump and then settled to a slow, rib-banging beat. The still, sultry morning suddenly seemed overwhelmingly hot. Abigail had driven out to Lintong; Harvey was up at headquarters; apart from the baby and the servants she was alone in the house. Why did Gene have to pick this, of all moments, to breeze back into her life?

For four months he'd ignored her existence, never a word from him to let her know if he was alive or dead, no sign that he knew or cared if her child was safely delivered, total silence, utter rejection. At first she'd been surprised; then in succession hurt, resentful, and finally resigned to the fact that he'd completely forgotten her. It was no use weaving fantasies about his handsome figure; she'd do better to look the truth in the face and put him out of her life – as he'd so obviously put her out of his.

It hadn't been easy. Too often she'd seemed to hear echoes of his voice as she sat daydreaming by the lilypool, or gazed with sudden hope at wavy dark hair and wide shoulders vanishing round street corners. But as each hope was dashed, the struggle to forget him became easier. Four months after he left her, she could look back with cool detachment on their moments together, and see him for what he was: a casual charmer to whom every pretty face was a lure and a challenge, every woman's heart a citadel to be conquered, and as easily abandoned.

So now he's back, she thought, trying to gather her wits and decide what to do. I suppose he thinks he has a perfect right to stroll in, kick the cat, pat me on the cheek and stroll out again. Well, he's got another think coming!

She drew a deep breath and said evenly, 'Please tell Mr Lyon I am not at home.'

'Velly good, Missee.' The boy gave her a puzzled glance and pattered away. She tried to concentrate on her letter to Sybil, but was annoyed to find Gene's face intervening between her eyes and the blank paper. Resolutely she jabbed her pen in the ink-well and wrote on:

The baby is much better and will soon be fit to travel. I have passages booked on the Empire Star, *and should arrive in England around the middle of October unless I decide to spend a few days visiting friends of my brother's in Boston. I will give you further details nearer the time of our arrival. I hope all goes well at Longmarsh . . .*

She paused. The Number Two boy had returned and hovered expectantly.

'What is it?'

'Mr Lyon say send message to Sian Guest House when Missee home. He waitee all-time.'

'Has he left the house yet?'

'No. Waitee all-time.'

Bother him! Why can't he take a hint? she thought. She didn't want to spend all day cooped up in her room for fear of bumping into him.

'All right. Tell him you'll give me the message and show

him out,' she said impatiently. 'Go on. Can't you see I'm busy?'

He lingered. Li Wan-ti, the Number Two boy, was a cheerful round-faced rascal, as different from his brother, the melancholy, industrious Li Li-san as chalk from cheese. Li Wan-ti had his eye firmly fixed on the main chance and had a lamentable habit of questioning orders which often brought Dr Lombard's wrath on his head.

'Well? What is it?' she said.

He said confidentially, 'Mr Lyon going in Shanghai tomollow. Wantee see Missee now.'

I wonder how much it cost Gene to get that information delivered? she thought, her annoyance mounting. She had an uneasy suspicion that Gene guessed she was hiding here, waiting till the coast was clear. Perhaps she should confront him after all . . . But the memory of those long months of silence stiffened her resolve. Why start the whole agony over again?

'Where did you say I'd gone?' she asked. If Li had blown the gaff already there was no point in further evasion.

'Say Missee going in temple, see ponee,' said Li Wan-ti.

She thought this over, wondering whether to believe him. He was certainly quick-witted enough to have thought up this excuse; on the other hand he might be lying to her just as she had told him to lie to Gene, and since she had ordered the one lie, how could she blame him for the other?

She sighed. Tiresome as it was, she had better make the story true. She had planned to visit the old temple outside Sian where she kept her two ponies this evening, anyway. Harvey had mentioned that he had a buyer for her fast dun gelding, a Mongolian 'griffin' which showed a good deal of promise for next season's races. One of the Young Marshal's officers might be persuaded to pay a good price for him. By now Romy knew Harvey's business methods well enough to be certain that a good deal of the Chinese officer's purchase price would end up in Harvey's pocket, but she didn't much care. If the pony went to a good owner it was enough for her.

Harvey had promised her the use of his car and chauffeur; all she need do to avoid Gene's afternoon visit was move the expedition forward a few hours. She would drive out to the temple right away; perhaps ride the pony this evening, spend the night there, and return in time for Clare's after-breakfast playhour. By then Gene would be on his way to Shanghai. The only snag was the absence of Harvey's chauffeur, who had driven him up to headquarters . . . Romy considered the matter and decided she wouldn't allow so small a drawback to spoil her plan. I'll drive myself, she thought, and take Li Wan-ti with me in case I get a puncture. I'm sure Harvey won't mind.

She waited impatiently until Li reported that Gene had driven away, then summoned Clare's *amah*, the cook, and her personal maid, and explained what she was going to do. She told them to put a picnic supper and clothes for the night in the boot of the big Lowland coupé. Then she collected her riding boots and whip, scribbled a note to Abigail, and was ready to leave within the hour.

Li Wan-ti viewed these preparations with disfavour. Though not normally troubled by conscience he was aware that Mr Lyon, who was large and strong and a barbarian at heart, no matter how civilized he might appear on the surface, had rewarded him handsomely for information about Missee Lo-mee's whereabouts and state of mind. He was unlikely to be pleased when he returned to the house this afternoon and found her still absent. He might even hold Li Wan-ti to blame for this state of affairs.

'Mr Lyon coming in house one-time,' he said earnestly. 'Wantee see Missee.'

'That's just too bad,' responded Romy. She felt strangely lighthearted, as if by refusing to see Gene she had shaken herself free of his domination. 'Mr Lyon will have to learn that I can't hang about all day waiting for him to turn up. I've got better things to do. Jump in the back now and be quick about it. I don't want you spilling the beans to him the moment I've gone,' she added in an undertone.

Li Wan-ti caught her meaning even if he didn't understand the exact words. Grumbling, he obeyed. The courtyard door swung open, the gatekeeper bowed, and the big car rolled into the street.

It was a long time since Romy had been behind a steering

wheel and she was surprised how strange it felt. This large, powerful motor was very different from the battered Hillman on which Stephen's gardener had taught her to drive. Never mind, all cars are *basically* the same, she told herself optimistically. When in trouble stamp on brake and clutch and you're bound to stop. I'll soon get the hang of the controls.

But in spite of this bold assurance she felt a distinct flutter of apprehension when a mere touch on the accelerator sent the big machine surging forward. It was like kicking a racehorse in the ribs in the mistaken belief that it would react like a riding-school hack.

Unprepared for this burst of speed, she shot round a corner too fast and was immediately obliged to stamp hard on the brake to avoid mowing down a bullock cart which was lumbering along taking up most of the narrow street. For a breathless second she feared that the Lowland wasn't going to stop in time. When it came to rest, its bonnet was a bare foot from the bullocks' affronted noses and Li Wan-ti, his face an Oriental mask of doom, was flung forward against the front seat.

'Oh, help!' said Romy.

While the bullocks bellowed their indignation and their driver, a hulking blue-clad peasant, cursed them and the devil-car impartially, Romy tried unavailingly to find reverse, but each time she selected a gear and cautiously engaged the clutch, the car inched forward towards the cart again.

'It's no good, you'll have to tell him to turn round. I can't go backwards,' she said to Li at last, pushing the damp hair back from her flustered face. 'Go on, tell him; or we'll be here all night.'

Very reluctantly Li Wan-ti descended and received the rough side of the driver's tongue. A crowd gathered, delighted by this unexpected sideshow, and began to offer conflicting advice. The driver's language became steadily more abusive. He had a shaven head and sinewy bare legs; it seemed likely that he might resort to physical violence.

Romy fumbled hastily in her purse. 'Here,' she called, winding down her window. 'You'd better give him this.'

At the sight of the strings of cash the bullock-driver changed his tone and became more civil; but in order to turn the cart it was necessary to unharness the bullocks. Romy waited, controlling her impatience as best she could while the yokes were removed, the animals led out and back past the cart, then the vehicle itself was heaved round by many willing hands to the accompaniment of an ear-splitting commentary by the crowd. Sweat trickled down her spine and she drummed her fingers on the steering wheel, trying to breathe as shallowly as possible because the combined odours of rotting vegetables, garlic-eating humanity and open drains which were trapped in the narrow street was enough to bring bile to her throat.

Since it had taken Li and two gardeners nearly ten minutes to swing the engine into life before she set off, she kept it running, although the noise was maddening and the exhaust fumes did nothing to improve the atmosphere.

'Tell them to hurry up!' she called to Li, who showed a strong desire to crawl back into the car and disassociate himself from the noisy proceedings. 'Tell the bullock-driver I'm going to drive on in two minutes and if he's not out of the way I'll squash him flat.'

This threat produced a tumult of protest but it had an immediate effect. The road cleared as if by magic and Romy drove forward, using the controls with exaggerated care. Once she had passed the Temple of the Recumbent Dragon the streets became wider and she found the big car easier to handle. She was gaining confidence rapidly when, to her consternation, she saw near the Bell Tower crossroads another vehicle nosing its way through the ruck of pedestrians: an unmistakable red sports car with the Stars and Stripes fluttering gaily from its bonnet. Gene's car.

Motors were still enough of a rarity in Sian for one driver to wave acknowledgement to another: Gene might not recognize Harvey's Lowland coupé but he was bound to give an interested glance at the person behind the wheel. She could not risk passing him.

She swung the wheel over hard, and bucketed down a street so narrow that the runningboards scraped the walls and children jumped into doorways like bolting rabbits.

Two more rapid turns and she was back by the Bell Tower, having avoided the crossroad. She risked a quick glance in the rear-view mirror. Yes, there was the red sports car, safely behind her and proceeding on its way. A moment later it, too, turned down a side street and vanished.

Romy breathed more easily but Li, whose nerve had been shaken by her latest manoeuvre, was calling on his ancestors to protect him in terms most unflattering to her skill as a driver. Still, they were past the worst of the traffic now; as each new hazard was conquered, Romy's confidence grew. Really, this was a marvellous machine. It took a little time to get used to having such power under the bonnet, but once you knew what to expect it could be handled as easily as a bicycle. When they were out of town she'd give it a real chance to show what it could do; after all, she'd need a car when she got back to England and it would be useful to compare performances with the Lowland. She might even buy one herself . . .

She glanced at her wristwatch: four o'clock already. She must hurry if she wanted to take her griffin out for a canter before his evening feed. Carefully she nudged her way through the traffic thronging the city gates and sighed with relief as the open road stretched ahead.

'Now we're off,' she said.

Li whimpered and cringed back in his seat.

'Do stop moaning,' said Romy. 'You're quite safe with me and we'll be there in no time.'

Despite this assurance he continued to whimper; some imp of devilment prompted Romy to give him something to complain about. Heavens, she thought, from the way he was going on you'd think he was being driven by Jehu himself! She trod firmly on the accelerator and the speedometer needle crept round the clock.

Forty, fifty, sixty – she had never driven so fast. A wild exhilaration gripped her. The car was a thunderbolt, built for speed; it was wasted in the winding streets of a town. Bending peasants looked up in astonishment as she rocketed past and she raised a hand to wave at them. Wind whipped her hair forward across her eyes and the steering wheel throbbed beneath her fingers. When she slowed for a corner it seemed as if they were crawling and she stamped the accelerator to the floorboards the moment she was back on the straight, glorying in sheer speed, wishing the temple was a hundred miles away instead of ten. She would like to drive like this all day, never slackening pace. I'll *certainly* buy a Lowland when I get back to England, she thought. At this speed I'd be able to nip up to London in a couple of hours and shake the dust of Longmarsh out of my hair. It'd make all the difference. Oh, if only English roads were as straight and empty as this!

But Chinese roads have their drawbacks, too. Motor traffic may be rare on them but livestock is very common. It was unfortunate that the widow Ng Sun-yi, who herded her white ducks on the irrigation channel running parallel with the road, should have decided to cross with her charges at the very moment when Romy came roaring round a gentle curve.

Seeing the road ahead blocked by the waddling quacking flock, Romy stamped desperately on clutch and brake together. The car slewed sideways in an explosion of dust and the ducks rose in a whirling white cloud. She could see nothing. For a moment she had the horrible sensation of plunging forward blindly in a snowstorm, then the wheels left the road and the heavy car ploughed through the willows fringing the irrigation channel. It upended itself with the bonnet in the water and the back wheels spinning helplessly in mid air.

Romy and the Number Two boy were catapulted skyward, he to land in the reeds on the far side of the channel, while Romy, after describing a slow parabola through the air, curled herself in a tight ball and landed on a half-made stack of rice straw on Ng Sun-yi's First Son's threshing-floor. Though shaken she was quite unhurt.

She lay blinking up at the clear blue sky, gasping for breath and trying to work out what had happened.

'Romy! Where are you? Are you all right?'

Before the wheels of the Lowland had stopped spinning, Gene was out of his own car, running towards the irrigation channel. He waded across and clambered up the opposite bank.

'Romy! Darling!'

She sat up and peered over the edge of the rick. Her face was white with shock and the rice straw in her hair gave her a curiously raffish appearance. When she saw who it was she groaned and sank back in her nest of straw. 'Oh, no!' Apart from the Lowland's owner, Gene was the last person she wanted to face just now.

He climbed the short ladder propped against the rick, scrambled across and took her in his arms. 'Oh, darling, are you really all right? I thought you must be a goner.'

To his surprise she pushed him away. 'Don't fuss,' she said crossly. 'I ought to know how to fall.' She stood up rather shakily on the yielding straw, smoothing her skirt and picking bits from her hair. She avoided looking at him.

'Glad to hear it, because you sure as hell don't know how to drive,' retorted Gene, taken aback by this cool reception.

Romy fired up at once at the criticism. 'What d'you mean? I was getting on fine until those birds started flying round the car. I couldn't see a damned thing, and Li was screaming . . . Oh!' She looked stricken. 'How awful! He was in the back. Is he. . . ?'

'He was lucky too. He's sitting over by those willows nursing his bruises,' said Gene tersely. 'I don't think you'll get *him* to come driving with you again in a hurry. Have you any idea how fast you were going when you hit those ducks? It's a wonder you weren't killed.'

'R – Rubbish,' snapped Romy, though her teeth had begun to chatter. How dare he nag at her, just as if he had a right to? 'It's none of your business anyway. I was just trying out the car –'

'Your car, I suppose?'

'Well, no. It's Harvey's.'

Gene whistled. 'He's going to be delighted. It looks to me as if some fairly extensive repairs will be needed before he drives it again.'

'Oh, *Lord*!' Romy bit her lip. 'Anyway, I'm *sure* he'll understand when I tell him how it happened. He knows what these roads are like. *He* won't go jumping to conclusions and assuming it was all my fault.'

'I admire your confidence. I wish I could share it.'

She gave him a defiant glance, but her trembling mouth showed him she was on the verge of tears.

'Come on,' he said more gently, taking her by the arm. 'It's no good crying over spilt milk.'

'I'm *not* crying.' But she allowed him to help her down the ladder and over the humped bridge that spanned the channel a little way further along the bank. She sat silent and subdued in the front of his car while he tried to persuade Li Wan-ti to climb in the back.

This the Number Two boy resolutely refused to do.

'All right,' said Gene at last, losing patience, 'if you prefer to take your chance of getting a ride home on a bullock cart, that's OK by me. I'll drive Missee back to Sian.'

'Oh, no,' said Romy, rousing herself from her abstraction. 'I ought to see my ponies now I'm here. That's why I came.'

'Where *are* the ponies?'

'We keep them in a temple just a mile or two on. I've got a man coming to buy one of them tomorrow morning.'

'You were planning to stay overnight?' Gene gave her a curious look, but she didn't notice.

'Yes . . . My case is in the car. Oh, and some food. But I don't want to trouble you,' she said uncertainly.

'It's no trouble. How else do you propose to get there – walk?'

Romy flushed. 'I don't mind walking.'

'Don't be a dope. You'd much better come with me.'

There was really no alternative to accepting his offer.

'All right,' she said slowly, 'but what about the car? We can't just abandon it.'

'Why not? It's not going to run away. It can stay where it is until we get together a bullock-team to pull it out of the ditch.' He turned to Li Wan-ti. 'You toddle on home and tell your master what's happened. Say we're going to pull his car back to the road tomorrow morning, if he likes to lend a hand. Otherwise we'll manage it somehow.'

Li nodded. 'Velly good, sir. Go home tellee Master. Come tomollow.' He shuffled off down the road, all the ebullience temporarily knocked out of him.

Poor Li, thought Romy. Poor Lowland. What a mess. She leaned her head back against the car seat and closed her eyes, waiting passively while Gene retrieved her belongings and heaved them into the back seat. Her attempt to avoid him had failed disastrously and she was back where she had started, fighting not to give in to the attraction that swamped her every time he came near her. I know what he's like now. I will not, not, *not* make a fool of myself again, she vowed. In silence they drove on to the temple.

CHAPTER EIGHTEEN

'Why did you run away from me? What's got into you?'

The questions took her by surprise. For the past few hours they had managed to maintain an appearance of casual friendliness and avoided clashes. They had inspected the stables and Gene complimented the head *mafoo* on the condition of his ponies in terms that made the old man's wrinkled face glow with pleasure. He bowed until his head nearly touched his worn black velvet slippers. Then Romy had cantered her dun gelding across to the pagoda crowning a neighbouring hill, leaving Gene to explore the temple and its surroundings.

She returned to find that Feng, the shaven-headed temple boy who waited on visitors, had installed their belongings in adjoining apartments. That wouldn't do at all. She told him to move hers over to the far side of the inner court.

'I enjoy watching the moon over that twisted pine tree when I can't sleep,' she explained hastily to Gene's raised eyebrows. 'Harvey always gives me that room.'

He nodded, his expression unreadable. 'Good idea. Will dinner at eight suit you? I've told Feng to put it on the terrace. There's quite a breeze, so the insects won't be too bad.'

'That'll be fine,' said Romy though she felt it was her

place, not his, to give orders to Harvey's servants. She wished most fervently that the evening was already over and she hadn't been manoeuvred into this embarrassing two-some. If only Abigail had been here! Even Harvey's sharp rebukes to the grooms and tiresome inclination to talk down to her would be better than a tête-à-tête with Gene. At least she wasn't afraid of Harvey . . . Was she afraid of Gene? she wondered. Or was it her own response to him that she feared? In a rare mood of depression she washed and changed, delaying the inevitable moment when she'd be alone with him.

'Come on, I'm hungry!' he called at last. 'What on earth are you doing over there – dressing for a ball? Dinner's ready. Now, what'll you have first? There's whisky, gin and tonic . . .'

'I'll drink water, thanks,' she said coolly, crossing to the long table which the boy had set with candles and fresh flowers on the snowy cloth.

'Nonsense. You need a bump start after a fright like that,' he smiled, splashing gin into a glass; when he tried to press it into her hand she shook her head.

'No, I mean it. I don't want it. Anyway, there wasn't time to be frightened. It all happened so quickly.'

'Then you were lucky. I was scared half out of my wits.'

'Oh, let's forget it . . . It's too *boring* to go over the same thing again and again.'

'Just as you like,' he said imperturbably. 'Well, since you're not drinking, let's eat. We don't want to disappoint Feng after all the trouble he's taken.'

As he moved from behind the drinks table her eye was caught in horrified fascination by the sight of his shorts. She supposed they were meant to be shorts, but they certainly didn't resemble the loose, respectable, below-the-knee garments which Englishmen favoured in this climate. Those allowed only a narrow strip of bare leg to show between their lower edges and the tops of high, ribbed socks. Gene's shorts were more like drawers, and exposed a disturbing expanse of muscled thigh from which she found it difficult to drag her gaze. She was glad when he sat down and his legs were safely concealed beneath the tablecloth.

Despite the lack of warning of their visit and the bare two hours he had had for preparing a meal, Feng had excelled himself. He took great pride in his cooking and to Gene, accustomed for the past months to the sparse diet of the Red areas, where eggs and meat and flour were practically unobtainable luxuries, the *Moo Shoo* pork, paper-wrapped fish, and spinach and beancurd soup he set before them were forgotten delights.

'This is really delicious!' he kept exclaiming, heaping his bowl from a dozen side-dishes; he seemed disappointed that Romy ate sparingly, without enthusiasm. He encouraged her to speak of Clare, but there is little one can say about a four-month-old baby to someone who hasn't seen her, and when this subject failed he kept up an easy flow of talk about his travels in the Red areas. He had secured the promised interview with Mao Tse-tung and been impressed by his mixture of idealism and down-to-earth pragmatism.

'A difficult man to live up to, though,' he commented. 'He has a way of fixing you with those hooded eyes which makes you feel about two inches tall. Chou's the one they all love – Chou En-lai. He has such a twinkle: he's everyone's favourite brother. I wanted to see the old warhorse, too: Chu Teh. They say he's a great raconteur. But he hadn't arrived from Sikang, though I gather he's on his way north now. Apparently he's got some new wonderboy who's a whizz at codes – a Comintern man, I suppose. They really rolled out the red carpet for me, and I've got all the material I need. I'm going to twist my editor's arm until he agrees to give Mao and his boys the newspaper coverage they want. The Kuomintang have hogged the West's headlines long enough.'

'So you're off to Shanghai tomorrow?'

His eyes narrowed. 'How did you guess? Or – wait a bit – that wasn't a guess, was it? I had a feeling this morning that you were hiding away in your room, sending that poor houseboy back and forth with messages. Tell me, Romy –' his hard brown hand moved unexpectedly across the table to close over her wrist – 'why did you run away from me today? What's got into you?'

'I don't know what you mean,' she said quickly. 'I don't

have to account for my movements to you – or anyone else. And now, if you'll be kind enough to let go of my wrist, I'd like to go to bed. It's been rather a *wearing* day.'

'Not so fast,' said Gene. His dark face no longer looked amused; it was sombre, almost menacing. His fingers tightened until she winced. 'I think you owe me an explanation, and I shan't let you go until I get it. Why did you send me a message to say you were out, then creep out of the house the moment I'd gone away and drive like hell in the opposite direction?'

'So you *were* following me! What a lowdown, dirty trick,' said Romy furiously. 'Snooping and prying and questioning the servants – you should be ashamed! Can't you see when you're not wanted?'

'We journalists make our living by snooping and prying,' he said dryly. 'It gets to be kind of a habit. We have to know what's going on, so we can't always afford your high-nosed aristocratic principles. Sure, I asked your houseboy a few questions – not that he told me much. Then I happened to see you in town, just by the Bell Tower. I thought you'd seen me, too, but you shot away down the next turning as if the devil was at your heels. So I turned around and came after you.'

'Then you know all about it. You've answered your own questions.' In the candlelight her colour was high and she met his eyes defiantly.

'Oh no, far from it. I know *what* you did and *how* you come to be here, but I don't know why. Come on, out with it. Tell me why I'm not wanted all of a sudden. You wanted me all right before I went north; what's happened to make you change?'

Romy said wearily, 'You've been away a long time. People do change, you know.'

'Some girls . . . I wouldn't expect you to, though – not without some good reason.'

'What's the use of hashing it all over again? It's finished, Gene – can't you leave it at that?'

He released her wrist and sat back, staring at her. Then he said with a kind of dogged dissatisfaction, 'No, I can't. I don't believe you. Until you give me chapter and verse of why you suddenly can't stand the sight of me, I won't accept that it's finished between us.'

'Very well,' said Romy. 'I'm not much good at explaining, but I'll try.' She hesitated. 'You're right. I did – find you attractive. I was lonely and worried. I couldn't face going home without Stephen, telling his family, spending the rest of my life rotting slowly away in that great gloomy house . . . I felt as if I was trapped in a long dark tunnel. I didn't want to go forwards, but there was no way out. Then, when you came, I thought I saw a way of escape . . . as if a window opened in the tunnel. When you were with me I felt alive again. It was like waking up after a long sleep.'

She paused and looked at him challengingly. 'Go on, laugh if you want to. I don't care.'

'I never felt less like laughing. What happened next?'

'You went away,' said Romy bleakly. 'That was when I realized I'd been a fool to dream that I meant anything to you. You see, I didn't know much about you then.'

'And now you've found out a lot more, am I right?' His voice was expressionless. 'Tell me, who was kind enough to fill in the gaps in your knowledge? Mrs Bentley?'

'She wasn't the only one. You haven't gone to any great trouble to keep your affairs secret, have you? The story of your marriage is common knowledge in Shanghai, I gather – and common's the right word.'

'So now you know that I quarrel with my wife, visit brothels, and wine and dine with the Marshal's mistresses. What else do they say about me? Go on, I find this fascinating.'

'You don't deny it, then?'

'Why should I? Anyway, what would be the use of denying it when Linda and the Shanghai grapevine between them have blackened my name so effectively? What *does* surprise me is that you should believe it without hearing my side of the case.'

'Is there another side?'

'Every story of marital disharmony has two sides, but don't worry – I'm not going to burden you with mine,' he replied dampingly. 'Linda's already filed for divorce, so that's a closed chapter. The less said about it now the better. Since you're not prepared to give me the benefit of the doubt –'

'Why should I take everything on trust?' cried Romy. 'What do you expect me to think when you tell me you're going away for a week and then disappear for four months? Not a word from you in all that time – are you really surprised that I've begun to believe the stories about you? Easy come, easy go: off with the old love and on with the new . . . It all *fits*.'

'Hey, wait a minute!' exclaimed Gene. His face lit up with sudden comprehension. 'You say you didn't hear from me? What about my radio messages? You mean they didn't reach you?'

'Not one. Not a single word.'

They stared at one another. Then Gene said slowly, 'My messages went out all right, because I stood over the radio-operator and watched him send them. But who do you think received them on her dinky little concealed receiver?'

Romy's hand went to her mouth. 'Abigail. But *surely*. . . ?'

'Mrs Bentley is going to have some explaining to do,' said Gene rather grimly. 'I wonder what other – editing – she's been indulging in lately, all on her own initiative? Oh, well, that clears up quite a few questions. If Mrs Bentley took it on herself to suppress all my messages, no wonder you thought I'd forgotten you.' He smiled warmly into her eyes and took her hand again. 'But I *did* send them, I swear. I was thinking of you all the time, wondering what you were doing, wishing you were with me. So now we know who's been putting spokes in the wheel, can't we start again? Forget the last four months . . .'

'No,' said Romy.

His smile faded. 'You don't believe me? Oh, darling, you must understand – you're the only girl in the world for me now. I knew it the moment I saw you – and Linda realized it too. That was . . . part of our trouble.'

'So you blame me for the break-up of your marriage? I must say, that's a bit thick,' said Romy indignantly.

'Of course I don't blame you. I see now that it would have happened anyway, given the kind of people we both are. You were only a contributing factor.'

'I don't think I like that any better.' She crumpled her napkin and pushed back her chair. 'Gene, I'm tired. There's no point in discussing this any further. You may be able to forget, but I can't. Anyway, I've got my own life to live now. In a few days' time I'm leaving for England; if the baby hadn't been ill I'd have gone months ago.'

'You can't leave now!' he exclaimed. There was a note of urgency in his voice that she hadn't heard before.

Her eyebrows rose. 'Who says I can't?'

'I do.'

'What gives you any say in the matter?'

'Listen, Romy, this is important. I'm not trying to pull a fast one or stampede you into anything, but it's vital for me, and for Mrs Bentley, that you shouldn't leave Lombard's house just now.'

'Don't be ridiculous. What difference does it make if I'm there or not?'

'You asked me once what I had against Lombard – remember?'

Romy nodded, puzzled.

'I suspected then that he was hand in glove with the Blueshirts, but I couldn't prove it. Now I can. We've got to keep a watch on him during the next few weeks, particularly when the Generalissimo visits Sian. The negotiations between Marshal Chang and the Reds are at a very delicate stage, and Lombard will kybosh them if he can. He's dangerous – you must believe me.'

She shifted restlessly in her chair. 'Harvey? I can't believe it. If you'd seen him when Clare was ill . . . He stayed up all night.'

'Some of the most dangerous criminals in history have been charming family men who loved children and animals,' said Gene drily. 'If you'd talked – as I have – to some of the prisoners he's tortured, you'd believe me all right. Did you know he has a direct telephone line to Governor Shao's headquarters?'

'Shao gives me the shivers,' she admitted. 'There's something about his eyes . . . But all the same I don't see why I should stay. It's got nothing to do with me.'

'If you leave Lombard's house, Mrs Bentley will have to go too. At the moment she's well placed to warn the Reds about his movements – it was a great stroke of luck getting her into the house. Please don't go just yet, Romy. It'll ruin all our plans.'

'What about ruining *my* plans?' She was suddenly angry. Why should she be expected to obey these peremptory orders issued from heaven knew where? 'What's your stake in this, Gene? I thought you were a journalist, not a political subversive. How did you get involved?'

'I'm not sure of that myself,' he admitted. 'All I know is that the Chinese peasant deserves a fresh deal and Mao looks like giving him one. Please, Romy, stick around just a while longer. It won't be long now before the whole affair comes to boiling point.'

'I'll think it over,' she said reluctantly and he smiled, apparently satisfied.

'I knew you wouldn't let me down.'

She immediately felt annoyed that she had given in so easily, and rose before he could think of any other tiresome little favours he wanted from her. 'I'm off to bed now,' she said firmly. 'Good night.'

'I'll see you across to your room.'

'Good lord, there's no need for that!' Hastily she picked up the torch which Feng had placed on the sideboard.

'Happy dreams,' drawled Gene. She felt his eyes on her as she crossed the flagged courtyard, but he made no move to follow.

She opened the door on blackness. Surprised, because Feng usually left a lamp burning, she swept the beam of her torch around, and gasped as the light picked out gleaming eyes in the middle of the room.

Before she could scream or retreat a hand was clamped over her mouth and she was propelled forward. Behind her a voice growled, 'Quiet, Missee. Be silent and do not struggle.'

A knife pricked her ribs. Romy kept very still, cursing her folly in shutting the door before making sure the room was empty. Bandits were commonplace in the wild areas around Sian, and she had heard chilling stories of wayfarers kidnapped or murdered. She heard the doorbolt click into place and her heart sank.

'What do you want?' she whispered.

A soft snigger was the answer. The knife dug deeper, pressing her tight against her assailant's short, sturdy body. He smelt rank, of grease and garlic, and there was something else, some body odour that was at once faintly familiar and wholly repellent. She felt a hard protruberance working against the back of her thighs, pushing them apart, and this frightened her even more than the knife. A Chinese so depraved as to consider raping a white woman was the lowest form of bandit. She forced herself to stay calm, knowing that if she struggled she would excite him even more. Instead, she feigned surrender, sagging in his arms so that he had to step back to support her. But far from releasing his grip as she'd hoped, he deftly wound a length of cord about her wrists, and tied a vile-tasting piece of cloth across her mouth. Then, with an ease surprising in so short a man, he picked her up and carried her over to the bed.

The moon had risen, and as her eyes adjusted to the dim light, she made out another moving shape in the room; a second man was systematically rifling the contents of her handbag and overnight case, giving little satisfied grunts as he transferred his haul into a sack.

She gave a strangled cry, trying to spit out the stifling gag, and immediately the knife jabbed her again.

'Quiet!'

At that moment footsteps rang on the flagstones outside, and Gene called, 'Romy, are you still decent? There's something I forgot to tell you.'

Both bandits froze into utter stillness. Romy prayed: Don't go away! Oh, please realize there's something wrong!

Silence. Then the door rattled. He called again in a puzzled tone, 'Romy? Are you all right? Why have you locked the door?'

She could imagine him pacing up and down, listening, staring at the door . . .

'Oh, all right. It doesn't much matter,' he said at last, and she heard his footsteps diminish as he moved away.

When they were sure he had gone, the bandits set about tying Romy's wrists and ankles to the legs of the bed. She kicked and fought like a wildcat, knowing that this was her last chance, but their combined strength was too much and before long she lay helplessly spreadeagled. With excited giggles the bandits began to tear off her clothes.

She fixed her eyes on the lighter square of the window, through which the twisted pine, silvered by moonlight, stood sentinel over the temple's curving roofs. She tried not to think what was about to happen to her, and kept her gaze on those stately, outspread branches, the noble span of the ancient trunk. Will they slit my throat when they've finished with me? she wondered, terror-struck. Will they leave me here like a trussed pig for Gene to find in the morning?

Over by the window a shadow moved among shadows. She hardly had time to think, Oh God, there's another of them! before she was blinded by two flashes in quick succession, and a double explosion rocked the stonewalled room. One body collapsed on top of her, shot through the head, and the other bandit gave a great leap at the wall before he, too, keeled over with a bubbling, choking gasp. The acrid fumes of cordite rolled across the room like a sea-fog. She couldn't grasp what had happened.

'Are there any more of them?' shouted Gene into the ringing silence. Getting no answer he heaved himself over the sill and strode across to the bed. 'My God, Romy! Have they . . .? Did they . . .?'

He took a knife from his pocket and slit the gag, pulling it from her mouth, then attacked the ropes binding her to the bed. Romy sat up slowly, massaging her jaws which ached so much that she could scarcely speak. Her throat felt raw from screaming into the gag.

'No,' she whispered. 'You were . . . you were in time. Are they dead?'

'Of course.'

He wrapped a blanket round her and moved briskly about the room, giving her time to recover. With slow, stiff fingers she pulled a dressing-gown over her torn dress, trying not to look at the bodies which Gene had dragged into a corner. She felt completely stunned.

After a time she said shakily, 'W . . . What will you do with them? I can't . . . can't . . .'

Gene considered, prodding casually at one of the corpses with the toe of his shoe. 'Ugly-looking customers. I'd say they're soldiers who've been turned off by the local warlord. You can see where the armband's been torn from their sleeves. I'd better ask Feng to dispose of them. Wait here a minute – I won't be long.'

'No, no. Please don't leave me.' She was shaking all over again; this second shock had come too soon after the car crash and she felt unable to control mind or body. She pleaded, 'Stay with me, Gene. I'm frightened.'

'Don't worry, I'll stay with you,' he said gently. 'You're quite safe now. We'll leave this mess as it is and find you somewhere else to sleep.'

He put his arm round her shoulders and she followed unresistingly to the room on the other side of the court which Feng had originally prepared for her. Gene put down the suitcase he'd carried and tucked her into bed. 'I'll get you something to help you sleep. There's some brandy . . .'

But she still clung to him like a frightened child and deep shudders shook her from head to foot. 'I – I don't need anything,' she insisted through chattering teeth. 'Just stay with me. I'll be all right soon.'

It was nearly an hour before the tremors allowed her to relax, and Gene held her patiently all that time. Every movement he made to ease his cramped limbs caused her to open wide, scared eyes. 'Don't leave me,' she whispered; and each time he answered reassuringly, 'Take it easy. I'm here. You can go to sleep.'

When at last she did, he padded across to his own room, leaving the door ajar. He placed his loaded revolver beneath the pillow and lay for a while listening intently to the noises of the night before he, too, turned on his side and slept.

Minutes or hours later he awoke, instantly alert, slipping his hand beneath the pillow to find the gun. 'Who's there?' he demanded into the darkness. 'Stay where you are or I'll blast you to pieces.' With his other hand he pressed the switch of his torch.

'It's only me,' said Romy.

She clutched a long-fringed silk shawl round her shoulders but her feet were bare and she was shivering. 'What's the matter? Can't you sleep?' he said resignedly.

She came and perched on the edge of his bed. In the torch-light her eyes looked large and brilliant in her pale face. 'I never thanked you for saving me,' she said.

'Thanks can keep till the morning. You should be in bed, not padding about with bare feet. You're frozen,' he scolded.

'I couldn't sleep till I'd thanked you,' she said again and he wondered if, in fact, she was properly awake now. There was something fey and somnambulistic in her manner. Perhaps she's in shock, poor kid, he thought, and instinctively his arms went round her to draw her close.

She lay beside him, tense and trembling. 'Whenever I shut my eyes I see those men's faces,' she whispered. 'They were going to kill me, you know. I could hear you outside and I tried to shout but I couldn't make a sound. I thought you were going to walk away and leave me to die. I was so scared . . .' her voice cracked in remembered fear. 'I kept thinking, this is all my own fault. If only I'd been nicer to you. If I hadn't tried to run away – if I'd let you come across the courtyard –'

'Stop thinking about it,' he said firmly. 'Those men are dead and you're safe and that's all that matters. It's no use tormenting yourself thinking of all the things that might have happened, and there's no sense in blaming yourself, either. One thing led to another, just as they always do.'

'You're only saying that because you want to go back to sleep,' she accused. 'You don't want to talk about it any more.'

'Mmm . . .'

It wasn't true. From the moment he'd drawn her in beside him, his desire for sleep had been retreating fast, and he was finding it increasingly difficult to hold her in a suitably relaxed, comforting, brotherly manner. Pressed against his warmth, the tense cold body he'd taken in his arms was melting into pliant desirability. Her hair brushed his cheek and the warm feminine scents of face cream and bath oil and talcum powder reminded him forcibly what a monk's life he'd led since Linda's departure. Before that, too. Linda could always rake up an excuse to prevent him starting what she referred to as 'all that nonsense'. Linda's femininity was a sham: her voluptuous figure and provocative manner were traps to entice unwary males into her power. Sexually she was cold, and since desire never touched her, she had learnt to use sex as a weapon, permitting it as a reward for behaviour that pleased her and withholding it as a sign of displeasure. Gene had soon decided to satisfy his own desires elsewhere. There were plenty of attractive Chinese girls in tea-houses and bored willing ex-patriate women who were fair game.

Romy was a different matter. If he gave in to temptation now, might she not – in the cold light of morning – accuse him of taking advantage of her in a weak moment? She had come to him for comfort: it was his responsibility to keep the situation under control.

Darn it, thought Gene. He raised himself on one elbow and listened to her quiet breathing. He was fairly sure she had dropped off to sleep. Cautiously he edged farther away so that her shoulders no longer pressed against his chest and there was a respectable space between her slim warm haunches and his groin. He began to think determinedly of chilly, metaphysical matters. Problems. How many angels could sit on a pin, for instance? If a glacier moved six inches a decade . . . If an express train collided at seventy-five mph with a truck doing fifty mph . . .

It was no use. He would have to decamp. He couldn't lie here without touching her a single minute longer. But the moment he stirred he heard a quick soft intake of breath from the other side of the bed – a listening silence. 'Where are you going?' she asked. This time she sounded fully awake.

'I think I'd better move into your bed for what's left of the night,' he said as casually as he could. 'You stay here in the warm.'

He saw the pale gleam of her face as she turned towards

him; for a moment she didn't speak. Then she said softly, hesitantly, as if searching for the right words: 'Is it because you want . . . what I want?'

There was no mistaking her meaning.

'Since you ask, yes.'

'Then, if we both want the same. . . ?'

'Ah, that's the question. Do we want the same? I admit your motives aren't crystal clear to me. A while ago you refused a perfectly good offer of marriage, and from the way you were talking this evening I thought the last thing you wanted was – er – proximity of this kind.'

'Will you listen to the man!' exclaimed Romy in exasperation that something that seemed so simple to her wasn't obvious to him. 'Of course I don't want offers of marriage and all the troubles that go with it. Must love always be such a heavy tedious business that you have to agree exactly what's due to you before you even begin?' Her fingers stroked the back of his neck, twisting the hair into little curls, her lips brushed his. 'Must it?'

Gene swallowed and said thickly, 'Tell me what you *do* want, then,' and she laughed.

'Oh, love without ties, of course. Freedom for both of us. Love without promises or responsibilities, or claims on one another.'

'You're fooling yourself, Romy. There's no such thing.'

A teasing smile hovered about her lips. Her eyes looked huge and brilliant, and the tantalizing softness of her breasts crushed against his chest roused him unbearably.

'But supposing there *was* such a thing, wouldn't you settle for it?' she persisted.

'I might – temporarily,' he said, and pulled her roughly to him. The suppressed savagery of his lovemaking startled her; it was so different from Stephen's wary, diffident approaches. Her blood thrilled with a primitive response; she felt there was nothing she could do or say that would shock this man or distract him from his purpose. There was no fear that he would suddenly withdraw into chilly politeness or apologize for handling her roughly. His hands were hard and demanding against her body and a matching wildness possessed her so that nothing hurt her, nothing mattered to her. She fought him for the sheer pleasure of feeling his strength matched against her suppleness, letting him know that he couldn't take her too easily and she could give pain and pleasure just as he could.

'Little wildcat!' he said, laughing. 'You'd better tell me if you're making any more conditions. I ought to know the worst before I commit myself any further.'

'*I'm* not making conditions!' she retorted, rather breathlessly. 'The only condition I ask is that there *are* no conditions between us.'

'What an attorney you'd make,' he said admiringly. 'You can twist the language into knots to suit your case and leave me no wiser than before. Oh no, you don't!'

With a quick grab he captured the hand she had raised to strike him and looked down mockingly on her attempts to prise his fingers apart. 'What will you give me to let you go?' he enquired.

Half laughing, half in earnest, she struggled to free herself.

'Nothing!' she gasped.

His dark gaze became more concentrated, almost remote, as if he was looking at her for the first time. He said something under his breath, some word she didn't understand, and then holding her easily with one hand he ran the other the length of her body, peeling off the thin silk nightgown so that she lay naked in the pearly dawn light that had begun to filter through the paper lattice.

Romy's lips parted. The strength ebbed from her suddenly and she lay passive, unmoving, as the slow-moving hand stroked firmly over her bare shoulders, slid across her breasts and down her flanks to her thighs. All the sensation in her body seemed concentrated on the path of that hand, and a tongue of flame seared her skin until her whole being was alight with an inferno of desire.

She made a small, incomprehensible murmur and rose to meet him with an ecstasy she'd never imagined. As the first ray of sun stole over the bed and lay like a yellow ribbon across the muscles in Gene's shoulders, they united with a passion which was all the fiercer for being so long denied, which needed neither words nor gestures. Locked in his arms, Romy felt herself a complete woman for the first time in her life: not subordinate but equal; not a wife to be classed with goods and chattels, but a free independent human who had the good fortune to be female, and the still better fortune to have encountered a man whose desires matched hers.

But underlying the physical joy a small chill breath of warning touched her like a strand of sea-fog clouding the golden sun. Back in England Longmarsh still waited to claim her, and nothing Gene could do would have the power to free her from its ancient clinging tentacles. For Clare's sake she would have to return, and that was when she would lose her lover.

CHAPTER NINETEEN

There's no better beauty treatment than love, thought Abigail, watching Gene and Romy cross the frost-rimed lily garden arm-in-arm, sharing a ricepaper cone of roast chestnuts.

In this first week of December the plum and almond trees were bare, but their branches, carefully trained along bamboo rods, were still eye-catching in their uncluttered elegance, and a few late-blooming roses made splashes of colour in the terraced borders.

The chestnut-eaters had been on a spending spree, she noted. Gene was carrying parcels and Romy's dark curls were crowned by a dashing white fur hat. Abigail was about to open the lattice and call to them when the two figures merged in an uninhibited embrace. Hastily she drew back. Really, the modern young! In broad daylight, too – what would the servants think?

The loving embrace did not last long. Suddenly it degenerated into a scuffle, pierced with giggles, shrieks from Romy and threats from Gene. She broke from him, darting heedlessly across the rosebeds and ducking under the sweep of willow boughs with Gene in hot pursuit. Abigail had to smile. They're like a couple of children, she thought. I only wish they'd get married, but Rosemary seems set against it, silly girl. I suppose an old fogey like me simply has to close her eyes to this very irregular relationship, but I can't approve of it. Dr Lombard's no help. He positively encourages them. Of course, he's got *no* morals . . .

'Abby! Save me!' Romy burst into the room, bringing a blast of cold air with her. She whirled round and tried to slam the door in Gene's face as he followed. 'He's going to throw me in the lilypond!'

'That's the least you deserve, after putting that rotten chestnut down my neck.'

'You looked so funny. You should have seen your own face!' Romy dodged back and forth round a lacquered table, clinging to the rim as Gene lunged in pursuit. Furniture went flying. She slipped on the polished boards and before she could rise again he pounced on her.

'Save me!' Romy shrieked. 'Abby, make him put me down!'

'Say you're sorry,' Gene growled menacingly, 'say it quickly or I'll dump you in the pond, just as you are.'

'I'm not s – sorry! You really looked ridiculous . . .'

'Right! You've asked for it.'

The door banged behind them and Abigail heaved a sigh of relief, but she noticed it was in the direction of Romy's bedroom rather than the frozen pond that Gene carried his struggling captive. Her laughter faded into the distance.

What behaviour! thought Abigail again. No wonder the Chinese call us barbarians. Still, it's nice to see them so happy together. I only wish I could shake off this wretched premonition of trouble. I must be getting old. . . .

But she knew in her heart that what she really feared was that her usefulness was coming to an end. It was galling to know that since Lu the tailor had taken charge of radio communications, the Reds in Sian hadn't lost a single agent. Lu assured her tactfully that this was because they were using improved codes, but to Abigail it seemed to prove that the job she'd enjoyed so much was being done better by her successor. I must go back to Shanghai soon, she thought. I'm really more use there. I'll go after the Generalissimo's visit.

Dissatisfied with the progress of his Anti-Red campaign, Chiang Kai-shek had announced his intention to arrive in Sian on the 7th December, and it was widely rumoured that he intended to relieve the Young Marshal of his command.

Harvey Lombard drew luxuriously on his second pipe of opium and felt his senses swim deliciously. The pale moon face of the concubine serving him came slowly back into focus, offering another pipe, but he waved her away. Two was exactly right. His brain was active but relaxed. A third inhalation, tempting though it now seemed, would fuzz the edge of his concentration and detract from his deductive powers. It was imperative tonight that those powers should be at their peak. If his reputation as the oracle who could see into the Red leaders' minds was to survive the Generalissimo's imminent visit to Sian, he must crack the codes in which the Reds were sending their messages; and at long last he thought he had the means to do so.

The lucky capture of a Red Army radio-operator had thrown new light on the codemaker's identity. Under torture, the prisoner had added a good deal to what they already knew about this mysterious figure. Other informers had described him as a white-haired, learned recluse, Ti-fen by name, with a bitter grudge against Chiang Kai-shek and his warlord allies who had killed Ti-fen's wife. Now a vital bit was added to the jigsaw: it appeared that Ti-fen was not Chinese.

'Is he Russian, German, Yanqui?' demanded Shao Li-tzu, the head of police, as his executioner applied the thumbscrews.

The prisoner shrieked pitifully but could shed no further light on the codemaker's nationality.

'Tell us the key to the code.'

This approach, too, proved useless. The codes were

frequently changed and only Ti-fen himself held the key. Harvey had not been present at the interrogation but before the prisoner finally expired one further nugget of information was gleaned from him. The call-signals for the various radio-stations were words in Ti-fen's native tongue. The dying prisoner had reeled them off with his last breath, the stenographer had copied them down, and a transcript of the statement now lay on Harvey's desk.

Transliterated, they read: Teh-No. P'i-t'an-iah. T'i-T'i. San-Chao. P'in-Weh. T'en. They were always transmitted in that order.

Now, thought Harvey, massaging his eyebrows to rid them of the lingering fumes of opium, there must be a reason for a man to choose an unconnected set of sounds like that. The words made no sense in Chinese or any other language he knew. He stared at them for a long time, then took a brush and drew out the Chinese characters. Gibberish, he thought, screwing up the piece of paper and throwing it on the floor. His calligraphy was getting stilted, too; to write beautiful characters one needed a heart at peace and fingers kept supple by constant practice. He considered calling back the concubine and telling her to prepare another pipe, but then a new idea occurred to him. Perhaps he was tackling this the wrong way. Perhaps the sense was phonetic.

He read the words aloud: at once a faint response tinkled like a distant bell in his memory. He tried to grasp it but it slipped away.

Dammit, thought Harvey, staring at the paper. It's something I've heard before: some kind of incantation. Now *where* . . . and *when*?

Again he repeated the syllables, faster this time, and they seemed to slip into a definite rhythm. A nursery rhyme? A slogan? A drinking song? Yes, that was more like it – a song.

Harvey seldom sang, but he was certain by now that he hadn't just listened to those words, he'd actually sung them himself. That limits the field, he thought with sudden excitement. He considered the occasions when he'd been obliged to sing. In church? No, he didn't think it was a hymn although the memory was now becoming clearer: men's voices raised in rowdy unison – rollicking reedy boys' voices . . .

Had it been at a scout singsong, then? He remembered some kind of gibberish being shouted around a campfire, but this wasn't it. All the same, he was getting warmer.

He said the words over and over again. There ought to be something between 'P'in-Weh' and 'T'en.' A beat was needed . . . A definite rhythm was beginning to emerge from his memory, a waltz tune.

Dreadnought, Britannia, Thetis,
St George, Prince of Wales, and Ten . . .

He hummed the names of the Eton boats aloud, remembering how fireworks had sprinkled trails of golden stars into the summer sky, and wine-flushed young oarsmen in flower-decked boaters had stood proudly and precariously to attention as their wobbling craft drifted past the cheering crowd.

Oh yes, Ti-fen would have enjoyed all that: King's Scholar, Captain of Boats, his moment of youthful glory. He would have enjoyed it a good deal more than his contemporary, Harvey Lombard, already under threat of expulsion. Harvey's lips drew back from his teeth. How typical of the arrogant bastard to assume that no one else in China would be capable of understanding his private joke!

Well, he who laughs last laughs loudest: Stephen Russell, alias Ti-fen, would soon regret the quirk which had led him to choose those names to identify his Red signallers. Triumph bubbled up in Harvey, more intoxicating than brandy, more heady than opium. He felt an irresistible urge to share the news of his discovery.

Clapping his hands to summon the pretty concubine, he ordered her to bring his fur-lined cloak, and then to rouse the chauffeur with the message that the master wished to be driven to police headquarters immediately.

Shao Li-tzu was not in his office. Harvey waved aside the ADC's offer of tea and went to find the governor in the long vaulted underground room which had once been the warlord Wei Jui-ching's dungeon and now served as the interrogation centre of Communist suspects. At first sight it looked like an enormous aviary. Naked bulbs shed a harsh light on rows of bamboo cages, their bars wound round with barbed wire to deny the inmates the small comfort of leaning against them. In each cage slumped the tattered remnants of a human being.

Harvey walked briskly down the centre aisle between the cages, giving each prisoner a keen, searching glance. He noticed several newcomers since his last visit, but it was plain that every one of them had already endured the attentions of Shao Li-tzu's interrogators, for all were battered and mutilated to a greater or lesser degree.

An old woman, bone-thin and parchment-pale, clutched the spiked bars, oblivious of her bleeding palms, and cursed Harvey through the dreadful black hole which had been her mouth before all her teeth were torn from it. The broad-shouldered young peasant in the next cage moaned continuously, turning his empty eye-sockets from side to side. Harvey ignored these two, but stopped to peer at the object in the cage opposite. It lacked arms and legs: only the head and trunk of what had been a man slumped heedlessly against the wired bars, waiting for death.

The background noise of moans and groans, bellows and wails, was interspersed with sharper screams of pain from the far end of the chamber where, behind a bamboo screen, the governor's interrogators were at work. The whole place smelt of blood and ordure, sweat and fear, like an abbatoir.

Shao Li-tzu was seated on a small dais behind the bamboo screen, watching with detached interest as a bald and brawny soldier, stripped to the waist and glistening with sweat, systematically prised the finger-nails off the hands of a dishevelled young woman, bound to a chair. She might have been pretty in other circumstances. She screamed on a single piercing note which lanced through Harvey's head like a surgeon's knife. It was astonishing, he thought, how impervious the Chinese are to high levels of noise. Neither Shao nor his subordinates seemed to notice the din.

The governor was something of a dandy. Though small and fat, he wore white gloves and an immaculate starched uniform, the trouser creases razor-sharp above his highly polished boots. When he saw Harvey he bowed courteously and signalled him to wait.

'One moment, please. I will be with you very soon.' He turned to the girl again. 'Now, I ask you once more. The names of your friends.'

The brawny soldier grinned. He picked up his tongs and fastened them on yet another delicate fingernail. The girl said nothing but went on screaming.

Harvey's eyes wandered to the overflowing baskets full of bloody human extremities – hands, feet, ears, noses, eyes – that had been casually dumped in a corner. They smelled rotten. Flies buzzed and crawled over them in a thick greeny-black blanket; he observed individual flies commuting freely between the gory mess in the baskets and the eggshell porcelain teacup at Shao's elbow. Harvey's hospital-trained instincts were offended. They've never heard of hygiene, he thought disgustedly. Why can't they clear that lot away? If there's an outbreak of typhoid in this putrid hole during next year's Tiger Heat, Shao Li-tzu'll have only himself to blame.

He said as much in strong terms to the governor when at last they were seated sipping a rare green tea in his office. Shao smiled politely.

'It makes no difference to the prisoners if they die from disease or live long enough to face public execution,' he pointed out.

'I'm thinking of you, not the prisoners,' Harvey insisted. 'Don't you see you're exposing yourself to infection every time you attend an interrogation?'

Shao's eyes crinkled into tiny crescent moons. 'I am fortunate to have the services of such a brilliant Western-trained doctor as yourself to protect my unworthy person from disease,' he murmured politely.

'All the same, prevention's better than cure. You'll have that room cleaned and disinfected daily, if you take my advice. And another thing,' he said with some irritation, 'you really should insist that those butchers of yours break the joint before trying to hack off a limb: it makes a much tidier job. I showed them how to do it last time I was here.

You'll find your prisoners last longer, too. You might even squeeze more information out of them before they give up the ghost.'

'I am always grateful for my elder brother's advice,' said Shao earnestly.

'Good,' said Harvey. He leaned forward confidentially. 'I didn't come here tonight to criticize, though. I've got news for you. Good news.'

The governor waited, relaxed yet watchful, his eyes slitted above his bulging cheeks. 'Tell me your news.'

Harvey said softly, 'I have discovered the identity of the Red codemaker, and have thought of a way by which we may lure him to Sian and capture him. But I will need your help.'

Shao's eyes gleamed. He spread his pudgy hands. 'Everything I have is yours, Eldest Brother.'

'Excellent,' said Harvey. 'Now this is what we have to do.'

As Chiang Kai-shek descended briskly from his private plane, immaculate in well-pressed uniform and glassy Sam Browne, the saviour of his country arriving like a *deus ex machina* on the wind-seared airstrip outside Sian, a mob of students waving banners who had been waiting for him since dawn burst through the surprised ranks of his bodyguard and tried to thrust a petition into his white-gloved hands.

'Arrest them immediately!' shouted the Generalissimo in a fury. 'How dare they lay hands upon me?'

The Young Marshal, saluting stiffly at the head of his own bodyguard of tall Northerners, was moved to protest as the Governor of Sian moved in with his police, clubbing the defenceless youngsters with rifle-butts and shoving them in the back of an open truck. Among them he recognized the teenage son of one of his Tungpei officers.

'They mean no harm, Excellency. They are Chinese patriots,' he said urgently.

'Is this the way you interpret my orders?' The Generalissimo's high-pitched voice was shrill with outrage. His eyes blazed. 'Do you allow Communist agitators to flourish openly in the areas under your command? These bandits have attempted to harm their Leader, and you do nothing to prevent them. I require an explanation immediately.'

Tight-lipped, the Marshal saluted again and the soldiers surrounding him exchanged sidelong glances. The rumours must be true. Never before had they witnessed such open disagreement between the Generalissimo and his second-in-command.

Without another word, Chiang Kai-shek stalked across the tarmac to the waiting black limousine and climbed inside. Engines revved, horns blared; armed soldiers sprang to the runningboards. The procession of motors swept forward along the special route that had been resurfaced and cleared of dwellings in preparation for the visit, clouds of gritty dust trailing behind as they drove at full speed to the Generalissimo's temporary quarters in the hotsprings resort of Lintong. For Chiang Kai-shek's visit the houses that lined the approach to the temple of Lintong had been razed to the ground, and armed guards posted to patrol the high walls surrounding the temple: the Generalissimo was well aware of disaffection among the Young Marshal's troops and he was taking no chances.

Stephen Russell's arrival in Sian the next evening was a very different affair. He rode into town in a Tungpei truck, wearing a well-used Tungpei uniform; his hair cropped and dyed near-black, his face and hands stained yellow. His right arm was wrapped in a dirty bandage and rested in a makeshift sling. With dark glasses to hide the telltale shape of his eyes, he would pass at first glance as a wounded Manchurian soldier, rather taller than the average Chinese, with larger hands and feet, but not dissimilar to many of the young Marshal's Northern men.

Accustomed as he was to the austere frugality of living conditions in the Red base, Stephen was dazed at first by the brightly-lit streets, garish shop-fronts and incessant noise. Seething humanity: thieving humanity, too. Hungry beggars surrounded him, flaunting their sores, plucking at his clothes, half-threatening, half-pleading. He had forgotten how importunate they could be: there were no beggars in the Red areas.

Celestial Sparrow, pattering at his heels, beat off the

mendicants with shrill cries. Stephen stared about, wondering how Romy would react to his resurrection. It was bound to be a shock for her.

The news that she was in Sian had shocked him, too. At first he'd found it hard to accept the evidence of the photograph which George Hatem, the American doctor now working at the Red base had been handed by a visiting French journalist. It was enclosed in an envelope addressed simply to *Ti-fen, Pao An Radio School*. Dr Hatem had grinned as he dropped it into the sunken court where Stephen and Celestial Sparrow were playing chess.

'Looks like you've acquired some fan-mail!' he joked.

It hadn't been fan-mail. When Stephen opened the envelope and drew out the contents his heart seemed to skip a beat. From the photograph Romy's face smiled at him, her dark curls wind-blown and dimples showing in both cheeks as she shared a joke with her companion on the steps of Sian's famous Bell Tower. The other woman posing with her was recognizable too. Beneath a solar topee which obscured the upper part of her face, he observed the unmistakable nose and lantern jaw of Mrs Bentley. Beneath the photograph was written in small neat capitals: YOUR WIFE AND CHILD ARE NOW LIVING AT THE HOUSE OF DOCTOR LOMBARD IN THE STREET OF TRANQUIL WISDOM. YOU WOULD BE WISE TO CONTACT HER AS SOON AS POSSIBLE.

Despite the anonymous sender's advice, Stephen's initial reaction was one of rejection. If Romy had a child it wasn't his. A lifetime seemed to have passed since the last night he slept with her on the slopes of the Great Snow Mountain, a lifetime in which Bright Treasure and River Pearl had lived and died. How could Romy's child be his?

Further thought obliged him to recognize that it was not impossible. If the child was, say, nine or ten months, old, it might very well be his, but he felt no particular desire to see it or even know if it was a boy or a girl. Why was Romy living in Sian? Why hadn't she taken her baby home to Longmarsh? Could it mean she nursed a lingering hope that her husband still lived?

There was no way of answering these questions, he realized reluctantly, other than going to Sian to find out for himself. Whether he liked it or not, Romy was still his wife and his responsibility, quite apart from the question of the child's paternity.

After a night spent in anxious thought, Stephen approached Chu Teh and asked his permission to leave the Red base. With a reluctance equal to Stephen's own, Chu agreed and wished him well.

'You have served us nobly, Ti-fen, and we hoped that the benefit of your wisdom would shine on us for many months to come,' he said courteously. 'But it is true that among strangers a man longs for his own people, and we have no right to detain you any longer.' He paused, then added with his engaging gap-toothed grin, 'Who knows? We may meet again. When you have found your First Lady you may wish to return to us. You will find us glad to welcome you.'

Stephen thanked him and took his leave with a fair degree of regret. Never again, he reflected, as the southbound truck jerked and bumped over the rutted tracks, was his life likely to be so simple and satisfying as in the past months. What had begun as captivity had become a strange sort of freedom, and while he worked with Pao's comrades and shared their hardships, the spirit of his Bright Treasure seemed to be constantly beside him. Would he lose her when he was back at Longmarsh, surrounded by servants and possessions? Would the reality of Romy ever diminish his longing for his lost Chinese love? He doubted it.

Stephen shook his head to dispel his forebodings and said softly to Celestial Sparrow, 'We'll try the silk-merchants first. Mrs Bentley loves buying silk; one of the merchants may recognize the photograph.'

Sure enough, the second shop they tried produced results. Celestial Sparrow emerged triumphant with directions for finding the house of the tall English *t'ai-t'ai*. She lived in the Street of Tranquil Wisdom. Only a few days before the merchant had called there to show her silks because she wanted a special pelisse made for the baby of the house. She had chosen a yellow silk, very heavy. The garment would be ready next week.

A few days ago! Stephen quickened his pace until Celestial Sparrow had to jog to keep up with him. He whispered urgently, 'More slowly, Ti-fen. Remember you are a soldier . . .'

At last they stood before sturdy red-lacquered double doors with lion's-head rings, set in a high, blank wall. She's in there, thought Stephen in a fever of impatience. Maybe Romy's there too. How can I get to them? He glanced up and down the quiet street: a few coolies chatted, resting on the shafts of their rickshaws, at the street corner; an old woman shuffled past carrying a load of firewood; curious children eyed them and edged nearer.

Some instinct of caution prevented him from hammering on that closed secret door. It was unlikely that the *k'ai-men-ti* would admit a soldier as scruffy as he and he did not wish to reveal his identity yet. He squatted down in the gritty dust to think the matter over. The tantalizing smell of fried millet cakes drifted to their nostrils. They had not eaten since dawn.

'I go to buy food,' said Celestial Sparrow importantly, and swaggered away in the direction of the alluring fragrance; but before he reached the corner where the cake-vendor was selling his wares, there was the roar of a motor engine and a sudden squeal of brakes. A large black car thrust its bonnet down the narrow street. Immediately the rickshaw coolies scattered to give it passage, but the cake-vendor could not move his cooking impedimenta quickly enough to avoid the shining monster. There was a splintering crash as the flimsy cart went under the wheels, and a tongue of flame shot from the overturned brazier, licking up the spilt cooking-oil. For a moment the bonnet of the car was enveloped in flame. Soldiers leapt from the running-boards to beat it out, and the single passenger alighted hastily. Stephen recognized Harvey Lombard.

The flames were soon extinguished. The soldiers turned their attention to beating and kicking the vendor instead, but only briefly. Their master was in a hurry. Doors slammed; the horn blared a warning. The motor rolled forward again, narrowly missing Celestial Sparrow, who had stood with mouth agape throughout the incident and only just managed to save himself by flattening his body against a wall.

The motor swung through the red-lacquered doors which opened to receive it, and the growl was muffled as its passenger was deposited inside. Celestial Sparrow pelted back along the street, hunger forgotten.

'Ti-fen – it is Lom-pa! The white-devil doctor who stole my Shining Moon!' He was shaking with excitement.

'What? Are you sure?' Stephen stared at him.

'It is – it is . . . I know him,' stuttered the boy.

Stephen frowned. 'You must be mistaken. You always say one white face is just like another to you.'

'No, no. It is true. I know him.' Celestial Sparrow bounced like the lid of a simmering kettle in his agitation.

'But that doctor was far away, in Shanghai. What did you call him?'

'I told you before, Lom-pa,' said Celestial Sparrow in the injured tone of one whose word is unjustly doubted. 'He is older now, as I am, but when I saw him I remembered as if it was yesterday.'

But Stephen wasn't thinking about Celestial Sparrow's old grievance: his brain was busy with another problem. He had thought of asking Mrs Bentley to break the news of his reappearance to Romy, but now it struck him that as a doctor, Harvey might have more experience of such matters.

He said, 'I hope you're wrong, because Lom-pa, as you call him, is an old acquaintance of mine.' He raised his hand to knock on the door, but with a moan of protest Celestial Sparrow caught his arm.

'No, no! He is a devil. Do not go in his house, Ti-fen.'

'Don't worry, I know how to deal with him,' smiled Stephen. 'We went to the same school, long ago.'

'Then you, also, are of the Green Gang?' The boy looked astonished and fearful.

'Of course I'm not! It was an English school. We didn't have secret societies – at least, not the kind you mean. What makes you think Lom-pa is one of the Green Gang?'

'It is known,' muttered Celestial Sparrow. He tried to pull away, his small face darkened by an expression of sullen misery. 'I will not go in that devil-doctor's house,' he announced, spitting to emphasize his point.

'All right, please yourself. But look here,' said Stephen coaxingly, 'let me go in and make sure everything's quite safe; then I'll come out and fetch you. How's that? You go and get something to eat, then wait by the corner with the rickshaw coolies. I won't be long.'

Without waiting for further objections he knocked firmly and was soon admitted to the outer courtyard. Rummaging in his pocket for pencil and paper, Stephen scribbled a few words, folded the note, and told the *k'ai-men-ti* to see it was delivered to his master at once. The red doors swung smoothly shut, leaving Celestial Sparrow staring at them blankly.

As Harvey read the note, jubilation bubbled up in him until he felt like shouting aloud. At last! The mouse had taken the cheese. What luck that Romy had complained of a sore throat and gone early to bed instead of joining him for a game of cards or chess after dinner. Mrs Bentley, too, had seized the opportunity to retire to her room to write letters: there would be no inconvenient witnesses when he sprang the trap.

He summoned Li and gave him a few quick instructions, then lifted the telephone that linked him directly with police headquarters.

'Hullo? Lombard here. I want to speak to Governor Shao. It's urgent.'

The flustered voice of a subordinate crackled in his ear. Harvey frowned. 'I don't care if he's sleeping with his *grandmother*: please fetch him immediately. No, it won't wait. It's urgent. Do you know the meaning of the word? Well, then, wake the Governor Shao and be sharp about it.'

He waited, drumming impatient fingers on the marble tabletop until Shao's voice, sleepy and petulant, came on the line.

'My dear Li-tsu – my apologies for dragging you from your new flame, but something important's come up. Our friend has arrived in Sian. Yes, at my house. I know, it's incredible, but there it is. I'm having him brought in . . . Yes, as soon as you can. I'll hold him here until you arrive.

He should be able to tell you quite a lot. Very well. *A bientôt, mon cher.*' He rang off and waited.

Soon there were soft shuffling steps outside. 'Come in!' he called. Li entered, followed by a shabby, crumpled Tungpei soldier.

Had it not been for the note he still held, Harvey would not have recognized his former schoolfellow. Thin to the point of emaciation, slouching bent-kneed in scuffed felt slippers, clothed in greasy grey cotton which hung on him like rags on a scarecrow, with shaven dark head, mahogany skin. 'Russell?' he said doubtfully.

The apparition removed its dark glasses and immediately Harvey's doubts vanished. It *was* Russell; vastly changed but undoubtedly the same man. He wondered fleetingly what Romy would think of her husband – that Savile Row tailors' dummy – if she could see him now. But that was the last thing he wanted.

He pulled himself together and forced a smile. 'My dear fellow, this is a most marvellous surprise. Forgive me if I seem a little bewildered, but I can hardly believe it even now. We'd all given you up for dead, you know.' He grasped Stephen's hand and shook it heartily, pumping the arm up and down. 'Li, whisky-soda, chop-chop,' he ordered. 'Do sit down, Russell old man. You look pretty done up and I won't ask a lot of questions, but I must know one thing – where have you sprung from? Have you been with the Reds all this time?'

Stephen nodded. His gaze wandered round the room as if he had difficulty in adjusting to his surroundings. After living in a peasant's hovel for so long, he felt as if he'd stumbled into Aladdin's cave. Incense from glowing braziers hung in the air. Screens, scrolls, rugs, lacquered cabinets bound with gleaming brass. Delicate rosewood furniture glowing in the lamplight. Ming vases, Tang figures with their wonderful triple glaze. A glass-fronted showcase was full of jade: white jade, translucent lavender jade, dark-green and palest leaf-green jade. Tigers and dragons and horses and turtles. Even an elephant. His gaze fastened on a magnificent howdahed beast of smooth black jade. Was that the one Celestial Sparrow had lost? Then he saw there were plenty of other elephants, flowers and phoenixes, a dazzling array of priceless treasures. Stephen suddenly felt tired.

'Yes, with the Reds,' he said and his words sounded rusty. 'It's a long story.' His voice trailed away as if he hadn't the energy to think back to the circumstances of his captivity.

'Well, I'm very glad to see you,' said Harvey heartily. 'Here, drink this. You look as if you could do with it.'

Stephen took a single sip and put down the glass. First he must ask about Romy. 'Harvey, I need your help,' he said carefully. 'Will you do something for me?'

'You've only to ask, old fellow. What's the trouble?'

'It's Romy. My wife. I'm afraid she's going to be pretty startled – shocked, even – to discover I'm still alive. I wondered if you'd tackle the job of breaking the news; gently, you know. You must have done that kind of thing before. You're probably an expert . . .'

He stopped because Harvey was shaking his head lugubriously.

'Oh dear. Mean to say you don't know? Better sit down. This is bound to be a blow . . . I hate to have to break it to you but . . . she never came back, you know. It's not much good hoping now.'

'But – but she's here!' Stephen blurted. He stared at Harvey blankly. 'I had a photograph. And a note telling me she was living here!'

'Someone's played you a dirty trick,' said Harvey. 'A photograph, you say? Sure it's not an old photograph?'

Stephen said slowly and deliberately, trying to keep a grip on his senses, 'The note told me she was living here, in your house, *with her baby.*' With trembling hands he pulled the envelope from his pocket and shoved it at Harvey. 'Look. Here it is. Romy with Mrs Bentley, *here in Sian.* It can't be a fake.'

'Very strange,' murmured Harvey, examining the picture with apparent interest. 'What makes it all the more peculiar is that as far as I know, Mrs Bentley's still living in Shanghai. She's never been up here – at least, not for years.'

He's lying, thought Stephen. He doesn't know we've had

corroborating evidence that Mrs Bentley's been here recently. Now why? And what's he listening for? Adrenalin pumped suddenly into Stephen's veins. He smelt a trap.

'Then I'm sorry I've bothered you,' he said curtly. 'I'll be on my way . . .'

Too late he heard approaching footsteps and grabbed for the door handle. Harvey was just saying with a trace of anxiety, 'But you mustn't go, you've only just come. Stay and have some . . . Ah, good evening!' he exclaimed, obviously relieved, as the door opened and a short, stout Chinese official bustled into the room. 'My dear Shao, I thought you were never coming. I've just been telling our friend Ti-fen how anxious you are to talk to him.'

Ti-fen!

So it had been Harvey who sent the snapshot and was now going to turn him over to the police like a lamb to the slaughter. Stephen had never felt less like a lamb. As more soldiers stamped into the room, looking at Shao, waiting for orders, he sprang at Harvey, getting one arm crooked about his neck and a knee in his back before he knew what was happening.

'Don't come any nearer,' he warned the astonished Shao. 'One move from you and I'll break the doctor's neck. *Put down that gun!*'

'Do as he says,' gasped Harvey, slowly turning purple as Stephen bent his neck steadily backwards, holding him like a shield as he manoeuvred towards the door.

'Get your men down on the floor. Lie down!' he snapped, and sheepishly the soldiers obeyed. The glass showcase of jade went over with a crash as Stephen and his unwilling partner backed into it; Stephen kicked the pieces aside. If he could reach the door, escape into the dark garden . . .

Too late he saw Shao's slitted eyes flicker as they saw something move behind him. Someone behind him.

Li, entering softly as usual, summed up the situation at a glance and sprang to his master's aid. He brought the urn of boiled water he was carrying down on Stephen's head. Dazed and scalded, he sprawled on the floor, losing his grip on Harvey.

'Get him!' hissed Shao Li-tzu.

The fight was furious but unequal. Though Stephen defended himself fiercely and landed some effective punches among his assailants, he was slowly overwhelmed by weight of numbers.

'Take him away,' snarled Harvey, rubbing his neck, when at last Shao's men had their prisoner securely trussed. 'He's all yours, Shao, and I never want to set eyes on the bastard again.'

'Of course,' agreed Shao. He had stood well back during the struggle and now swaggered forward, unruffled, to spit in the prisoner's face. 'We will go now. I look forward to improving my acquaintance with the celebrated Ti-fen. I am sorry my men and I were not able to protect you better from this dangerous bandit.'

Harvey surveyed the devastated room, littered with broken glass and splintered furniture. His neck felt as if it had been stretched on the rack. He could scarcely turn his head and both eyes were closing fast as a result of Stephen's assault.

'Mind you make him pay for everything, in full!' he added with controlled venom.

'I will do so, have no fear,' Shao assured him as Stephen was dragged away.

CHAPTER TWENTY

The Almond Blossom Concubine was waiting patiently, covering her pretty red mouth with her hand to hide yawns, when Shao Li-tzu came back to the tea-house to resume his interrupted pleasure. When Clouds had met Rain with results satisfactory to him and the Peony had blossomed for the second time that night, the governor lay in a pleasantly relaxed torpor, his head pillowed on Almond Blossom's pointed breasts, and began to explore in his mind ideas for extracting the maximum information from his captive while inflicting the most prolonged pain. He had never before had the pleasure of questioning a white suspect.

He would use nothing crude like the slicing process for this very special victim: Doctor Lombard had insisted that when he had finished no trace of Ti-fen must remain – no inconvenient white hand or European foot must be left to identify the prisoner.

Shao turned the matter over in his mind for some time before the ideal solution presented itself. Then he giggled aloud and roused the sleepy concubine so that she might share his pleasure in his own ingenuity.

'Wake and listen, Joy-of-My-Soul. I have a new captive and for him I shall revive a traditional punishment, one which our venerable ancestors used in the old days.'

'Who is your prisoner, Lord-of-My-Heart?' she asked dutifully, smothering another yawn. Her only hope of escaping the drudgery of the tea-house lay in Shao's continued interest, but she did wish he were not so active late at night.

'An important bandit called Ti-fen,' he said impressively. 'He is a dangerous Communist and can give me much information.' He knew the name would mean nothing to her, but the capture of a foreign devil might stick in her mind: he restrained himself from adding further details.

'What will you do with him?' she asked without interest.

'I have decided he shall "stand in the tub",' said Shao happily. 'It is an ancient method used to loosen the tongues of most determined criminals. I have never tried it, but the results are said to be effective. Do you know how it is done, Soul's-Delight?'

He described the process in careful detail. Despite her sleepiness the girl's eyes widened and she shivered.

The city of Sian was like a cauldron, beneath whose tightly clamped lid steam was rising, waiting to explode as soon as the pressure was removed. Romy was aware of suppressed excitement in the streets as she climbed the steep ramp of the North Wall and shielded her face against the stinging wind as she stared out across the yellow-brown plain, hoping to catch a glimpse of Gene's car driving back to the city.

Gone, now, was the vivid patchwork of neat plots intersected by silver threads of irrigation channels. The landscape had turned a pale, uniform sepia, drained of colour; vegetation had shrivelled under the dry wind from the Gobi desert, and was now brittle and lifeless. Against the dull background the temples and pagodas of the plain stood out in brave contrast as the sun glinted on blue and yellow tiled roofs, red and green columns.

From her vantage point she could see the seven tiers surmounted by an onion dome of the Big Wild Goose Pagoda, one of Sian's landmarks. Nearer the city centre, the tall Bell Tower kept watch over a huddle of smaller buildings, and far away to the north-west she could see the hazy blue hills that sheltered the Communist bases.

Out in the dusty yellow plain, movement attracted her attention and she shaded her eyes against the light. A long, straggling blue-clad procession, carrying banners, was marching away from the city. It was the demonstration Gene had gone to watch. She wished now that she had accepted his offer to take her with him, but even after a year it still sickened her to see Chinese boys and girls, thin and unresisting, being beaten and flung into trucks to be driven away to the prison camps from which few would ever emerge. There seemed to be an inexhaustible supply of these volunteer martyrs, but she hated being unable to help them when the dreaded Blueshirts moved in on them with their clubs and whips.

Today's demonstrators planned to march out of Lintong and present a petition to Chiang Kai-shek; she doubted if many of them would reach their destination. Tailing the procession, some way behind, was a small cloud of dust which might be Gene's car. Even the thought of him out there in the plain was enough to bring a smile to her lips and a lift to her heart. This is love, she thought. A feeling of happiness, excitement, uncertainty . . . as if all one's senses were tuned to a higher pitch, making colours brighter, sounds louder, smells more tantalizing, and feelings so sensitive that a single touch from Gene is enough to send delicious shivers over my skin from head to foot.

The thought occurred: *it was never like this with Stephen*, but she pushed it firmly away. It seemed disloyal to make comparisons; besides, she mused, if all love affairs were the same they'd soon lose their fascination. Look at those millionaires who'd married six or seven times, always trying someone new in the hope of finding perfect happiness. Look at Chinese emperors with all their concubines!

She walked on, registering with one corner of her mind that the ragged child a few yards behind her looked very like the one she'd noticed on the corner of the Street of Tranquil Wisdom as she set out. Odd that he should have followed her. He was probably a beggar, though most beggars stayed in the main streets rather than pursuing possible benefactors up to the city wall. She increased her pace. The boy did the same. That settled the matter: he *was* following her. After rounding one of the deserted watchtowers, she stopped suddenly and, as the boy blundered past the corner, head down to prevent his over-large cap being blown off, she stepped out and confronted him.

'What do you want?' she asked. 'Are you hungry? If you come back to the house the servants will give you rice.'

The boy raised a grimy, tear-stained face and looked at her with puffy eyes. 'Don't you know me, Lo-mee?'

The reedy, high-pitched voice sent a shock through every nerve. She stared at him, unable to believe what she saw.

'Celestial Sparrow!' Her voice was a whisper, a mere thread of sound. A sudden fit of shaking seized her. She sat down hurriedly on the parapet, both hands outstretched to steady herself, staring at the well-remembered impudent face as if she'd seen a ghost. Was he a ghost? 'I – I thought you were dead,' she said unsteadily. 'They told me you were killed when – when Stephen . . .'

He nodded solemnly. 'I fell, off mountain. Ti-fen saved me then. I save him now.'

'What? You mean he's . . . still alive?'

Her teeth chattered wildly. She could hardly take in what he was saying.

'Bad trouble for Ti-fen,' said Celestial Sparrow mournfully. 'Shao Li-tzu came with soldiers to take him from doctor's house. I saw him go. Lom-pa is . . . very bad man. Very bad devil-doctor.'

'W – Wait,' she stammered. 'I don't understand. Where is Stephen? What doctor? Why has Shao Li-tzu arrested him?'

Slowly, with many repetitions, he recounted the whole story; as her initial shock faded her brain begun to function coldly and calmly, working out what she had to do.

Gene, she thought. First I must find Gene. He'll know who to ask and how to make them let Stephen go. But the small dustcloud in the plain had vanished into the distance. She had no vehicle in which to chase after him, no way of sending a message. Then she remembered Abigail's car.

She took Celestial Sparrow by the hand and said, 'Come back with me to the house. We will find Mrs Bentley and ask her to help.'

But the boy refused absolutely to go anywhere near 'Lom-pa's' house. He seemed to have a pathological fear of the doctor, and at last she gave up trying to persuade him. She had no time to spare. After much argument he agreed to meet her and Mrs Bentley on the wall in an hour's time; she left him there and hurried back to the Street of Tranquil Wisdom.

When she got there, breathless and exhausted from running in her heavy fur coat, the servants met her with the news that Mrs Bentley had driven out in her car a few minutes earlier, without leaving word of when she would return.

I'm on my own, then, thought Romy. There's no one else I can trust. Somehow I've got to get him out of the hands of those devils. She seemed to hear an echo of Gene's voice saying: 'Lombard's dangerous . . . If you'd even seen one of the prisoners he's tortured, you'd believe it all right . . .' Oh God, she thought, what am I going to do?

Cramped in a bamboo cage four foot high by two foot wide in the dank chill of an underground cell, Stephen spent the most miserable night of his life, his physical discomfort increased tenfold by the anguish of anticipation. What would they do to him tomorrow? Why had he been fool enough to trust Harvey Lombard, even after Celestial Sparrow's warning?

The questions mocked him through the bitter dark hours, revolving in his tired brain as he shivered and shifted from one painful position to another, listening to the swift scuffle of rats and far-off screams.

He was light-headed with hunger and scarcely able to move at all when at last the cell door squeaked open and he was dragged from the cage. As he stumbled along dank passages, his attempts to communicate with his guards provoked only hostile stares and agonizing upward jerks on his bound wrists. This further evidence that he was in Kuomintang hands frightened him. If only they'd been Tungpei soldiers he might have been able to get them to listen to him, as so many of the Young Marshal's officers had responded to Red propaganda. But these were hardline Kuomintang, chosen for their unswerving loyalty to the Generalissimo which had probably secured them their positions. Their ears were deaf to the blandishments of propaganda.

He expected to be taken to one of the notorious 'interview rooms', but instead, he was puzzled to find himself hustled into the fresh cold air, across several courtyards and into a walled enclosure like a vegetable garden in which coolies had just finished digging a large round hole some eight feet deep.

Was he to be buried alive? The very thought brought waves of claustrophobia pressing in on him. In the crisp winter morning, the delicate tracery of bare branches was outlined against a sky the clear pale blue of a blackbird's eggshell. The world looked more beautiful than he'd ever seen it. They couldn't kill him on such a morning.

As he stood peering into the grimly suggestive hole, Shao arrived with a smartly-uniformed escort, and behind the soldiers another gang of coolies struggled with an enormous barrel. A man-size barrel. Stephen's heart seemed to miss several beats; he felt very cold.

'Governor Shao,' he said as loudly and firmly as he could, though his teeth were chattering with fear and cold, 'my name is Stephen Russell and I am a British subject. You must release me at once. There has been a mistake. The British Government will be angry when it hears how I have been treated. If you let me go I will make no complaint to them.'

Shao giggled delicately and slapped his prisoner in the face with the white gloves he carried. 'You are so generous, Mr Russell,' he said in excellent English. 'However, I regret to inform you that appeals to your respected government will never be heard . . . unless you are prepared to co-operate with me.'

Co-operate? A chance to haggle? In China there was always a chance to haggle. Stephen breathed more easily. 'What do you want?'

'I believe, if you think hard, you will know what I mean.' Shao's bland smile was infuriating. Stephen wanted to pick him up and shake him until his gold teeth rattled. He said nothing.

'I want to know the codes.' Shao's voice cracked like a whip.

Stephen's heart sank. 'I know nothing of codes,' he said automatically.

'Only the key to the codes can open your prison.'

'But I don't know them! I was a prisoner of the Reds. They told me nothing of their codes.'

'Do you take me for a fool, Ti-fen?' hissed Shao. 'Think hard before you refuse, because I will give you no more chances.'

Stephen felt suddenly tired. Even if he told Shao everything he wanted he would not be released. The governor was playing with him, hoping to have his cake and eat it. There was no point in betraying any secrets because his fate was already decided. He shook his head. 'I know nothing.'

The coolies had been busy lowering the big barrel into the hole and now they proceeded to tip several bags of a chalky, powdery substance to form a thick layer at the bottom. Stephen's nostrils caught a sharp familiar whiff that brought a vision of damp brown fields, white-dusted.

'That is unslaked lime, Ti-fen,' said Shao conversationally. 'You may be wondering the purpose of our preparations. I will enlighten you. You will stand in that barrel on a pile of bricks, seven in number. I am a traditionalist, you see, and seven is the proper number of bricks to use for this purpose. Each day one brick will be removed. In seven days you will be dead – perhaps less.' The gold teeth twinkled. 'Now will you tell me your codes?'

Stephen's mouth was dry. He swallowed with difficulty, and said, 'I warn you, Shao, you will regret this. I am a British subject and I demand that you release me.'

The twinkle became a broad beam. 'Exactly the answer I hoped to receive. I am interested in experiments, Ti-fen, and have gone to some trouble to arrange this one. It would have grieved me if you had cheated me of this chance to try out my little experiment. Perhaps, tomorrow, you will give me another answer.'

He barked an order. Stephen was seized and dumped feet-first in the barrel, still with his hands tied behind him. For a panicky instant he struggled to balance on the precarious heap of bricks that raised him above the level of the lime, but as soon as he was up on it a heavy wooden lid with a rough hole cut in the centre was clapped on top of the barrel, imprisoning him. With his head protruding through the hole and the rest of his body encased in this infernal prison, he scraped the soles of his felt shoes quickly against the sides of the barrel, fearing that the lime collected during his scramblings would burn through the soft material.

He was only just in time. With a look of diabolical pleasure, Shao approached the barrel and tipped a small pan of water through the lid. Most of it soaked into Stephen's clothes, but enough reached the bottom to set the lime sizzling and clouds of searing fumes rose through the lid, half-choking him.

'Let me out!' he screamed, then realized that screaming was the worst thing he could do as the lime fumes scorched his throat. He froze into utter stillness, trying not to breathe until the fumes subsided. A terrible burning pain spread through his feet and tears from his watering eyes streamed down his face.

The soldiers and Shao were roaring with laughter at the sight of his torment. The governor bent down to shout something in his ear but Stephen was in too much pain to listen.

'You'll pay for this, Shao!' he sobbed. 'You'll regret this.'

The podgy figure surveyed him benignly, his slitted eyes still twinkling with merriment. 'On the contrary, Mr Russell, it is you who will regret it,' he simpered, and vanished through the archway, leaving his helpless prisoner alone with a single guard in his private hell.

Chiang Kai-shek had flown into Sian on the 7th December. By the evening of the 11th, his anger against Marshal Chang was common knowledge. The Marshal's imminent dismissal was an open secret. The merchants and mandarins discussed it in their offices and tea-houses, the hard-worked singsong girls knew of it from their army clients. The rickshaw men, who know everything first, spoke of it freely as they waited shivering for fares, or trotted with heaving chests through Sian's rutted streets.

The only person who seemed unaware of his impending doom was Chang Hsueh-liang himself. He continued about his duties, cheerful and unruffled as ever. He had brought his Leader's wrath on his head by intervening in the big student demonstration, and presenting their petition to the Generalissimo with his own hands. It was like presenting a red rag to a bull: Chiang Kai-shek had been furious.

Now the question was no longer whether Marshal Chang would lose his command, but when. One by one his officers had been summoned to Lintong and offered glittering promotion if they would transfer their allegiance to Chiang Kai-shek himself. One by one they had refused, knowing well that refusal meant the end of their military careers. The Young Marshal's successor had even been named: those in the know whispered that General Chiang Ting-wen would soon be taking over as chief of the Bandit-Suppression Commission.

Doctor Lombard, calling at Tungpei headquarters to give the Young Marshal his weekly medical check-up, found his former patient composed and cheerful, apparently oblivious of the storm gathering round his head. His pulse and respiration were normal, his complexion healthy. He had even gained a little weight and showed no sign of the nervous depression that used to afflict him in his drug-taking days.

'Pretty fit, eh?' he asked, smiling, as the examination was concluded.

'You're in excellent health, sir,' replied Harvey, putting away his stethoscope. 'Sleeping well? No headaches?'

'Nothing that a young concubine can't cure. Oh, by the way, Lombard,' said Chang Hsueh-liang with sudden enthusiasm, 'I've sent Captain Wei up to Mongolia to choose some new ponies. He's bringing them over next month, and you must see them and take your pick. I want to get a really top-class polo team together as soon as the ground's fit to play on.'

Ponies and women! He either doesn't know, doesn't care, or doesn't believe he's about to get the Order of the Boot, thought Harvey in some puzzlement as he took his leave. A fourth possibility occurred to him a little later: or else he doesn't trust me any more.

He hung around headquarters for a while, hoping to glean further intelligence, and learnt from a chance remark by a friend on the telephone switchboard that a joint meeting of divisional commanders had been called by the Young Marshal at ten o'clock that night.

A farewell beano, Harvey diagnosed. They'll all be high as kites by midnight, weeping on each other's shoulders and vowing death and destruction to Japan. What a bunch! I suppose I'd better drop by when they've finished and see that nothing of interest comes out of the meeting. He sighed. The life of a spy could be very wearing.

I'll have to tackle him myself, thought Romy. It's the only way. She paced her room like a caged wolf. Her stomach muscles were cramped into a hard knot and her fists so tightly clenched that the nails dug into her palms. She hadn't been able to eat or drink at supper, waiting with taut nerves for the sounds that would herald Harvey's homecoming: the shrill shouts of the servants and his heavy, purposeful tread over the tiles.

But suppertime passed and Li reproachfully cleared the untasted dishes; still Harvey did not appear.

'Call me when the master comes in. I want to speak to him. It doesn't matter how late it is,' she said, walking about the room, picking things up and putting them down again.

'Velly good, Missee.' Li surveyed her anxiously as she went across the courtyard. The door of her bedroom slammed.

Midnight passed; one o'clock struck, two. Shivering in an armchair, fully dressed, Romy dozed uneasily, and woke, and dozed again. Through her dreams she heard footsteps and was suddenly wide awake. Why hadn't Li called her? Harvey was back, going past his bedroom, heading for the study.

Silently she padded after him down the trellised walk. Now that the moment had come she didn't know what to say. He might laugh at her and deny everything Celestial Sparrow had said . . .

Trying to gauge his frame of mind, she pressed her face to the paper lattice. The blurred outline of Harvey, enormous in a fur coat and hat, swam into focus. He sloshed liquor into a glass, she heard the bottle clink against the rim as if his hands weren't steady. Then he pulled out the middle drawer of his desk and reached inside.

A moment later he pulled out a gun and levelled it towards the window. For a heartstopping moment she feared he'd seen her shadow outside. She kept completely still, holding her breath, but he lowered the gun without discharging it, and when she looked again she saw that he'd broken it open and was loading it.

Where was he going so late, and *armed*? Romy's breath came in shallow gasps. Wherever it was, she was determined to follow. Without allowing herself to think of what might happen, she fled back down the covered passage, across the courtyard and the water-garden, making for the 'peace gate' – the small back exit used by Chinese families in times of emergency. Romy knew the key was often hidden in a niche by the gatepost. With trembling fingers she fitted it into the lock, turned it, and slipped into the silent alley.

To reach the front entrance, Harvey would have to cross the outer court and rouse the *k'ai-men-ti*. Before he got there, she hoped to have time to smuggle herself aboard his car. Her ribs were heaving when she had run round two sides of a square to the front gate, but there, sure enough, was Harvey's long black limousine, successor to the Lowland, and the driver's seat was empty. Her guess had been right. On this clandestine errand, whatever it might be, Harvey intended to drive himself.

As she hesitated, wondering whether she dared slip into the back seat and risk premature discovery, the beam of a torch shone under the lacquered doors with their brightly-polished lion's head rings. He was coming: she'd left it too late.

Sick with disappointment, she shrank back in the shadow of the wall just as Harvey strode out, pulling on a pair of driving gauntlets. He climbed into the front seat and slammed the door. The engine whirred, spluttered, and died. Over and over again the sequence was repeated: whirr, splutter, silence. Romy waited, her nerves tingling, for the moment when he would either call for help or get out himself to use the starting handle.

Don't let it start, she prayed. Oh, don't let it . . .

He was out, cursing, fumbling in the boot for the starting handle, kneeling on the freezing ground to manoeuvre it into position. The handle engaged; he put down the torch.

Now!

Like a patch of moving shadow Romy slid alongside the car and softly pressed down the back door handle. She waited until Harvey, grunting with effort, began to swing the engine, then opened the door and crept inside the car. Huddling down on the floor between the seats, she pulled the car-rug over her and waited, holding her breath, for any sign that her stealthy entry had been observed.

Harvey still struggled with the starting handle. The whole car shook as he swung the engine over repeatedly, but it was several minutes before the motor caught properly.

Then he flung himself behind the wheel and revved noisily. Romy heard his laboured breathing and caught the tang of sweat.

'Damn,' he muttered. 'Damn, damn, damn.'

He dropped the starting handle on the floor and slammed shut the glass partition behind the front seats. She relaxed and allowed herself to ease into a more comfortable position. He wouldn't hear her now above the hum of the engine. The car began to move.

Harvey drove as if the devil was at his heels. For what seemed an eternity Romy was bumped and banged as the vehicle hurtled over rough roads. She dared not put aside the smothering rug for fear that the driver would catch a glimpse of movement in the mirror, but she knew they must have left the city because even Harvey wouldn't dare drive so fast among houses. Steadily her hopes grew that he was heading for one of the out-of-town camps where Communist suspects were impounded. She felt more and more certain that this furtive journey was connected with Stephen's disappearance. If I can get a glimpse of where they've hidden him, I can come back in the daylight with Gene, she thought. Then Harvey can't deny it all. Faced with my evidence and Celestial Sparrow's, he'll *have* to admit that Stephen's alive. She forced the grim possibility that he was already dead from her mind. Instinct told her that every turn of the wheels was bringing her nearer her husband. Not for the first time in her life, instinct was completely wrong.

The Almond Blossom Concubine had chosen the dress she would wear and left the rest on the floor for her servant to pick up. Now she concentrated on painting her face in preparation for entertaining her customers.

First she applied a thick mask of white foundation, rubbing it well into the skin to conceal the pitted scars of *hua-ping*, the flower disease which had killed her mother and three young brothers, and led her father to sell her at the age of nine to the Fragrant Tree tea-house. Now she was twelve years old, and much in demand with Kuomintang officers for her slight graceful body and the sweet high voice with which she would sometimes sing for favoured clients. Since Shao Li-tzu had singled her out for patronage her prospects had improved. There was even a possibility that he would one day install her in his family house, give her a courtyard of her own and servants to wait on her.

Ho-sen, the toothless old *amah* who attended her, often scolded Almond Blossom for not trying harder to secure her future with Governor Shao.

'You are a fever in his blood now, but it will not always be so,' she shrilled. 'Your youth and beauty will soon fade as mine did, and one day Shao Li-tzu will lust for younger flesh than yours. Then you will regret that you did not flatter him as he liked.'

Almond Blossom paid little heed to these gloomy predictions. She hated Governor Shao just as she hated all the other men who fondled and abused her. Dreaming of the day when the Red bandits would sweep into Sian and women would unbind their feet and no longer be the helpless playthings of men, she outlined her plucked brows, sweeping the brush in an upward curve like the wingtips of swallows. Then she painted her mouth deep scarlet, applied a thick layer of powder, and repeated the process.

The child's face vanished under a simpering, featureless mask.

'I am prepared. Leave me now and admit the English *t'ai-t'ai* who waits at the peace gate,' she ordered Ho-sen. 'I have business with her.'

'Business! While your customers drink tea and call for you? You are growing too presumptuous, with your talk of foreign devils and book-learning,' grumbled the old woman. 'Evil will come of it.' All the same, she left the room and invited Abigail to enter.

Almond Blossom bowed gracefully over folded hands. 'How may I serve the honoured *t'ai-t'ai*?' she enquired politely, dismissing the muttering Ho-sen.

Abigail waited until she was sure the woman had gone. Then she said quietly, 'I have come from Mr Lu. He tells me you have important news concerning Ti-fen.'

The girl cast a quick look round. Her painted face could

express no anxiety, but her movements were nervous as she went to the door and jerked aside the leather curtain. The passage was deserted. She moved close to Abigail and spoke so softly that the rattle and click of *mah-jong* counters in the tea-house nearly drowned her words.

'Ti-fen has been arrested, here in Sian.'

'What?' exclaimed Abigail sharply. 'Who told you that?'

Almond Blossom put a finger to her lips. 'Not so loud,' she begged. 'Ears are always listening.' She drew a deep breath and said, 'Ti-fen came to Sian secretly. Governor Shao heard of it and arrested him. He has put him to stand in the tub. This he told me himself. If Ti-fen is not rescued he will soon die.'

She watched her information sink in.

'But who –?' began Abigail. She was interrupted by the long-drawn-out wail of a horn sounding in the outer court, and the strident voice of the doorman proclaiming, 'Guests have honoured us with their presence! Three distinguished officers and Governor Shao! Make haste to greet our honoured guests!'

All along the dark corridor curtains were drawn aside and pretty, painted girls in their evening finery tripped and rustled from their rooms to welcome the visitors.

'I regret, I must leave you now,' whispered Almond Blossom. Hurriedly she adjusted the seams of her stockings and clipped on sparkling earrings. Her simple silk dress, slashed to the thigh, moulded her supple figure gracefully, in stark contrast to her stiff masklike face and frizzed hair. With a slither of silk she was gone, hurrying after the other girls, leaving Abigail staring worriedly at the heaps of discarded clothing and spilt face-powder.

CHAPTER TWENTY-ONE

As Abigail hurried through the cold, windy streets in search of Lu the tailor, part of her mind noticed that the military were extra busy that night. Staff cars sped noisily to and fro.

Patrols roamed the streets, bayonets fixed, faces grimly expectant. A convoy of army trucks rumbled out of town.

She passed the Sian Guest House where most of Chiang Kai-shek's general staff was billeted, and saw to her surprise that the guards on duty were tall Northerners wearing Tungpei uniforms. It seemed odd that the Young Marshal should have more men in the streets now than for months past. She wondered fleetingly if the order for his dismissal had been revoked. Allegiances changed so fast in China. While she worried about Ti-fen's fate whole new alliances might have been made or broken, yesterday's tyrant executed and tomorrow's welcomed with banners.

At last, tired and footsore, she reached the Street of Coloured Clouds of Spring where Mr Lu lodged, and was admitted by his thin little maidservant who stared at her with frightened eyes and said that Lu Fu-ch'un had gone out before dark and not returned.

Abigail consulted her watch. It was already past midnight.

'I will wait for him,' she said.

She sat sipping tea, trying to believe that Ti-fen was not Stephen Russell and the concubine had been wrong about the torture planned for him. Mr Lu did not come home and by two o'clock Abigail was extremely worried for his safety. She had just made up her mind to return to the Street of Tranquil Wisdom in case he had left a message for her there, when an outbreak of firing close at hand brought the maid running into the room. It came from the direction of the Sian Guest House.

'Whatever's that?'

Abigail went to the door and peered into the dark street.

'No, no, Honourable Venerable Lady, come back!' sobbed the maid, pulling at her sleeve. 'Do not go out, you will die!'

The sharp crackle of rifle-shots, nearer now, convinced Abigail that this was sound advice. A moment later an explosion rattled the door and leaping flames outlined the dark houses opposite. Feet thudded down the street; there were loud shouts and more shots, then farther away they heard crashes and thumps as if a building was being rammed by a heavy vehicle. Clearly it would be madness to venture into the streets just now, but she longed to know what was going on. Who was fighting whom? Was this a surprise attack by the Reds?

Swiftly Abigail went through into Mr Lu's study and dismantled his radio transmitter. She hid it in the hollowed out base of a large sewing machine. Then she told the maid to bring more tea, bolted the street door, and sat straining her ears for the tramp of feet outside and the dreaded knock of police come to search the house.

The big car slowed and stopped. A torch-beam shone through the driver's window, hesitated on the heap of rugs that covered Romy, and moved slowly away. Harvey's voice rumbled. A moment later he drove gently forward, bumped over paving stones, halted . . . The engine was switched off and a rush of icy air blew under the seat as Harvey opened his door.

Romy lay perfectly still until she heard his steps fade in the distance, then very carefully she put aside the rug and knelt to peer out. A dim grey light was filtering into the courtyard where the car was parked. It must be nearly dawn. If anyone took more than a casual glance into the back seat she would surely be discovered.

It hadn't occurred to her that Harvey meant to drive so far afield, but clearly she couldn't remain where she was. After a quick glance round to make sure that the courtyard was deserted, she opened the back door and crept out; then on impulse reached through the open window to remove the ignition key. She didn't want to be left stranded miles from Sian.

Cautiously she made her way through the nearest archway and stopped short, staring in bewilderment at the sweeping branches of willow surrounding a small lake off whose gleaming pewter surface vapour was rising like the steam from a bath. She knew where she was at once, and tears of disappointment stung her eyes. She'd been so sure he was driving to the place where Stephen was concealed, but instead he had brought her to Chiang Kai-shek's headquarters in Lintong. Her journey had been in vain.

But why the loaded revolver, and why at such an hour? Surely Harvey didn't intend to threaten the Leader? Well, she could do nothing now but wait until he emerged from whatever secret business he had with Chiang, then ask him to drive her home. It would be awkward explaining her presence here; he would be angry to know that she had spied on him. She would face that problem when it arose; first she turned to practical matters. She must find a way out of this maze of courts and temples. At the moment all was quiet and still, but Chinese are early risers and she knew the outer gates were guarded by Chiang's bodyguards. The rear of the temple where the outer wall met the mountainside seemed to offer the best chance of an exit.

Harvey had vanished up a flight of steps. She followed, working her way slowly uphill, and eventually reached the perimeter wall, set with small towers. By standing on a handy heap of rubble she was able to reach up and grasp the parapet; with a struggle she heaved herself to sit astride it. On the inside the wall was no more than six feet high, but a deep ditch yawned blackly on the outside separating the temple from the rocky slopes beyond. Although it wasn't a sheer drop it was impossible, in the dim light, to see quite how deep it was; after a brief survey she rejected the idea of launching herself into such a blind abyss. There must be a better way out.

She was about to scramble down to the rubble-heap again when the rumble of heavy engines came to her ears. Instinctively she looked down towards the road and saw the lights of a convoy scything through the gloomy dawn. Faint shouts sounded far below; then a machine gun began to chatter furiously, like an angry squirrel.

The lights of the leading truck swung round and she distinctly heard the crash of metal as it rammed the gates which the guards were struggling to close.

Torn between fascination and fright, Romy eased herself along the wall until she reached the shelter of one of the watchtowers. There was a platform inside on which she crouched, straining her eyes to see what was happening in the outer courtyard. Silent and deserted a moment ago, now it was suddenly full of dark figures scurrying antlike from the surrounding pavilions, pulling on clothes and shouldering guns. Orange flame spat from the weapons, and white puffs of smoke drifted lazily upward before the crack of the report reached her.

More men sprang from the convoy of lorries, stabbing, slugging, shooting at the dazed guards and other defenders, who ran here and there with no apparent purpose except to escape.

From her vantage point above the layers of golden-tiled roofs, their tilted eaves adorned with protective birds and beasts, she could see into half a dozen courtyards linked by flights of steps which led down to the willow-fringed hot lake and bath-houses. The invaders swarmed purposefully in and out of the buildings, shouting to one another in high, cracked voices. They looked, at this distance, like children engaged in a game of hide-and-seek.

Where was Harvey? She suddenly felt cold with fear. For the past few minutes she had forgotten his presence in the temple. Now she remembered, but far from reassuring her it presented another puzzle. Had he come to warn Chiang Kai-shek of an impending attack, or was he himself the attack's spearhead?

Then she saw him, revolver in hand, creeping out of a small plain pavilion at the rear of the temple, almost directly beneath her. There were two flights of steps leading out of that courtyard, and she could see – though Harvey couldn't – that a party of soldiers was ascending the right-hand one. The other was empty and she prayed that he would choose it.

For a moment he hesitated, listening. His big fur coat evidently hampered him for he slipped out of it, leaving it crumpled on the flagstones. Stealthily he began to descend the right-hand flight of steps. He was going to run straight into the soldiers.

'Harvey!' she screamed. 'Go back!'

He looked up and saw her. His upturned face was dead white beneath the copper thatch of hair and wore a look of blank amazement. The hand holding the revolver dropped to his side.

'Go back!' She gestured urgently. He didn't move.

She waved him back again and suddenly he seemed to understand. He spun on his heel: too late.

The soldiers rounded the angle of the steps and bayed like hounds viewing their fox. At once they opened fire. The shots slammed Harvey against the stone wall before he could even raise his gun. He slumped to the ground.

Romy covered her face with her hands and shrank back into her refuge with waves of giddiness threatening to overwhelm her.

When she looked up again, a movement farther along the wall caught her eye. Someone – no, two people – were trying to scramble over. The smaller figure crouched on all fours to let his companion stand on his back, then slowly hoisted him until he could heave himself on to the parapet, just as Romy had done. For a moment he, too, contemplated the drop. He wore a loose, light-coloured robe and slippers; his close-cropped hair stood up spikily as if he had just been roused from sleep.

Evidently he had no intention of joining the fight below but planned to save his own skin. His shorter companion hopped frenziedly against the wall, trying to grasp the parapet, but the first climber didn't extend a hand to help him up. Selfish pig, thought Romy, staring at him, willing him to remember his partner. Instead he swung his legs over the drop, hung suspended for an instant at the full stretch of his arms, then let go.

She saw him crumple like a parachutist as he hit the slope, feet, knee, hip, shoulder – and rolled out of sight to the bottom of the ditch. One slipper remained to mark the spot where he'd landed.

Romy peered into the shadow beneath her. She heard groans and wondered if he was injured. However a few moments later the fugitive appeared, limping, and began to scramble up the hill on all fours. Any thoughts she had entertained of following his example she put firmly aside. She couldn't take that way out leaving Harvey wounded, possibly dying. Unwillingly, she looked back at the scene within the temple walls. Harvey still lay where he'd fallen, but she thought his position had changed.

She longed to climb down and drag him into shelter, but

dared not while sporadic bursts of gunfire still echoed from different parts of the temple complex. Here and there members of Chiang's bodyguard were still being dragged from their hiding places and hustled away to the waiting lorries. She was scared that she, too, would be discovered, but time passed and no one approached her refuge.

It was now full daylight. The limping fugitive had made surprisingly good progress up the hillside. She could just make out a flutter of light-coloured cloth where he rested in the rocks high above; then that, too, vanished as he dragged himself into a fissure in the cliff.

Why? How? Questions were pounding in her head but there was no one to answer them. Soldiers still quartered the buildings like gundogs flushing birds from covert, and presently she saw a platoon in Tungpei uniform come round the perimeter wall and fan out to search the hillside. She hoped that the fugitive would have the sense to stay where he was. She remembered her own desperate flight in the twilight after Otto's plane had crashed, and felt a wave of pity as the soldiers closed steadily in on his hiding place, imagining his pounding heart and starting eyes as he waited for the moment of discovery.

They were level with him. They had passed him! No: almost before she had time to rejoice she saw a man hesitate, turn back . . . Then they were on him, a pack of hounds closing in for the kill. Romy shut her eyes, waiting for a cry, a shot . . .

Neither came. When she could bear the suspense no longer she looked again. To her amazement she saw the fugitive being ceremoniously hoisted on to the back of the officer leading the platoon. Not a common soldier – *the officer!* His men fell in behind at a respectful distance as he bore his burden down the hillside. The little procession filed along the narrow path just below Romy's tower, and for the first time she saw the fugitive's face. There could be no mistaking that close-cropped head with its square jaw, hollow cheeks and high forehead, the deeply-scored lines about a tight mouth and burning, deep-set eyes.

Dishevelled and slipperless, wearing nothing but a nightshirt and all too plainly in a furious temper, Generalissimo Chiang Kai-shek was being carried like an infant on the young captain's brawny back, and suddenly as she registered the significance of this surprising sight, Romy understood all that had happened that night. Young Marshal Chang's loyalty to his 'Elder Brother' had finally been stretched too far; with one brilliant stroke he had captured the Generalissimo and made himself master of China's fate.

Stephen drifted in and out of consciousness. Sometimes he seemed to be hovering above his own tortured body, looking down curiously at the wooden barrel in which a man hung motionless, supported by his chin which rested on the edge of the lid to take weight off his numbed feet.

Even when he was aware of being that man, he could feel nothing below the knees – for this he was grateful. The searing agony of scorched skin had subsided into a dull, continuous torment, creeping gradually higher. When he thought the pain in the soles of his feet had become unbearable and he had neither voice nor strength left to plead with his indifferent guard, he had realized it wasn't his soles that were registering pain any longer. That had been transferred to his insteps, then ankles, shins, knees. Though he tore at the cord binding his crossed wrists behind him, he couldn't free them and had to support his weight with neck and chin, feeling his strength ebb and with it his willpower.

Two days and a night had passed since Shao put him in this hellhole, and although no one had carried out the threat of taking away the bricks on which he perched, the guard had several times amused himself by directing a stream of urine past Stephen's head into the barrel. Even this small quantity of moisture was enough to provoke a chemical reaction and bring fresh clouds of choking fumes to scorch his lungs.

'Die, die, foreign devil! Die, mother-defiling bandit!' chanted the guard, swinging his rifle like a club close to Stephen's head.

Strangely, the curses and small malicious additions to his pain stiffened Stephen's resolve not to die. Anger and a stubborn determination not to give his tormentor the satisfaction of seeing him succumb had borne him up until today. That and the faint hope that Celestial Sparrow was still at liberty; that he might finally pluck up courage to find Mrs Bentley and tell her what had happened . . . It was a forlorn hope but he couldn't altogether suppress it. Grimly he recited all the poetry he could remember, trying to separate his mind from his tormented body. Shakespeare, Chesterton, Donne, Belloc, Keats, Coleridge, Catullus, back to Shakespeare again.

But as darkness closed in for the second time and his guard changed yet again, despair engulfed him and he prayed for death. He couldn't last another freezing, burning night. Would it be better to unhook his chin and sink down where the fumes would suffocate him? He closed his eyes. Pao was near him again; he hadn't lost her. 'If I am in your heart I will be safe,' she had said. 'Wherever you go I will stay with you.' She had kept her promise, but surely she'd understand if he gave up now? Her own death had been swift: she wouldn't blame him for putting an end to this lingering torment.

He groaned aloud and the soldier laughed delightedly.

'Still alive, foreign devil? You've lasted longer than I expected. I've bet my mates you'll be dead by morning, so mind you don't lose me my money. When you're good and dead we're going to shove you down into that lime and there won't be a morsel left to show what's become of you. Neat, eh?' He chuckled again.

I won't die, thought Stephen grimly. I'll stay alive till the next change of guard. Never say die. *Nil desperandum.* While there's life there's hope. I won't die for just a few hours more. *Tomorrow and tomorrow and tomorrow, Creeps in this petty pace from day to day, To the last syllable of recorded time* . . . I won't die yet. I won't.

The last truck roared out of the temple courtyard in a swirl of dust, heading back to Sian with the illustrious prisoner, and a surge of curious villagers ran through the open gate, chattering shrilly as they stared at the sprawled bodies of the guards who had died defending Chiang Kai-shek.

Now that the immediate danger was over, Romy felt dazed and sick. Shakily she climbed down from her eyrie and stumbled across the rear courtyard to where Harvey was lying in a spreading pool of blood. He was alive, but his breathing was harsh and laboured; his skin had a blue, drained look. He was slumped in the angle of two walls, where the light was poor. As she debated whether she dared move him, his eyes flicked open.

He stared at her blankly.

'Harvey?' she said uncertainly. 'Can you hear me, Harvey?'

'I was shot.' His hoarse voice held astonished indignation. 'They fired on me – those treacherous rats. Young Marshal's treacherous rats. Thought he could fool me. I saw his game. Came to warn the Gen . . .' He broke off, breathing heavily. 'Romy? What are you doing here?'

'Don't worry about that. Save your strength. I'm going to get help,' she said urgently. The pool of blood was spreading at an alarming rate. It was clear that he was sinking fast.

'Don't go.' His hand caught her arm in an icy grip. She thought he muttered, '. . . beyond help,' then there was silence, broken only by the painful rasp of his breath and a slight whistling as of a punctured tyre. She guessed that a bullet had pierced his lung. He might die at any moment; it was now or never.

She gulped and said 'Harvey . . . there's something you must tell me. Something I've got to know.'

'Wha – what's that?' he mumbled.

'Is Stephen alive?'

The blurred gaze seemed to sharpen momentarily at the name, and she knew he'd understood; but the silence stretched on and on with only the whisper of his whistling, sighing breath growing rapidly fainter.

'Harvey, tell me, please!' she pleaded.

'Don' . . . know . . . wha' you're . . . talking about.'

She knew he was lying. His eyes closed as if the effort of talking had exhausted him. Down in the courtyard engines rumbled and staccato voices shouted orders, but she and

Harvey seemed to be in another world, locked in a private duel for the secret he meant to take with him to the grave.

His grip on her wrist slackened. He was winning, slipping away from her into unconsciousness. She seized his shoulders and shook him, but his head rolled slackly from side to side.

'Tell me. Tell me!'

'Done for,' whispered Harvey, and she thought he was trying to laugh. A moment later he shuddered all over, struggled briefly to rise, his outspread hands clawing at the walls, then lay still.

He had won.

When Abigail returned to the Street of Tranquil Wisdom soon after dawn she was alarmed to discover that Romy wasn't there. The servants reported that her bed had not been slept in; and the master of the house was missing too.

They must be together, thought Abigail, somewhat reassured. Dr Lombard must have anticipated last night's trouble and taken Romy somewhere safe, out in the countryside, perhaps. But in that case, objected her reason, surely she'd have taken the baby with her? She wouldn't have left the child to take its chance with a lot of looting, trigger-happy soldiers on the rampage?

Deeply worried, she called the rickshaw to take her to see Captain Ng, the Tungpei officer in charge of this sector of the city, but the handsome young Manchurian could throw no light on the double disappearance. He was, moreover, extremely busy. News of the Generalissimo's capture had spread through Sian like wildfire. All the members of his general staff who'd been staying in the Sian Guest-House had been caught as neatly as rats in a trap; but there had been a fierce struggle when the Young Marshal's men stormed Governor Shao's headquarters. Now the old fortress, too, was in Tungpei hands, and the surrounding streets resembled a shambles.

Abigail realized it was useless to press him to search for Romy amid such chaos, and turned to the question of relief work. At least that would keep her from worrying.

Captain Ng, however, was loath to dissipate any of his slender resources of manpower or medicine for the benefit of wounded soldiers and peasants who would probably die anyway.

'Do not concern yourself for them, Honourable Lady,' he said soothingly. 'The problem of injuries is not great and we will deal with it in due course.'

'Don't you realize they're lying in *rows* out there? No one is doing a thing to help them,' protested Abigail. 'I'm offering to organize relief work for you – I'll take the problem off your hands.'

'All that will come in good time,' repeated the young officer. He was in a euphoric mood and preferred to brush aside such mundane matters. 'As you see, we are very busy now with important affairs. Young Marshal Chang and General Wang have invited the Red Army to send representatives to discuss the fate of the Generalissimo. No doubt they will demand his immediate execution,' he added happily. 'It is a great day for China.'

'It won't be such a great day if Nanking sends bombers to smoke you out,' pointed out Abigail. 'You can't leave the streets littered with wounded while you consider what's to be done with Chiang Kai-shek. You'll have an epidemic on your hands.'

Captain Ng's smile faded. He wished the Honourable Old Nosy Parker would go away and leave him his moment of glory. Why must she spoil it with nagging talk of wounded and epidemics? Didn't she see that this was China's finest hour, when the tyrant was overthrown and the glorious struggle against the Japanese invader could begin in earnest? He thought she had come to offer her congratulations on his part in the night's brilliant coup; he should have guessed that all she wanted was an opportunity to harrass and annoy him.

True to his Confucian code, Captain Ng allowed none of these peevish thoughts to show on his smooth face. He said politely, 'Although the wounded are only peasants and soldiers, you are right to think of their welfare, Venerable Friend. If it should be in my poor power to assist you, I will gladly do so.'

'That's very kind of you, Captain.' Abigail's tone was brisk. 'For a start, I'd like your signature to an official document authorizing me and my helpers to requisition public buildings as temporary hospitals. Also blankets, medicines, and medical supplies, in particular bandages. Then I'd be grateful for a platoon of your men to help collect the wounded from the streets, rickshaw coolies, buckets, cooking utensils, basic foods . . .'

Why doesn't she ask for the moon as well? thought Captain Ng as the list of Mrs Bentley's requirements grew and grew. He knew as well as she did that he'd end up by giving her some of the things she wanted, if only to get rid of her, but in order to preserve face it was necessary for him to hum and haw a little, to raise certain difficulties.

He assumed his most judicial expression, placed the tips of his well-tended fingers together as he had seen American actors do on the silver screen, and said weightily, 'That is a very large requirement for the welfare of a few worthless soldiers and peasants, Honourable Lady. Our resources, you must realize, are not unlimited. However, if you are prepared to modify your quantities a little, I may be able to supply some, at least, of your needs.'

'Excellent. I knew you were just the man to help me.'

Abigail, who from long experience had asked for three times as much of everything as she expected to get, smiled graciously. She lifted her teacup and drained it as a signal that she would now remove her unwelcome presence and leave Captain Ng to more important matters.

Armed with his authority, she spent the rest of the grey, bitter morning organizing her makeshift hospital. Soon Mrs Han, a fat, amiable Belgian woman married to a Chinese engineer, Miss Muller and Mrs Windt from the German Missionary Society, and Gene Lyon arrived to offer assistance. Like Abigail, he was deeply worried by Romy's disappearance. 'She wouldn't go off without telling you – without taking the baby along!' he said tensely. 'It doesn't make any kind of sense.'

'All we can do is wait and hope.'

'There must be something we can *do*,' he said with a kind of suppressed savagery. 'The suspense of not knowing is driving me crazy. Those damned servants of Lombard's won't say a thing, even if they know where she is, which I doubt.'

He flung himself into the work of clearing wounded from the streets with frantic energy, and by early afternoon they were ready to turn their attention to the grim old fortress where Shao's police had their headquarters. Gene and Abigail were standing in the outer court, directing stretcher-bearers, when a long black car, its coachwork thick with dust, swung through the gates and braked to a halt.

'That's Lombard's car!' exclaimed Gene. He began to run towards it.

'Li told me where to find you,' said Romy numbly. She sat in the driver's seat as if unable to summon the energy to move, and when Gene pulled open the door she almost fell out into his arms.

'My dear, where have you been?' exclaimed Abigail.

'Where the hell did you get to? We've been worried sick!' Gene demanded with the anger of a man who has lived through a torment of anxiety.

She shook her head dazedly. 'Harvey's dead,' she said, as if that explained everything. 'He was shot by the Tungpei – the Young Marshal's bodyguard. He was trying to warn Chiang Kai-shek. He –' she choked on a sob, putting her hand over her eyes.

'You mean, you were at Lintong this morning – both of you?' demanded Gene incredulously. Abigail gave him a warning shake of the head. She could see from Romy's trembling lips and ashen face that she was in no state to answer questions.

Together they supported her to a marble bench set in a sheltered corner. She walked between them stiffly, like a sleepwalker. Tremors shook her from head to foot.

'Easy, honey, easy. Take your time. You're safe now and that's all that matters.' She relaxed into the security of his arm about her shoulders. She felt very tired.

A Tungpei officer approached Abigail and signalled urgently. She rose and went to meet him. 'Yes? What is it?'

'You come now, please, Honourable Lady. You will come and see this man.' He was plainly nervous; his fingers twisted against the seams of his uniform trousers.

'A prisoner? A wounded man? Well, bring him out, then. Take him to the hospital. You have your orders.'

'Please, I do not like this responsibility. We are afraid we will be blamed. You come, please.'

'Stuff and nonsense! Oh, very well, then. I'll come if you insist.'

As she turned to follow him she glanced back at the marble bench. Romy's head was turned sideways, her cheek pressed against Gene's fur coat. Her eyes were closed.

She'll be all right now, thought Abigail with deep relief. He'll look after her.

'This way,' said her guide nervously. She followed him through an arch and across an overgrown courtyard where huge magnolia trees showed pale buds in the winter sunlight. On the farther side was a small gate into a walled enclosure. Abigail cast a quick glance round and stopped with a gasp of horror.

Once before, on an expedition to a backward village in Sinkiang, she'd seen something similar: a robber punished by confinement in a slatted wooden crate from which only his head protruded. It had been high summer, and a thick crust of flies, like a moving black balaclava helmet, had eaten away most of the robber's face so that only his dull, piteous eyes were recognizably human. She had been sickened then; this time there were no flies but the sight was even more horrifying, because this grey, shrivelled caricature of a man was someone she knew. For a moment she feared she was going to faint, then disgust and anger surged in to replace the dizzying black void.

'Get him out,' she ordered sharply.

The body hung motionless, head bowed, weight supported on the chin. It was impossible to tell if it was alive or dead. The soldiers moved forward reluctantly and two of them prised the heavy lid from round the captive's neck. As the support was removed he sagged into the bottom of the barrel, raising a cloud of vile, throat-catching fumes.

'Dear heaven, that's lime!' she cried. 'Pull him out as fast as you can. What devil can have done this?'

The officer snapped an order and two husky soldiers leapt into the barrel. Gently they lifted the bundle of rags and charred flesh and laid him on the ground. As she stooped to examine his injuries she saw his lips twitch as if he was trying to speak.

The coolies ran away to fetch rugs and a stretcher, and while she waited she removed her heavy tweed coat and laid it over the ghastly figure. His lips moved again, though his eyes were closed. She bent closer and caught the words he was muttering. '*Tomorrow and tomorrow and tomorrow* . . .' like a wornout fibre needle slipping in a record's groove. '*Tomorrow and tomorrow and tomorrow* . . .'

If she'd needed any more proof that Ti-fen and Stephen Russell were one and the same, this was it.

'I love you, Romy,' said Gene quietly, his lips pressed against her curly dark head. 'Oh, I know this is a hell of a time to say so, but you can't always wait for moonlight and roses. When I went to the house this morning and they told me you'd vanished, I nearly went mad. Don't ever give me such a fright again. I want you with me, always, for the rest of my life.'

'That's what I want, too,' said Romy. They sat in silence, her head on his shoulder, an island of calm in the bustling courtyard. Presently two coolies trotted purposefully towards the archway through which Abigail had vanished.

'It looks as if they've found some other poor devil in there,' said Gene. 'I'd better go and give a hand.'

'Don't go.' She clung to him, shivering from some vague premonition. 'They can manage without you.'

Gently he disengaged her hands. 'You stay right here, honey. I won't be long. Here, you're cold. Put this over you.'

He draped his fur coat round her, smiling as she huddled into its folds. Her happiness of a moment ago had vanished and been replaced by a deep chill which seemed to penetrate the marrow of her bones. Without Gene she felt lost, frightened; threatened by some ancient evil in this grim fortress. 'Come back!' she whispered. 'Don't leave me alone.'

He reappeared in the archway a few minutes later, advancing with wavering, uncertain steps like a sleepwalker. For an instant she saw how he would look in twenty years' time; the curves of cheek and jaw transformed into sharp planes and angles; the dark gaze narrowed and wary; the smiling mouth drawn tight with deep grooves between nose and chin.

She jumped up and ran to him. 'Gene! What's happened?'

Even his voice was unrecognizable as he said harshly, 'Don't go in there, Romy. Wait while I tell you. She sent me to tell you. Oh, God –'

She'd never known him at a loss for words. She said fearfully, 'Tell me what, Gene? What are you trying to say?'

For a long moment he was silent, gazing at her as if he wanted to concentrate all his memories into this one instant, then he squared his shoulders and said in that harsh, srained voice, 'There's no way to wrap it up. You'll have to brace yourself for a shock. They've found your husband. He's – he's still alive, but he's in a bad way. They're bringing him out now.'

Romy's whole face drained of colour and she stared at him with huge, stricken eyes. She swayed on her feet and one hand went to her mouth.

'Stephen?'

She made a movement towards the archway but he caught her arm.

'No – you mustn't. There's nothing you can do. Come on, I'm taking you home.'

But with a twist she broke from his grip and ran to bar the path of the stretcher-bearers. Her hand shook as she drew aside the coat covering the face, gazing down in stunned horror at this wreck of a man – her husband.

'Stephen!'

Faint though it was, the sound of his name reached down to pierce the mists of unconsciousness. Stephen's eyes fluttered open and their dull, unfocused depths lit up with sudden recognition. 'My Treasure,' he said huskily, 'so you've come back to me. I thought you'd gone for ever. Please don't leave me again.'

He knew her. He loved her. Tears blurred Romy's eyes and she gave a strangled sob.

Watching from the archway, Gene's shoulders slumped under a sudden weight of despondency. Turning on his heel he went to call an ambulance.

CHAPTER TWENTY-TWO

Days of rumour and uncertainty followed. While Stephen hovered between life and death, the fate of Chiang Kai-shek and all China hung in the balance.

Gene Lyon left the city. He bribed his way aboard a southbound truck the very day of Chiang's arrest. No matter what his personal feelings about leaving without Romy might be, news was news and he foresaw a clampdown on communications between Sian and the outside world. There was no point in having a story unless you could print it.

The Generalissimo's arrest had provoked a furious reaction among members of his government. From the safety of Nanking, fiery General Ho, the war minister, threatened to bomb Sian flat. Rumour reported that Madame Chiang had a hard job to talk him out of blowing up her husband along with his captors.

Among Tungpei officers feelings ran high. Most of them had lost lands and kindred because of Chiang's refusal to fight the Japanese in North China. These were loudest in demanding the Generalissimo's execution.

'Wait till the Communist delegation arrives,' they said jubilantly. 'They'll back us up. Chou En-lai would have faced a firing squad during the Shanghai massacres if the officer commanding it hadn't known his father. He's got plenty of cause to hate Chiang Kai-shek. This is the Red Army's chance to get even with him for all the suffering he's caused them.'

'That's all very well,' replied the cooler heads, 'but with Chiang dead, who's going to keep the warlords from one another's throats? Who's going to charm money from the foreign bankers? We mustn't kill him. We must bring him round to our way of thinking. He must lead us all to victory. Alive, he can still be of use; if he dies, we'll be at the mercy of every jumped-up officer who likes to call himself a warlord. The revolution will be put back twenty years while the Japanese help themselves to the rest of China. Who wants that to happen?'

'All the same, he deserves to die,' grumbled the fire-eaters. 'Look how he's behaving now, refusing to show respect for Marshal Chang! They shouldn't treat such a man with honour. They ought to take him out and shoot him tomorrow . . .'

The man at the centre of all this speculation was indeed giving full rein to his natural intransigence and behaving like a sulky child, making negotiations as difficult as he possibly could for his captors.

Three days after his arrest, Chiang Kai-shek was still in a state of profound rage and shock. He refused to rise from the bed of the comfortably-furnished room he'd been given in Marshal Chang's headquarters; refused to dress, eat, speak or have any dealings with Chang until he was freed. He lay staring blankly at the calligraphy scrolls on the wall and didn't turn his head even when the door-curtain was pulled aside. Anger beat in his temples like a dozen red-hot hammers, clamouring for blood, for vengeance. How dare they confine him here – the great Generalissimo, leader of the Northern Expedition, saviour of China! How dare that treacherous, Red-loving son of a bandit Chang Hsueh-liang whom he had trusted, seek to placate him now with talk of a Kuomintang-Communist alliance! How dare he ask forgiveness for his action in arresting his leader? Mutiny was the supreme military crime. There could be no question of forgiveness – ever. Nor would he negotiate with a man who had made him lose so much face. He groaned and beat his clenched fists against his head.

Heels tapped briskly across the parquet and a cool hand touched his forehead. 'My lord! you are ill! How can these animals treat you so? I shall make Marshal Chang rue the day he raised his hand against his Elder Brother,' scolded a soft, familiar voice.

Chiang Kai-shek was so astonished that he forgot his sulks and sat up. 'Mei-ling! What are you doing here?' he exclaimed.

She knelt submissively before him, smooth hair shining, a touch of gold at the neck of her dark, high-collared dress. She looked as fresh and elegant as if she'd just stepped out of a Paris couturier's, but the long black eyes in her creamy face snapped with indignation.

Though he encouraged his officers to keep their wives in the subjection recommended by Confucius, Chiang was secretly rather in awe of his own clever, beautiful wife. He couldn't forget that she was a millionaire's daughter who had known power and riches when he was only a gangster's *compradore*. The three Soong sisters: Ching-ling, widow of Sun Yat-sen, Ei-ling, wife of Chiang's minister of finance, and Mei-ling herself formed a powerful triumvirate. Their combined intelligence was high and their information network second to none. He was uneasily aware that Mei-ling was a better judge of character than he was.

'Doing? I've come to make them set you free, of course! Marshal Chang's behaved disgracefully. He deserves to kneel before you with a boulder on his neck, and he will if I have my way. Never mind, we'll soon have this affair sorted out. TV is talking to him now, and when the Yenan delegation arrives we'll be ready to strike a bargain.'

TV Soong was her brother, and President of the Bank of China. Chiang was comforted to know that allies were rallying to his support. Nevertheless he groaned again.

'A Red Army delegation? Just as I feared. I might as well shoot myself now and be done with it.'

'What rubbish! Pull yourself together, my husband,' said Mei-ling sharply. 'Don't you see? This is your chance to bring those Communist dogs to heel. Your heel. They're planning to ask you to lead a Red-White alliance against the Japanese. All you've got to do is agree – on your own terms, of course.'

'What sort of terms, my flower?' asked Chiang cautiously.

He didn't want to appear naive but he still saw no way to emerge from this affair with his face intact. It was a mystery to him where Mei-ling got her information, but he had to admit she was usually right. 'I am a prisoner of my own army. I have lost face. How can I bargain with these Communists?'

'You must insist on being appointed Commander-in-Chief of the combined Anti-Japanese Alliance,' said Mei-ling with vigour. 'That, and certain other things.'

She rose and paced the room for a moment, sleek head bent, brow furrowed in thought. Then she said, 'Most important of all is that you should regain face after this . . . unfortunate incident. That is the first necessity. To achieve it Marshal Chang must be punished. He has despatched a plane to fetch the Red negotiators – let us hope they send Chou En-lai.'

'But Chou is my enemy,' groaned Chiang. 'I gave orders for his execution. I put a price on his head.'

'Nevertheless, it will be possible to deal with him, for he was a gentleman once,' declared Mei-ling with confidence. 'Mao Tse-tung has no breeding at all. Now listen carefully, my husband, and I will tell you exactly what you should do. . . .'

I am a wicked, sinful woman, thought Romy. I ought to be glad he's alive. I ought to thank God for saving my husband instead of wondering why the soldiers had to search that courtyard first. Another hour and he would have been dead . . .

Stephen was still very ill. His arms and legs were a mass of oozing sores. His throat and lungs were badly affected by lime fumes, reducing his voice to a whisper, and the long pressure on his spinal column had thrown so many muscles into spasm that he could hardly move. But his mind seemed clear and when he held Romy's hand and smiled weakly at her she knew that dreams of escaping to a life of adventure with Gene were doomed – if they had ever been more than dreams. Stephen needed her now as he never had before. She could not abandon him.

'We'll go home soon,' she told him gently. 'When you're strong enough we'll go home to Longmarsh. We'll make a new start.'

His eyes brightened at the mention of Longmarsh and his fingers tightened on hers; but when he replied she had an odd feeling that he spoke not to her but to someone standing immediately behind her.

'It's such a long way. Will you be able to come with me?' he said anxiously. 'Will you come and bring my son?'

'Of course I'm coming too,' she soothed. 'But you haven't a son, but a daughter. Now you're so much better I'll bring her to see you.'

A flicker of the old exasperation crossed his face but he said no more. When she brought Clare to him later that day he seemed curiously uninterested in the baby, turning his face away and closing his eyes. 'Not River Pearl,' he mumbled.

He's tired, thought Romy, trying not to feel disappointed. She'd hoped that the sight of his daughter would rouse him to some show of enthusiasm. Into her mind's eye, unbidden, came an image of Gene, stroking the baby's soft cheek and saying wonderingly, 'Gee, she's pretty. She's almost as pretty as her mother.'

Angrily she pushed the recollection away. None of Gene's compliments or assurances meant a thing. When she found out that he'd left Sian the very day Stephen was rescued, she felt bitter and betrayed. Once again he'd vanished just when she needed him most. That's what life with him would be like, she told herself. He's utterly unreliable. Here today and gone tomorrow. You can't trust him. I'm lucky to have discovered before it was too late.

It was over a week later that Li pattered into the nursery where she was supervising the *amah* giving Clare her bath. With a smile cracking his lugubrious features, he announced, 'Mr Lyon askee see Missee.'

This time there could be no question of avoiding the encounter, but her heart sank. She managed to say with a fair degree of composure, however, 'All right, Li. Show him into the drawing-room. Tell him I won't be very long.'

The temptation to fly to her room, put on her most seductive dress and brush her hair to a shine was almost irresistible, but she quelled it. With iron self-control she waited until the baby was dried and powdered and tucked into her cradle before kissing the peach-like cheek and going slowly over to the drawing-room.

He was standing by Harvey's desk, his dark head bent to examine a fine tiger carved in green jade, but when he heard her come in he put it down quickly and crossed the room in two strides. Before she could say a word, he pulled her into his arms and kissed her passionately.

From the doorway she heard Li's shocked gasp and the patter of retreating feet. It was just the stimulus she needed to blow her smouldering resentment into flames. Wrenching herself free she faced him with blazing eyes.

'Let me go! How dare you do such a thing?'

He released her and stepped back, as startled as if a kitten had clawed him. 'Hey, Romy, don't be mad at me!' he protested.

'Mad? You're the one who must be mad, kissing me like that in front of the servants. Haven't you any sense of decency?'

He said with his easy smile, 'The servants think we're barbarians whatever we do. In my view it's only fair to give them something to back up their prejudice now and then.' He looked more closely at her white, strained face and said seriously, 'Come on now, Romy, what's the trouble? Tell me all about it. You're all wound up about something and ready to pick a fight with the first person who crosses you. You'd better get it off your chest right away.'

Was it possible he didn't realize?

'You know what the matter is as well as I do, so don't pretend,' she said in a low, controlled voice. 'I can't think how you have the nerve to come back here and ask to see me after – after running away and leaving me when my husband was dying –'

'Your husband's *died*?'

'No, but he might have. Small thanks to you that he didn't. But you wouldn't have cared, would you? Why should a thing like that worry you? All you mind about is getting your name plastered on the news hoardings. *Gene*

Lyon Reveals Secrets of China Coup. So long as you get your headlines you don't give a damn what happens to anyone else.'

She knew she was being unfair but she didn't care. She wanted to hurt him so that he would take his handsome face and the smile that made her heart twist inside her right out of this room and out of her life for ever. She struck out wildly, saying things that made no sense, blaming him for everything that had happened since she met him; and he listened silently, with a queer, absorbed look as though he was trying to interpret everything she said into quite a different language.

When at last she stopped for want of ammunition, he said quietly, 'That's quite an indictment, Romy. I'd no idea you were bottling all that up against me. I can see you've been working up a fair head of steam over the last few days and I'm glad you've blown it all off and cleared the air, because now perhaps you'll listen to what I have to say. No . . .' as she tried to interrupt, 'it's my turn. I'm sorry I had to leave you so unexpectedly, but there were a number of things down South that needed attention and they wouldn't wait. But I'm glad, really glad, to hear that your husband's making a good recovery, because I don't want to give him any shocks until he's strong enough to stand them. All the same, I'm very eager to get matters sorted out between the three of us, and the sooner the better, since my editor in his wisdom has decided to recall me to the States. I want you to come with me.'

She gazed at him, open-mouthed. At last she said, 'Now I *know* you're crazy! How can you even suggest such a thing after what's happened? Stephen's very ill. You can't seriously expect that I'd leave him?'

'Not right now when he's sick,' replied Gene with a touch of impatience. 'I mean later on, when he's well again. I had a word just now with old Winterhalter down at the club – I understand he's been attending your husband – and he told me there's no reason he shouldn't make a complete recovery. That's why I was surprised when you said he was dying, right after the doctor said he was on the mend.'

The admission that he'd been interfering in her business

again, encouraging the old German doctor to gossip about his patient, added fuel to Romy's wrath.

'Oh, you did? Instead of asking me you prefer to go behind my back and squeeze information out of Stephen's doctor. You really are the limit!'

His eyebrows rose. 'I'm sorry if you object. I wanted an informed opinion . . .'

'By which I suppose you mean mine's uninformed! Well, whatever Dr Winterhalter may tell you, you can take it from me that Stephen needs me and I'm not leaving him for any snooping, prying gossip-mongering newshound. It's no good, Gene. It's all over between us and the sooner you realize it the better.'

He said calmly, 'You don't mean that, Romy.'

'How do you know what I mean?'

'You're just saying it because you've had a worrying time and you're all worked up. Now let's sit down and talk this over quietly. If you think it's too soon to break the news to Stephen, I'll respect your judgement. Pick your own time. I'm not trying to rush you.'

'Can't you understand? It's not a question of picking the right time,' she said desperately. 'There'll never be a right time.' Since that didn't seem to get through, she made it even plainer. 'I'm not going to leave Stephen. I love him.'

'You love him?' For the first time he sounded shaken. 'You mean that?'

'I'm not in the habit of saying things I don't mean, although you seem to think I am.'

'That's no answer. Are you telling me that you want to stay with him and be a slave to that great gloomy house – your own words, I'd remind you – for the rest of your life?'

Oh, why must he rub it in? 'Yes,' she said miserably.

Gene's eyes narrowed. 'But why this sudden change of heart? In our previous conversations on the subject I formed the impression that you'd rather live in a tent or a teepee or a turfcutter's cabin with me than in a palace with anyone else in the world. Do you deny that you said that?'

'No,' she whispered.

'Well, then?'

'Stop it, Gene,' she said, close to tears. 'I can't bear any more of this. Stop bullying me.'

He took a quick step towards her but she backed away. 'Don't touch me.'

He moved away, saying with sudden violence, 'You don't love the guy – I know you don't.'

'I never told you I didn't love him. I never said a word about not loving him.'

'No,' said Gene rather drily, 'it was what you didn't say that gave me that idea. In my job one gets a habit of reading between the lines.'

'Then it's a rotten habit and no wonder you're always barking up the wrong tree,' she said with a flash of spirit, but she was careful to keep her face averted.

'You'd sound more convincing if you looked me in the eye as you said that. Come on,' he challenged, 'look at me and tell me you never want to see me again.'

Reluctantly she turned to face him. Tears sparkled on her eyelashes. 'I – I can't . . .' She drew a deep, shuddering breath. 'Yes, I can. Go away, Gene. Stephen needs me and you don't. You can talk till you're blue in the face but you won't make me leave him.'

'But I love you.'

'Stop saying that,' she said fiercely. 'You don't even know what love is.'

His dark eyes were unfathomable. 'Tell me. I'd like to know what I'm missing.'

'Love,' said Romy slowly, 'is something that lasts. It's not something you can put on and off like a suit of clothes. To love someone you need staying-power. Stamina.'

'You think that's something I don't possess?'

'Yes,' she said sadly. 'You're a five-furlong man, Gene. Very good in a sprint, but you'll never last out a mile.'

Gene's mouth tightened. 'Staying-power's an overrated virtue. I think it's more important to know when to quit. When to make a clean break with the past. Even if the sprint was short, think what fun it would be! We'd roam the world together, have a life full of adventure, romance . . .'

'Go away,' she said tightly. 'Every single thing you say is

making it worse. I wish I'd never set eyes on you. I never want to see you again.'

His hands dropped to his sides as the broad shoulders slumped. 'Is that really what you want?'

'Yes.'

The monosyllable lay between them like a huge chasm which nothing could cross.

'All right, Romy, I'll go. I won't bother you any more.' He suddenly sounded tired. 'I know what you mean about wishing we'd never crossed paths. It would have saved both of us a lot of heartache.'

'Both of us?' she asked involuntarily.

Gene smiled crookedly. 'Had we never met nor parted, I would not be broken-hearted,' he quoted softly.

He went quickly out of the room.

Visitors to Longmarsh Park in the summer of 1937 often remarked to one another that Stephen Russell was a very lucky fellow. As they relaxed in deckchairs on the terrace, with the mellow sun-warmed wall of the house behind them, the climbing roses bright pools of colour against the soft yellow stone, watching sleek horses graze knee-deep in summer grass below the ha-ha, with the misty panorama of the Vale of Evesham unrolling in the distance, older guests would reflect that Longmarsh was one of the few country houses where one could imagine oneself back in the halcyon days before the Great War.

Staff shortages, money shortages, the Depression and the hectic pace of modern life had forced the owners of many big houses to economize, cutting down on entertaining and installing machines to do the work of servants, but at Longmarsh the old life went on in the old serene way. A maid or valet was always there to unpack for you if you happened to travel without servants; the morning papers were still ironed before they appeared at the breakfast table, and lawnmowers were still drawn by fat retired ponies wearing felt boots.

Of course, Russell was a rich man, although he'd been known as a bit of a Lefty in his Oxford days; but that was when his brothers were alive, long before this China business . . . No doubt a spell in a Chinese gaol made a man appreciate home comforts.

What caused more general surprise was the change in his wife. Time was – the County remembered – when it had thought Stephen's marriage to that strange Irish girl would be the death-knell of Longmarsh's ordered tranquillity. With shudders the matrons recalled young Mrs Russell's first attempts at entertaining: the crowd of wild, unsuitable, thoroughly fast young people who'd seemed drawn to her like moths to a flame, their reckless stunts and all-night parties.

She showed no inclination, now, to set the countryside by the ears, and though sons and daughters might secretly regret Romy Russell's new sobriety, the older generation was delighted. Adela Mountbutler's gel had turned out all right in the end. Her experiences in China had done her the world of good. It was refreshing, in these days of smoking, swearing, slack-wearing females, to find a young woman who dressed as a lady should. It was better still to see a young couple who treated one another with courtesy, instead of hanging their linen on the line for all to see in the regrettable way of so many moderns. You didn't see the Russells hugging and kissing in public, and if they had disagreements these took place behind closed doors, as they should.

Yes, said his friends, there was no doubt that Stephen was a very lucky fellow. There was only one man who could have told them how wrong they were, and he had been sworn to silence.

'I still say you ought to tell her,' he'd said, turning away to wash his hands as Stephen rebuttoned his waistcoat. 'It's hardly fair to keep her in the dark any longer. Sooner or later she'll have to know.'

'Not yet,' said Stephen.

'All the same –'

'Look here, old man,' said Stephen with his rare smile, 'allow me to know best about this, there's a good fellow. Why do you suppose I've slogged all the way to Harley Street and paid five guineas to consult you when old

Macarthy in Gloucester could have told me the same for five bob? We've been friends a long time, Simon; I hope I can rely on you to keep your mouth shut.'

'All right, if you insist, but I don't like it,' said Dr Cockburn unhappily. 'I want to see you in a month's time, anyway. Make an appointment with my secretary as you go out.' But he knew, and Stephen knew, there was little chance of the appointment being kept.

Walking away down Harley Street in the weak autumn sunshine, Stephen knew a wonderful sense of freedom. He had lost her for the moment, but it wouldn't be long now. He turned his head to watch a woman with smooth dark hair and a slender figure in a high-collared dress descend from a taxi. She was Chinese, but her face was older than the one he sought, flat-nosed and full-lipped with heavy, frowning brows. She glanced up suspiciously, feeling his gaze on her; after a second he sighed and moved on.

Romy waited until she was alone before settling down to read Abigail's letter. Since they arrived back in England she had tried hard not to regret her decision, but she feared that anyone watching her face as she read might guess the true state of her feelings.

As you see, I am back in Sian. I don't know how much you have heard of the changes here since you left, but I still don't trust the Shanghai Blueshirts and besides, I've started a new 'dig' on Mount Li – a real one this time! More about this later.

The Generalissimo is back in power after the ups and downs of the past months. The only man to suffer for his part in the 'Sian Incident' (as they call it) is the unfortunate Young Marshal. Poor Chang! He is the only person to emerge with his honour unsmirched and I am sorry I used to dismiss him as a mere playboy. He was persuaded to surrender to Chiang Kai-shek, to restore the Leader's 'face', and I fear this public-spirited action will cost him dear. The Generalissimo is very vindictive – like his idol in Germany – and I doubt if the Young Marshal will ever set eyes on his homeland again. His army is furious, and no wonder.

You will be amused to hear that I've met your friend Celestial Sparrow at last. What a character! He swaggered in one morning, dripping with weapons, and asked very civilly to be shown the late Dr Lombard's jade collection. (There is some confusion over what is to become of this, since no heirs have yet claimed it, and I am its temporary guardian.) I was very much taken aback, as you may imagine, when your young friend calmly laid claim to one of the finest pieces: a black jade elephant, which he called The Shining Moon, and alleged that Dr Lombard had stolen it from him several years before.

I said he must be dreaming, or words to that effect, whereupon the lad produced a little gold key from around his neck, inserted it in the elephant's eye, if you please, and caused a panel in its howdah to slide back, displaying a tiny clock inside. You could have knocked me down with a feather!

Of course, after that, I had to admit it must be his, and he carried it off in triumph. It is hard to imagine how such a valuable piece came into his possession, and he clearly had no intention of telling me. I cautioned him severely to take better care of it in future, and let him go. I have an idea that boy will go far.

I hope my god-daughter is well and growing fast; I much look forward to seeing her when I come to England next year . . .

Not a word about Gene: she wondered why she'd expected news of him. Gene was probably back in America by now, pursuing new stories and new girls. She couldn't imagine him broken-hearted or even downcast for long. He wasn't the type. He'd been right about one thing, she reflected. Stephen's recovery had been rapid: his dependency on her short-lived. It was dispiriting to find how little her husband had changed. His reserve was as impenetrable as ever and he was disappointingly reticent about his missing months in China.

'To be honest, I remember practically nothing about it,'

he said apologetically. 'I get the odd flash of memory now and then, that's all. It may piece itself together later on, I suppose.' He didn't seem to care much either way.

'Surely you remember places . . . people . . . Where did you *live* all that time?' she insisted.

His face took on the old shuttered look she knew so well. 'Unfortunately, I really can't remember.'

Another disappointment was his lack of interest in Clare. Perhaps he'd have preferred a son, thought Romy, but as the months passed and he said nothing about adding to their family, she was forced to the conclusion that small babies had no attraction for him.

All the same, I made the right decision, she thought fiercely. I know I did. She wished she could feel more convinced that the sacrifice had been worthwhile. Once or twice she even considered telling Stephen about Gene; but what, after all, would be the point? She imagined the brief exchange:

'I've been meaning to tell you . . . Before we left China, I thought of running off with Gene Lyon. I was madly in love with him.'

A frown from Stephen. An effort to recall the name. 'Lyon? You mean the journalist? Oh.' A pause, perhaps, then: 'What stopped you?'

'You. I thought it . . . wouldn't be fair to leave you.'

Would he then clasp her in his arms and say, 'Oh, my darling, I love you so much. You're the most wonderful girl in the world. Don't ever dream of leaving me!'?

She doubted it. Much more likely he would look a little embarrassed and say abstractedly, 'Very sensible of you, my dear. Now, about the arrangements for the Hunt Ball, I thought that this year . . .' and her moment of drama would be overlaid by the usual blanket of domestic trivia.

Village fetes, charity dances, point-to-points, the continual struggle to keep up standards at Longmarsh . . . Her life had become a meaningless mosaic of wasted time that filled her days without satisfying the hungry craving of her heart. There must be more to life than this, she thought. Doesn't he feel it too? But Stephen had slipped back into the old routine as if he'd never left it, apparently content, apparently oblivious of the stormclouds that were gathering over Europe for the second time in twenty-five years.

In August, 1939, they left Longmarsh under its summer dustsheets and travelled north to Lord Strathnairn's grouse-moor on the purple hills above Golspie. It had been a golden summer, but a storm blew up in the second week of their visit and Stephen, soaked to the skin for the third day in succession, developed a heavy cold.

'You can't go out today,' said Romy, when she heard him coughing and sneezing. 'Better spend a day in bed.' She was bound for a day's fishing, well bundled up in waders and a waterproof jacket, her dark curls hidden beneath a sou'wester.

'All right,' he agreed, rather to her surprise. 'I'll take a couple of aspirins and stay by the fire. Tight line, darling. Don't stay out too long.'

She bent and kissed him.

For a startled instant he seemed to see Pao bending over him, just as she had when they pulled him from that hellish pit. Her full lower lip curved; her almond eyes held a secret smile. He drew in his breath sharply: so she hadn't left him for good! Then he blinked and the vision was gone; there was only Romy bending over him, fussing with the bed-clothes.

'Watch out, you'll catch my cold,' he warned. He was impatient to see Pao again.

Romy hesitated, puzzled by a certain look on Stephen's face, wondering when she'd seen it before. She considered whether she should stay with him, but he hated being fussed or pitied, and after all there was nothing she could do. It was only a cold.

'Off you go,' he said cheerfully, waving her away. He looked happier than he had for a long time.

The river was rising and she caught two salmon, but towards evening she had a nagging worry about Stephen, and decided to pack in the fishing for the day. She was remembering another time when Stephen had worn that particular withdrawn, almost furtive, expression. It had been soon after their marriage, in his steeplechasing days. He had broken his collarbone in a bumper, but concealed the fact because he wanted to ride over fences later on in the afternoon.

What had he been hiding from her today? She drove faster, bumping over potholes, worry now smothering every other thought.

Lights blazed from the lodge windows as she braked to a stop on the gravel sweep. Her host was at the door to meet her, his face drawn, his voice unsteady. Behind him hovered the butler with a bottle of brandy.

'Romy, my dear, I'm afraid there's the most awful news . . . I hardly know how to tell you. You must be brave. It's a terrible blow to us all . . .'

She stared at him and knew with absolute certainty what he was about to tell her.

EPILOGUE, 1945

Romy and her sister-in-law sat at the long kitchen table, stringing beans and arguing in a desultory way over whose turn it was to salt the pig. Neither of them enjoyed descending the damp, slippery cellar steps, torch in hand, to confront the pale corpse they had known since it was a piglet.

'I did it yesterday. It's your turn,' said Romy.

Sybil frowned. 'I did it three times running when you were busy,' she objected. 'Once when Clare fell in the nettles and then again when you were taking the pony to be shod. It's your turn.'

'Surely it won't matter if we miss a day?' Romy wheedled. 'I don't much mind doing it in daylight, but it's dark now and the cellar's so spooky. I'll do it tomorrow, I promise.'

They thought it over, tempted.

'We'll curse ourselves if all that meat goes bad,' said Sybil heavily. 'I told you we shouldn't have had it killed before the frost.'

'But we'd run out of pigmeal coupons and anyway there often isn't a frost till Christmas.'

Six years of war had brought great changes to Longmarsh. It had served first as a training camp for commandos and later as a convalescent home for officers.

The staff was gone, the gardens were a jungle, and the park wall badly in need of repair when Romy and her daughter moved back into the Park itself, after spending the war years with old Lady Russell in the Dower House. She had invited Sybil and her husband, bombed out of two London flats in succession, to join them; but even with five in the family they seemed to rattle around the huge delapidated house like a handful of peas in a bucket.

Now the governors of a boys' school were showing interest in the property.

'I think you should sell,' said Sybil, shelving the matter of the pig. 'After all, they'll keep it in good repair, which is more than you can.'

'A boys' school? Stephen would be horrified.'

'I'm not so sure . . . I don't think he'd have minded. You've got Clare to think of, too,' said her devoted aunt. 'A great crumbling ruin won't be much use to her when she grows up. You can hang on to the Dower House, after all, and the land. I'd sell, if I was you.'

Far away the doorbell jangled. They groaned simultaneously.

'At this hour! Who on earth. . . ?'

'I'll go, Mummy,' called Clare faintly from her bedroom over the porch.

'She should have been asleep hours ago. Any excuse!' said Sybil, raising eyes to heaven. They listened to Clare's quick footsteps pattering across the landing and down the left-hand side of the double staircase. Tap-tap-tap . . . thud! as she jumped the last three steps.

'I bet she's not wearing her slippers,' said Sybil. 'Now, the pig . . .'

Neither of them moved.

'Let's finish the beans first, then do it together,' Romy suggested. They worked in silence, stringing and slicing.

'Mummy,' said Clare. She stood in the doorway, dark curls tangled, dressing-gown trailing its cord.

'Where are your slippers?' asked Sybil automatically.

Clare ignored her aunt. 'It's a man, Mummy,' she said excitedly. 'He wants to see you. He told me to tell you he's lasted more than five furlongs.'

Romy sprang up from the table. A bowl of beans went flying. 'He said . . . five furlongs?'

Clare nodded solemnly. 'What does he mean? Is it a joke?'

But her mother was gone, speeding out of the kitchen and down the long passage to the hall, where a dark head and broad shoulders were outlined against the porch light. He opened his arms and she ran into them.

Sybil watched her go, and bent to pick up the scattered beans before she answered the puzzled child. 'No, darling, I don't think it's a joke. Mummy'll tell you about it later.' She caught Clare to her in a hug. 'There, now. Off you go back to bed and straight to sleep. I don't want to hear another yip out of you before the morning.'